THE UNITED STATES AND PERU

COOPERATION AT A COST

THE UNITED STATES AND PERU

COOPERATION AT A COST

Cynthia McClintock
&
Fabián Vallas

Routledge
Taylor & Francis Group

NEW YORK AND LONDON

Published in 2003 by
Routledge
29 West 35th Street
New York, NY 10001
www.routledge-ny.com

Published in Great Britain by
Routledge
11 New Fetter Lane
London EC4P 4EE
www.routledge.co.uk

Routledge is an imprint of the Taylor & Francis Group.
Printed in the United States of America on acid-free paper.

10 9 8 7 6 5 4 3 2 1

Library of Congress Cataloging-in-Publication Data
McClintock, Cynthia.
    The United States and Peru : cooperation at a cost / Cynthia
McClintock, Fabian Vallas.
        p. cm. — (Contemporary inter-American relations)
Includes bibliographical references (p.) and index.
    ISBN 0-415-93462-1 (hardback) — ISBN 0-415-93463-X (pbk.)
    1. United States—Foreign relations—Peru.   2. Peru—Foreign
relations—United States.   I. Vallas, Fabian.   II. Title.   III. Series.
    E183.8.P4 M37 2002
    327.73085—dc21
                                                                2002008960

To my daughter, Alicia;
my sister, Jeannette;
and my brother, Kelly

CM

To my parents

FV

CONTENTS

<pre>
┌─────────────────────────┐
│ ACKNOWLEDGMENTS   │
└─────────────────────────┘
</pre>

We were very pleased when Jorge Domínguez and Rafael Fernández de Castro invited us to write this book for their series. The project conferences in Mexico City in 1998 and 1999 were extremely stimulating, and we are grateful for the very thoughtful and knowledgeable input from conference participants.

At that time, however, we did not anticipate the intensity of the drama of Peru's 2000 elections and the critical questions about U.S. support for Latin American democracy that would be posed by these rigged elections. It was due to the invitation of Jorge Domínguez and Rafael Fernández de Castro that we were poised to research and analyze U.S.-Peruvian relations during the tumultuous events of 2000, and we are most appreciative.

The cliffhanging drama of U.S.-Peruvian relations during 2000 engaged a broad and wonderful community of U.S. and Peruvian scholars, and we were proud to be active members of this community. In large part through the efforts of the Peru Section of the Latin American Studies Association (LASA), chaired at the time by Catherine Conaghan and Julio Carrión, this community worked to support democracy in Peru as best we could; in Peru and on the Section listserve, we shared our experiences and debated our interpretations. In Lima, led by Rafael Roncagliolo with the assistance of James Rudolph and Rudecindo Vega, Transparencia organized an invaluable pre-election conference in February 2000, and Transparencia also made possible a LASA Peru Section election-monitoring delegation for the first round of the elections. In Washington, Coletta Youngers at the Washington Office on Latin America was pivotal to the organization of numerous conferences and meetings that yielded information essential for this book. Support for these gatherings from colleagues at George Washington University—in particular Peter Klarén and Marie Price—was also fundamental.

We are also grateful to the many interviewees for this book who not only gave of their time and knowledge but also trusted us to be fair in our analysis of a complex *coyuntura*. Among these, we would particularly like to thank Alberto

Bolívar, Karen de Young, Luigi Einaudi, Morton Halperin, Dennis Jett, Salomón Lerner, Ricardo Luna, Enrique Obando, Angel Paez, Ted Piccone, Anthony Quainton, Peter Romero, Sharon Stevenson, Carrie Thompson, Arturo Valenzuela, and John Youle. Given the sensitive nature of key questions in the book, some interviewees requested their comments to be off-the-record, and we are particularly grateful for these interviewees' confidence.

This book is much the better for the comments and corrections made on earlier drafts by several persons. We would especially like to thank Rubén Berrios, Jeremy Bigwood, Richard Dawson, Coletta Youngers, and an anonymous reviewer for Routledge Press.

We would like to note briefly the division of labor between the book's co-authors. Cynthia McClintock was the lead author for Chapters I-II, IIIA, and IV-VIII; Fabian Vallas was the lead author for Chapter IIIB and the Postscript. In 1998 and 1999, McClintock and Vallas conducted most interviews in Lima jointly; after 1999, interviews were by McClintock. In 2001, transcripts of the "vladivideos" were secured by Vallas. McClintock also gratefully acknowledges expert research and survey assistance in Lima at numerous intervals by Mónica Villalobos.

This book is dedicated to members of our families. The book is dedicated by Fabián Vallas to his parents. In spite of a large family of eight children and limited economic resources, his parents made major sacrifices to provide education for them. He would not have been able to study without the daily sacrifice of his mother and the responsibility and commitment of his father. Cynthia McClintock dedicates the book to her daughter, Jeannette Alicia McClintock, who has bountiful warmth, keen insight, and exceptional common sense—not conventional teenager attributes—and has made her mother very proud. Cynthia dedicates the book also to her sister, Jeannette, and brother, Kelly. Cynthia, who is the youngest of the three siblings, has throughout her life enjoyed warm, enthusiastic support for her endeavors from her brother and sister. She feels very fortunate for the love and encouragement of her work that she has received from Alicia, Jeannette, and Kelly.

The transition from authoritarian rule to constitutional government.

The continentwide economic depression of the 1980s and the subsequent shift toward more open market-conforming economies.

The end of the Cold War in Europe.

The transformation of relations with the United States.

Each of these major events and processes was an epochal change in the history of Latin America and the Caribbean. More striking is that all four changes took place within the same relatively short time, though not all four affected each and every country in the same way. They became interconnected, with change on each dimension fostering convergent changes on other dimensions. Thus, by the beginning of the new millennium, we had witnessed an important transformation and intensification in U.S.-Latin American relations.

This book is part of a series of ten books on U.S. relations with Latin American and Caribbean countries. Each of these books is focused on the fourth of these four transformations—namely, the change in U.S. relations with Latin America and the Caribbean. Our premise is that the first three transformations provide pieces of the explanation for the change in U.S. relations with its neighbors in the Americas and for the changes in the foreign policies of Latin American and Caribbean states. Each of the books in the series assesses the impact of the epoch-making changes upon each other.

The process of widest impact was the economic transformation. By the end of 1982, much of North America, Western Europe, and East Asia launched into an economic boom at the very instant when Latin America plunged into an economic depression of great severity that lasted approximately to the end of the decade. As a consequence of such economic collapse, nearly all Latin American governments readjusted their economic strategies. They departed from principal reliance on import-substitution industrialization, opened their economies to international trade and investment, and adopted policies to create more open market-conforming economies. (Even Cuba had changed its economic strategy by the 1990s, making its economy more open to foreign direct investment and trade.)

The regionwide economic changes had direct and immediate impact upon U.S.-Latin American relations. The share of U.S. trade accounted for by Latin America and the Caribbean had declined fairly steadily from the end of World War II to the end of the 1980s. In the 1990s, in contrast, U.S. trade with Latin America grew at a rate significantly faster than the growth of U.S. trade worldwide; Latin America had become the fastest-growing market for U.S. exports. The United States, at long last, did take notice of Latin America. Trade among some Latin American countries also boomed, especially within subregions such as the southern cone of South America, Venezuela and Colombia, the Central American countries, and, to a lesser extent, the Anglophone Caribbean countries. The establishment of formal freer-trade areas facilitated the growth of trade and other economic relations. These included the North American Free Trade Agreement (NAFTA), which grouped Mexico, the United States, and Canada; the MERCO-SUR (southern common market), with Argentina, Brazil, Paraguay, and Uruguay; the Andean Community, whose members were Bolivia, Colombia, Ecuador, Peru, and Venezuela; the Central American Common Market (CACM); and the Caribbean Community (CARICOM). U.S. foreign direct and portfolio investment flowed in large quantities into Latin America and the Caribbean, financing the expansion of tradable economic activities. The speed of portfolio investment transactions, however, also exposed these and other countries to marked financial volatility and recurrent financial panics. The transformation in hemispheric international economic relations—and specifically in U.S. economic relations with the rest of the hemisphere—was already far reaching as the twenty-first century began.

These structural economic changes had specific and common impacts on the conduct of international economic diplomacy. All governments in the Americas, large and small, had to develop a cadre of experts who could negotiate concrete, technical trade, investment, and other economic issues with the United States and with other countries in the region. All had to create teams of international trade lawyers and experts capable of defending national interests, and the interests of particular business firms, in international, inter-American, or subregional dispute-resolution panels or "courtlike" proceedings. The discourse and practice of inter-American relations, broadly understood, became much more professional— less the province of eloquent poets, more the domain of number-crunching litigators and mediators.

The changes in Latin America's domestic political regimes began in the late 1970s. These, too, would contribute to change the texture of inter-American relations. By the end of the 1990s, democratization based on fair elections, competitive parties, constitutionalism, and respect for the rule of law and the liberties of citizens had advanced and was still advancing throughout the region, albeit unevenly and with persisting serious problems, Cuba being the principal exception. In 2000, for example, for the first time since their revolution, Mexicans elected an opposition candidate, Vicente Fox, to the presidency, and Alberto Fujimori was compelled to resign in Peru, accused of abuse of power, electoral fraud, and corruption. In each instance, the cause of democratization advanced.

Democratization also affected the international relations of Latin American and Caribbean countries, albeit in more subtle ways. The Anglophone Caribbean is a largely archipelagic region, long marked by the widespread practice of constitutional government. Since the 1970s, Anglophone Caribbean democratic governments rallied repeatedly to defend constitutional government on any of the islands where it came under threat and, in the specific cases of Grenada and Guyana, to assist the process of democratization in the 1980s and 1990s, respectively. In the 1990s, Latin American governments also began to act collectively to defend and promote democratic rule; with varying degrees of success and U.S. support, they did so in Guatemala, Haiti, Paraguay, and Peru. Democratization had a more complex relationship to the content of specific foreign policies. In the 1990s, democratization in Argentina, Brazil, Uruguay, and Chile contributed to improved international political, security, and economic relations among these southern cone countries. Yet, at times, democratic politics made it more difficult to manage international relations over boundary or territorial issues between given pairs of countries, including Colombia and Venezuela and Costa Rica and Nicaragua. In general, democratization facilitated better relations between Latin American and Caribbean countries, on the one hand, and the United States, on the other. Across the Americas, democratic governments, including the United States and Canada, acted to defend and promote constitutional government. Much cooperation over security, including the attempt to foster cooperative security and civilian supremacy over the military, would have been unthinkable except in the new, deeper democratic context in the hemisphere.

At its best, in the 1990s, democratic politics made it possible to transform the foreign policies of particular presidential administrations into the foreign policies of states. For example, Argentina's principal political parties endorsed the broad outlines of their nation's foreign policy, including the framework to govern much friendlier Argentinean relations with the United States. All Chilean political parties were strongly committed to their country's transformation into an international trading state. The principal political parties of the Anglophone Caribbean sustained consistent long-lasting foreign policies across different partisan administrations. Mexico's three leading political parties agreed, even if they differed on specifics, that NAFTA should be implemented, binding Mexico to the United States and Canada. And the George H. W. Bush and William Clinton administrations in the United States followed remarkably compatible policies toward Latin America and the Caribbean with regard to the promotion of free trade, pacification in Central America, support for international financial institutions, and the defense of constitutional government. Both administrations acted in concert with other states in the region and often through the Organization of American States (OAS). Democratic procedures, in these and other cases, establish the credibility of a state's foreign policy, because all actors would have reason to expect that the framework of today's foreign policy would endure tomorrow.

The end of the Cold War in Europe began following the accession in 1985 of Mikhail Gorbachev to the post of general secretary of the Communist party of the Soviet Union. The end accelerated during the second half of the 1980s, culminating with the collapse of Communist regimes in Europe between 1989 and 1991 and the breakup of the Soviet Union itself in late 1991. The impact of the end of the U.S.-Soviet conflict on the hemisphere was subtle but important: The United States was no longer obsessed with the threat of Communism. Freed to focus on other international interests, the U.S. discovered that it shared many practical interests with Latin American and Caribbean countries; the latter, in turn, found it easier to cooperate with the U.S. There was one exception to this "benign" international process. The United States was also freed to forget its long-lasting fear of Communist guerrillas in Colombia (who remained powerful and continued to operate nonetheless) in order to concentrate on a "war" against drug trafficking, even if it undermined Colombia's constitutional regime.

The process of ending the Cold War also had a specific component in the Western Hemisphere, namely, the termination of the civil and international wars that had swirled in Central America since the late 1970s. The causes of those wars had been internal and international. In the early 1990s, the collapse of the Soviet Union and the marked weakening of Cuban influence enabled the U.S. government to support negotiations with governments or insurgent movements it had long opposed. All of these international changes made it easier to arrange for domestic political, military, and social settlements of the wars in and around Nicaragua, El Salvador, and Guatemala. The end of the Cold War in Europe had an extraordinary impact on Cuba as well. Whereas the sharp conflict between the U.S. and Cuban governments continued, the latter was deprived of Soviet support, forcing it to recall its troops overseas, open its economy to the world, and lower its foreign policy profile. The United States felt freer to conduct a "Colder War" against Cuba, seeking to overthrow its government.

Two other large-scale processes, connected to the previous three, had a significant impact in the international relations of the Western Hemisphere. They were the booms in international migration and cocaine-related international organized crime. To be sure, migration and organized crime on an international scale in the Americas are as old as the European settlement, begun in the late fifteenth century, and the growth of state-sponsored piracy in the sixteenth. Yet the volume and acceleration of these two processes in the 1980s and 1990s were truly extraordinary.

Widespread violence in Central America and Colombia and economic depression everywhere accelerated the rate of emigration to the United States. Once begun, the process of migration to the United States was sustained through networks of relatives and friends, the family-unification provisions of U.S. legislation, and the relatively lower costs of international transportation and communication. By the mid-1990s, more than twelve million people born in Latin America resided in the U.S.; two-thirds of them had arrived since 1980. The number of people of Latin American ancestry in the United States was even larger, of course. In the 1980s, migrants came to the U.S. not just from countries, such as Mexico, of traditional emigration, but also from countries, such as Brazil, that in the past had generated few emigrants. As the twentieth century ended, the United States had become one of the largest "Latin American" countries in the Americas. It had also come to play a major role in the production and consumption of the culture, including music, book publishing, and television programming, of the Spanish-speaking peoples. All of these trends are likely to intensify in the twenty-first century.

Had this series of books been published in the mid-1970s, coca and cocaine would have merited brief mention in one or two of the books, and no mention in most of them. The boom in U.S. cocaine consumption in the late 1970s and 1980s changed this. The regionwide economic collapse of the 1980s made it easier to bribe public officials, judges, police, and military officers. U.S. cocaine supply interdiction policies in the 1980s raised the price of cocaine, making the coca and cocaine businesses the most lucrative in depression-ravaged economies. The generally unregulated sale of weapons in the United States equipped gangsters throughout the Americas. Bolivia and Peru produced the coca. Colombians grew it, refined it, and financed it. Criminal gangs in the Caribbean, Central America, and Mexico transported and distributed it. Everywhere, drug-traffic-related violence and corruption escalated.

The impact of economic policy change, democratization, and the end of the Cold War in Europe on U.S.-Latin American relations, therefore, provide important explanations common to the changing relations of the countries of the Americas with the United States. The acceleration of emigration, and the construction and development of international organized crime around the cocaine business, were also key common themes in the continent's international relations during the closing fifth of the twentieth century. To the extent pertinent, these topics appear in each of the books in this series. Nonetheless, each country's own history, geographic location, set of neighbors, resource endowment, institutional features, and leadership characteristics bear as well on the construction, design, and implementation of its foreign policy. These more particular factors enrich and guide the books in this series in their interplay with the more general arguments.

As the 1990s ended, dark clouds reappeared on the firmament of inter-American relations, raising doubts about the "optimistic" trajectory that seemed set at the beginning of that decade. The heavy presence of the military within civilian society was significantly felt in Colombia, Venezuela, and Peru (until the end of Alberto Fujimori's presidency in November 2000). In January 2000, a military coup overthrew the constitutionally elected president of Ecuador, although the civilian vice president soon reestablished constitutional government. Serious concerns resurfaced concerning the depth and durability of democratic institutions and practices in these countries. Venezuela seemed ready to try once again much heavier government involvement in economic affairs. And the United States had held back from implementing the commitment to hemispheric free trade that presidents George H. W. Bush and William Clinton had both pledged. Only the last of these trends had instant international repercussions, but all of them could affect adversely the future of a Western Hemisphere based on free politics, free markets, and peace.

This Project

Each of the books in the series has two authors, typically one from a Latin American or Caribbean country and another from the United States (and, in one case, the United Kingdom). We chose this approach to facilitate the writing of the books and ensure that each would represent the international perspectives from both parties to the U.S.-Latin American relationship. In addition, we sought to embed each book within international networks of scholarly work in more than one country.

We have attempted to write short books that ask common questions to enable various readers—scholars, students, public officials, international entrepreneurs, and the educated public—to make their own comparisons and judgments as they read two or more volumes in the series. The project sought to foster comparability across the books through two conferences held at the Instituto Tecnológico Autónomo de México (ITAM) in Mexico City. The first, held in June 1998, compared ideas and questions; the second, held in August 1999, discussed preliminary drafts of the books. Both of us read and commented on all the manuscripts; the manuscripts also received commentary from other authors in the project. We also hope that the network of scholars created for this project will continue to function, even if informally, and that the Web page created for this project will provide access for a wider audience to the ideas, research, and writing associated with it.

We are grateful to the Ford Foundation for its principal support of this project, and to Cristina Eguizábal for her advice and assistance throughout this endeavor. We are also grateful to the MacArthur Foundation for the support that made it possible to hold a second successful project conference in Mexico City. The Rockefeller Foundation provided the two of us with an opportunity to spend four splendid weeks in Bellagio, Italy, working on our various general responsibilities in this project. The Academic Department of International Studies at ITAM hosted the project throughout its duration and the two international conferences. We appreciate the support of the Asociación Mexicana de Cultura, ITAM's principal supporter in this work. Harvard University's Weatherhead Center for International Affairs also supported aspects of this project, as did Harvard University's David Rockefeller Center for Latin American Studies. We are particularly grateful to Hazel Blackmore and Juana Gómez at ITAM, and Amanda Pearson and Kathleen Hoover at the Weatherhead Center, for their work on many aspects of the project. At Routledge, Melissa Rosati encouraged us from the start; Eric Nelson supported the project through its conclusion.

Jorge I. Domínguez
Harvard University

Rafael Fernández de Castro
ITAM

INTRODUCTION

CHAPTER I

THE EARLY 1990S WERE A CRITICAL TURNING POINT IN THE relationship between the United States and Peru. Whereas from the 1960s to the 1980s the relationship between the governments of the two countries had been contentious, in the 1990s the relationship improved dramatically. Elected in 1990 and governing through November 2000, President Alberto Fujimori sought to cooperate with the U.S. government on most components of the bilateral agenda, including security threats, free-market reform, and narcotics control. For the most part, however, President Fujimori's government did not meet international standards for democracy and human rights, and on this component of the bilateral agenda the two governments clashed. Still, overall the bilateral relationship was more cooperative than it had been at any time since the 1950s.

The U.S. attitude toward the Fujimori government recalls the adage about U.S. policy toward Latin America that is widely attributed to President John F. Kennedy: "An embrace for the democrat, a handshake for the dictator." This adage highlights the long-standing U.S. preference for democratic government in Latin America, but also that nation's long-standing willingness to cooperate with nondemocratic governments on substantive issues.

At the same time, the application of a 1960s adage to U.S. policy toward Peru in the 1990s raises important questions. Was democracy not a greater priority— for the United States, international organizations, and Latin Americans themselves—in the 1990s than in the 1960s? Was U.S. cooperation with a president arguably best described as a *caudillo* (the Latin American "man on horseback" or strongman, either military or civilian, who usually enjoys popular support for a time) in the long-term, overarching interest of the U.S. or Peru as of the 1990s? Especially when President Fujimori's éminence grise was the increasingly blatantly depraved Vladimiro Montesinos (the de facto head of Peru's National Intelligence Service)?

The U.S. government continued to shake President Fujimori's hand until, from Japan, he faxed what he thought would be his resignation from the presidency in November 2000. This was the case despite the fact that the Organization of American States (OAS) and all other international and domestic election-observation groups judged that Peru's April–May 2000 elections did not meet international standards for freedom and fairness. However, after Montesinos was publicly implicated in the smuggling of guns from Peru to Colombia's guerrillas in August 2000, the U.S. government decided to withhold its handshake to him. The U.S. government did not expect that this decision would be an important catalyst in the downfall of Fujimori, but ultimately it was.

In private today, many U.S. officials concede that the Clinton administration extended its hand too enthusiastically for too long to the Fujimori government. In other words, they concede that, in the test of U.S. policy priorities posed by Peru in the late 1990s and 2000, they did not sufficiently prioritize democracy and human rights. Not surprisingly, this view is virtually unanimous among Peru's current government—led by President Alejandro Toledo—which was freely and fairly elected in 2001.

Accordingly, the underlying question of this book is: Why did the Clinton administration place a relatively low priority on democracy and human rights in Peru? In our conclusion to this book, we integrate material from previous chapters to try to reach some answers. Of course, to resolve the question definitively, more documents will have to be made publicly available.

A critical context for this explanation—and a good part of the explanation itself, however—is the extent to which the U.S. relationship with Peru improved under the Fujimori government. In Chapter II of this book, the tensions between the United States and Peru virtually throughout the Cold War are described. In the first section of most subsequent chapters, the acrimony between the U.S. and the government immediately preceding Fujimori's, the elected government of Alan García (1985–1990), is indicated. For the United States, the Fujimori government was a welcome change from Peru's historical pattern—and a change that U.S. officials were not particularly confident would be maintained by its successor. For its part, the Fujimori government appeared to play shrewdly on U.S. doubts about the maintenance of bilateral cooperation under any successor.

The bulk of Chapters IV, V, and VI of this book describes the cooperation that evolved between the U.S. and Fujimori governments on key components of the bilateral agenda: (1) national security, (2) free-market reform, and (3) narcotics control. We believe that the cooperation on security issues was most pivotal to the bilateral relationship and have accordingly placed it first. It was in the context of cooperation on security issues that there was the development of the relationships among U.S. and Peruvian actors—namely, among Central Intelligence Agency (CIA) agents and Vladimiro Montesinos—that appear to have been fundamental to the policies on narcotics control. It was the CIA that took the lead in downplaying issues of democracy and human rights at interagency meetings on U.S. policy toward Peru in the late 1990s and 2000 (see Chapter VII). Further, it was in the context of a scandal on security issues that the relationship between U.S. officials and Montesinos frayed, an estrangement that was one of the various catalysts of the Fujimori government's eventual demise.

Free-market reform was also very important, however, and is described in Chapter V. For most of the nineteenth and twentieth centuries, economic issues tended to top the bilateral agenda (see Chapter II). Also, economic issues were arguably at the top of President Clinton's own agenda; the influence of the Treasury Department increased markedly during the Clinton administration, and its highest officials were among Clinton's closest colleagues on international affairs (see Chapter III). Clearly, the Fujimori government's shift to the free market was a sine qua non for the improvement in the bilateral relationship.

Narcotics control, described in Chapter VI, was very important as well. Of course, narcotics control is an issue of great salience to the U.S. public. In the late 1990s and 2000, the issue engaged a wide spectrum of U.S. agencies in Peru, in particular the CIA and U.S. Southern Command (SOUTHCOM). Peru's apparent success in narcotics control was vital to these agencies' raison d'être. It seems possible that the U.S. and Peruvian military presence in the Amazonian areas of northeastern Peru was advantageous not only for narcotics control but also for counterinsurgency.

In short, the shift from bilateral acrimony to bilateral partnership was dramatic. Although no Peruvian government from the 1960s through the 1980s considered itself Communist or even socialist, leftist political currents flowed strongly in Peru during these decades. Socialist and nationalist attitudes were common not only among lower strata and the growing middle class but also— and unusually in Latin America—among military officers. Especially during the military government (1968–1980) and the government of Alan García, Peru rejected free-market principles: U.S. companies were nationalized, tariff barriers were raised, and international debt obligations were not serviced. At the same time, Peru purchased significant quantities of arms from the Soviet Union, and Peru's previous relationship with the U.S. military was disrupted. Peru was an active participant in the Movement of Non-Aligned Countries and other regional blocs that excluded the United States; Peru rarely voted with the United States in the United Nations.[1]

When the Cold War ended, leftist political currents ebbed in Peru. Of course, the end of the Cold War was interpreted as the victory of capitalism over socialism and of U.S.-style democracy over Communism. Peru would no longer enjoy moral or material support from the Soviet Union. Also, the leftist policies of the García government appeared to have led to disaster: Peruvians' living standards were plummeting and the Sendero Luminoso (Shining Path) insurgency was expanding relentlessly. Still, Peru's coalition of pro-Marxist parties, Izquierda Unida (United Left), was the strongest electoral left in South America during the mid- to late 1980s.

Peru's 1990 elections were held about six months after the fall of the Berlin Wall. Whereas until 1989 it had appeared that Izquierda Unida might win the 1990 presidential election, the coalition ruptured and secured less than 10 percent of the first-round presidential tally. The presidency was won by Alberto Fujimori, whose nonideological platform "Work, Honesty, Technology" was appropriate to the nascent post-Cold War era. Also, Fujimori's Japanese heritage was an asset for the candidate; in an era of globalization, Peruvians were aware of Japan's economic progress and respected it, and hoped for support from that country. A plurality of seats in the legislature was won by the coalition of parties called the Frente Democrático (FREDEMO, Democratic Front), led by the staunchly pro-free-market and pro-U.S. novelist Mario Vargas Llosa.

At the time of Peru's 1990 elections, the bilateral U.S.-Peruvian agenda was full—fuller than what might have been expected for a medium-sized country on the west coast of South America. The García government had sought to lead a regional challenge against the debt-service and free-market policies of the international financial community; a shift in Peru's economic policies was an important U.S. priority. Security issues were high on the bilateral agenda as well: In the late 1980s and early 1990s, the Shining Path posed a more serious threat than any other Latin American insurgency at the time, and in 1995, Peru and Ecuador went to war. Also, from the mid-1980s to the mid-1990s, Peru produced more coca for export to the United States than any other Latin American nation, and as a result was a priority theater in the U.S. war against drugs.

With such a full agenda, the U.S. government of course hoped that—despite Fujimori's center-left political platform during the 1990 campaign—his new government would shift toward cooperation, and it quickly did. Before his inauguration, Fujimori traveled to Washington, D.C. and to Tokyo and listened carefully to officials' advocacy of debt service and free-market reforms; the new president began to implement these reforms less than two weeks after his inauguration. Within its first year, the Fujimori government also increased collaboration with the United States on problems of internal security (such as the expanding Shining Path insurgency). The development of cooperation on narcotics control was slower, proceeding in fits and starts, but was firm by 1995.

The shift toward cooperation is evident in three sets of indicators. The first set is UN voting patterns. Whereas during 1986–1989, only about 15 percent of Peru's votes in the United Nations coincided with U.S. votes, during 1995–1998 the figure was roughly 40 percent (about the Latin American average).[2]

A second set of indicators is changes in international air travel to Peru. These changes were both quantitative and qualitative and highlight broad trends in

Peru's international relations. First, travel increased dramatically: The number of air passengers between the United States and Peru soared. The tally in 1998 was more than quadruple the figures of the mid-1970s.[3]

Second, the national bases of key carriers changed considerably. In the 1960s and most of the 1970s, U.S. carriers (in particular Braniff) and the German airline Lufthansa dominated travel to Peru. Then, in the late 1970s, the Peruvian government established the state carrier AeroPerú. As AeroPerú sought to extend its flights in the United States, air-travel disputes erupted between the Peruvian and U.S. governments. Astoundingly, for more than a year during 1984–1985 direct flights between Peru and the U.S. were suspended; passengers had to change planes in Jamaica or elsewhere. The relatively strong relationship between Peru and Communist nations was also evident at the Lima airport: While Eastern Airlines (which had replaced Braniff) was at one end of the airport, the Soviet carrier Aeroflot was at the other. The Cuban airline also maintained regular flights to Peru.

In the 1990s, the variety among international and Peruvian carriers declined considerably as U.S. airlines came to dominate the market. In 1990, Eastern Airlines collapsed, and its Miami gates and Latin American routes were acquired by American Airlines, which expanded aggressively in Peru.[4] One of the reasons was a personal relationship between American's chief executive Robert L. Crandall and President Fujimori; in 1997, Crandall presented a helicopter to Fujimori, and a few months later the Peruvian government gave American a coveted new route.[5] In 1998, AeroPerú and the private Peruvian airline Faucett, which had also enjoyed routes to Miami, were in dire financial straits; both airlines closed. For considerable time spans between 1998 and 2001, no Peruvian airline maintained flights to the United States.

A third set of indicators is U.S. aid to Peru. As Table I.1 indicates, the percentage of U.S. aid to Latin America and the Caribbean allocated to Peru jumped from an average of 5 percent during 1962–1979 and 4 percent during 1985–1989 to 17 percent in 1994–1999. Even during the controversy of Peru's 2000 elections, no U.S. aid was suspended. In real dollars (1982 = $1.00), U.S. aid increased from roughly $67 million annually in 1985–1989 to about $106 million annually in 1994–1998, an exceptional trend for the region.[6] Whereas previously U.S. aid to Peru had been a small percentage of its total aid to Latin America and the Caribbean, for the period 1993–1997 Peru was the recipient of more U.S. aid than any other Latin American or Caribbean country.[7] After the election of President Andrés Pastrana in Colombia in 1998 and the development of Plan Colombia, U.S. aid through the U.S. Defense Department increased dramatically to Colombia, however, and Colombia surpassed Peru as a recipient of U.S. aid.[8]

One caveat is necessary here. After the mid-1990s, it became more difficult to calculate U.S. aid allocations to Latin America. Whereas in previous decades U.S. military aid to the region was generally reported by the U.S. Agency for Inter-

TABLE I.1

U.S. AID TO PERU, 1962–1999*
As reported by the U.S. Agency for International Development

	Current Dollars (in millions)	As a Percentage of Total U.S. Aid to Latin America and the Caribbean
Annual Averages		
1962–1979	38	5
1980	57	11
1981–1984	104	9
1985–1989	75	4
1990–1993	147	13
1994–1999	147	17
Annual Allocations		
1990	93	4
1991	199	14
1992	123	8
1993	171	12
1994	156	16
1995	132	18
1996	104	15
1997	127	17
1998	168	18
1999	197	15

Sources: U.S. Agency for International Development, *U.S. Overseas Loans and Grants and Assistance from International Organizations, July 1, 1945-September 30, 1999* (Washington, D.C.), as well as previous editions, and U.S. Agency for International Development, *U.S. Overseas Loans and Grants: Series of Yearly Data, FY 1946-FY 1985, Vol. II Latin America and the Caribbean* (Washington, D.C.).

*Does not include counternarcotics assistance allocated through the U.S. Department of Defense's "Section 1004" or "Section 1033" accounts. The amount of this assistance surpassed $20 million annually in 1998; also, after the election of Andrés Pastrana in Colombia, larger sums were allocated through the U.S. Department of Defense for *Plan Colombia*. See Adam Isacson and Joy Olson, *Just the Facts: A Civilian's Guide to U.S. Defense and Security Assistance to Latin America and the Caribbean* (Washington, D.C.: Latin American Working Group, 1999), 102–105.

national Development (U.S. AID), by the mid-1990s it was not. Narcotics assistance was classified as "economic" assistance by U.S. AID; increasingly, however, narcotics-control assistance was provided to Latin American security forces under the auspices of the U.S. Department of Defense. Beginning with fiscal year 1996, U.S. military and police assistance to the region has been researched and reported by the Latin America Working Group. However, figures from different U.S. agencies are often inconsistent; indeed, there are major discrepancies in the figures provided by U.S. AID in its hardcover report and on its Web site.[9]

Table I.2 indicates the types of aid that the United States provided to Peru between 1981 and 1999. The table indicates that, especially during the 1980s and early

TABLE I.2

U.S. AID TO PERU BY CATEGORIES, 1981–1999*
Millions of Current Dollars

Year	Total Allocated Via U.S. AID	Economic	Military (Via U.S. AID)	Narcotics	Total Allocated Via the U.S. Dept. of Defense (Available only after 1995)
1999	197	121	0.5	75	26
1998	168	136	0.5	32	19
1997	127	100	0.5	26	27
1996	104	87	0.4	16	0
1995	132	117	0.3	15	
1994	156	148	0	8	
1993	171	153	0	18	
1992	123	111	0	13	
1991	199	155	25	19	
1990	95	83	2	10	
1989	68	54	3	11	
1988	71	63	0	8	
1987	64	55	0	8	
1986	59	55	1	4	
1985	88	77	9	2	
1984	175	161	11	3	
1983	98	91	5	2	
1982	59	52	5	2	
1981	84	77	4	3	

*The figures for the first four columns of the table is the U.S. Agency for International Development, *U.S. Overseas Loans and Grants and Assistance from International Organizations* (Washington, D.C.: U.S. Aid, annual editions through 1999). These figures are higher than those reported for recent years at the U.S. AID Web site (www.usaid.gov). The source for the figures in the final column of the table is Adam Isacson and Joy Olson, *Just the Facts: A Civilian's Guide to U.S. Defense and Security Assistance to Latin America and the Caribbean* (Washington, D.C.: Latin America Working Group, 1998 and 1999), 102–105. Figures may not add up due to rounding.

1990s, as much as 80 percent of U.S. aid was economic; a considerable amount of the economic aid was through the "Food for Peace" program, and some was also for structural adjustment programs. By the late 1990s, however, as much as 40 percent of U.S. aid was for narcotics control to the Peruvian military and police, provided through the U.S. Department of Defense, as stipulated in Sections 1033 and 1004 of the National Defense Authorization Act.[10] U.S. aid for democracy initiatives was about $3 million per year between the late 1980s and the late 1990s; this aid was not provided its own category in U.S. Department of State data.[11]

Although the figures on U.S. aid to Peru clearly demonstrate the overall favor in which U.S. officials held the Fujimori government and overall U.S. support for bilateral programs, it would be seriously incorrect to label the bilateral relationship entirely cooperative. As indicated above, the U.S. and the Fujimori governments shook hands, but they did not embrace. Chapter VII indicates that, although U.S. officials did not prioritize democracy and human rights in Peru as in retrospect they wish they had, many U.S. officials—in particular, numerous U.S. State Department officials—sought a higher priority for these concerns and raised them with Fujimori government officials. Conflict was especially tense twice: first in 1992, when President Fujimori executed the *autogolpe* (self-coup, which suspended the constitution and disbanded the congress), and then in 2000, when the election that would enable his third consecutive term was judged neither free nor fair by international observers. Ultimately, at both intervals, the U.S. government decided that it should not risk the demise of its new cooperation with Peru on security issues, free-market reform, and narcotics control to maintain high democratic standards in the hemisphere; but this decision was made amid bureaucratic conflict and uncertainty.

As mentioned above, in the conclusion to the book, we will offer reflections about the pattern of the U.S.-Peruvian relationship during the 1990s—the overall maintenance of bilateral cooperation despite the tensions on issues of democracy and human rights. The Postscript considers the prospects for U.S.-Peruvian cooperation under the newly elected government of Alejandro Toledo (2001–).

CHAPTER II

U.S.-PERUVIAN RELATIONS PRIOR TO 1990

THE UNITED STATES HAS BEEN AN IMPORTANT INTERNATIONAL actor in Peru since the country's independence in 1821, and the preponderant international actor since the end of World War I. In general, the relationship between the two nations was cooperative—until the Cold War period.

Overall, the primary U.S. interest in Peru was economic: U.S. companies sought to develop Peru's considerable petroleum and mineral resources. For the most part, until the 1960s the development of these resources was welcomed in Peru. It should be noted that, although traditionally agriculture was the major source of employment in Peru, during most of the decades since Peru's independence petroleum and minerals—silver, copper, lead, and zinc—were its primary exports, and U.S. companies were often the best positioned to exploit these resources.[1]

A second important interest for both the United States and Peru was the resolution of geopolitical tensions among Peru and its neighbors. These tensions were primarily the results of disputes over national boundaries, which were not clearly demarcated under Spanish rule and became contentious after independence. During and after the 1879–1883 War of the Pacific that pitted Peru and Bolivia against Chile, Peru sought U.S. support for its position; a measure of diplomatic support was forthcoming, especially during the 1920s when Peru's government was staunchly pro-American. Also, after Peru's 1941 defeat of Ecuador amid the two countries' border dispute, Peru achieved the support of the United States and other international mediators for its ownership of most of the contested region. While Peru's concern was its territorial integrity and its national security, the U.S. objective was stability and peace among its southern neighbors.

The overall pattern of cooperation on economic and geopolitical concerns did not extend to the issue of democracy promotion. In general, U.S. interest in democracy promotion in Peru was minimal. U.S.-Peruvian relations were most cooperative under authoritarian Peruvian governments, in particular Augusto

Leguía (1919–1930) and General Manuel Odría (1948–1956)—who were more supportive of the U.S. agenda than most democratically elected presidents. At times, U.S. disinterest in democracy provoked considerable popular backlash in Peru.

During the Cold War, the pattern of cooperation ended. After the Cuban revolution in particular, nationalist and leftist political currents flowed in Peru, and the relationship between Peru and the United States was tense. To the dismay of the United States, from approximately the early 1960s through the end of the 1980s, under both civilian and military leaders, the Peruvian government challenged the U.S. on key economic issues. Also, Peru purchased more weapons from the Soviet Union, and its military established greater technical cooperation with the Soviet Union than was the case with any Latin American nation save Cuba. Further, in most Peruvians' views, the United States was disinterested in the advancement of democracy in Peru. The U.S. government did not support several Peruvian presidents who were democratically elected but advanced nationalist economic policies—José Luis Bustamante (1945–1948), Fernando Belaúnde (1963–1968), and Alan García (1985–1990). Peruvians were especially dismayed by the U.S. focus on the fate of U.S. companies, not the fate of democracy, during the 1963–1968 Belaúnde government—a government that had been widely expected to be a Latin American model for the Alliance for Progress.

However, in contrast to the relationship between the United States and various Latin American nations during the Cold War, the relationship between the U.S. and Peru was not significantly affected by U.S. reaction (or overreaction) to the expansion of a Marxist revolutionary movement. Such a movement did expand in Peru, but only in the late 1980s, as the Cold War was ending.

FROM INDEPENDENCE TO WORLD WAR I: THE UNITED STATES AS A SECONDARY INTERNATIONAL POWER IN PERU

The trajectory of international power relations in Peru between the country's independence and World War I was similar to that in the region as a whole. Great Britain was the most important international power in Peru for the first ninety-odd years after independence; its predominance ended amid World War I. Two other European nations—France and Germany—were also significant international powers in Peru at this time. However, by most criteria the United States was the second most important nation in Peru after Great Britain, and its influence was on the ascendance during these ninety-odd years. For the most part during this period, Peru's elites perceived these foreigners' roles positively, believing that the development of the country's natural resources was critical to its future and that large-scale foreign investment was necessary to this development.[2] Many perceived North Americans especially positively, as frontiersmen who were overcoming geographic challenges in their own country and could do so in Peru as well.

Of course, Peru's declaration of independence in 1821 opened new opportunities for contacts between Peru and the United States. By far the most visible interactions between North Americans and Peruvians were economic. First, during the decade-plus of the war for independence, U.S. traders—typically sailors searching for sperm whales in the Pacific—sold muskets, textiles, and flour and other foodstuffs in exchange for Peru's silver and gold. Then, after a period of negotiation over debts incurred by Peru during the war, U.S.-Peru trade soared at midcentury with the exploitation of Peru's guano, an excellent fertilizer. Simultaneously, the U.S. sought to open the Amazon River and its tributaries to international navigation, a step opposed by the Peruvians and Brazilians.

Although economic issues were at the top of the bilateral agenda during these ninety-odd years, U.S. and Peruvian leaders expressed some common ideals. Of course, in 1823 President James Monroe declared the closing of the Western Hemisphere to further European colonization and argued that the Western Hemisphere was a region distinct from Europe in which Europe should not interfere. Although most Americans were skeptical about the prospects for democracy in predominantly nonwhite, illiterate, Catholic countries such as Peru, they did hope for new partnerships based on the Western Hemisphere concept.[3] For their part, pro-democratic groups in Peru looked to the United States as a model for republican and federal government.[4] Moreover, as the U.S. industrialized, Peruvian economic elites were increasingly impressed and hoped that Peruvians could emulate the competitive, adventuresome spirit of the North Americans.[5]

In the 1860s and 1870s, two American entrepreneurs initiated major investments in Peru, and for the most part their capital and know-how were welcomed by Peruvians.[6] William Russell Grace established a successful business selling provisions to the guano fleets, and then expanded into his own shipping line as well as sugar haciendas. Henry Meiggs promised an ambitious railroad network that would open up Peru's mineral-rich mountainous interior; however, Peru's guano reserves were rapidly becoming exhausted, and Meiggs's plans foundered as Peru defaulted on its foreign-debt service in 1876.

While North Americans' concerns were primarily economic, Peruvians' hopes were also on the diplomatic and even military role that the United States might play in Peru's various border conflicts. When most of Latin America had been under Spanish rule, there had been no need to demarcate borders precisely; after independence, disputes multiplied. In particular, Peru sought U.S. support during the War of the Pacific (1879–1883), which pit Chile against Peru and Bolivia for control over the guano- and nitrate-rich Atacama Desert region shared by the three countries. While the British for the most part supported Chile in the war, the Garfield administration in the U.S., encouraged by U.S. investors such as William R. Grace and led by Secretary of State James G. Blaine, supported Peru. However, the U.S. government was willing to provide rhetorical and diplomatic support only—not the military support that many Peruvians wanted.[7]

Peru suffered a devastating loss to Chile. In the Treaty of Ancón ending the war, Peru ceded its southern province of Tarapacá in the Atacama Desert to Chile and agreed to Chilean occupation of two smaller provinces just north of Tarapacá, Arica and Tacna, on the condition that a plebiscite be held after ten years to determine ultimate sovereignty in these two territories. Despite the failure of the United States to help Peru achieve a more favorable outcome—indeed, many analysts, Peruvian and otherwise, believed that the U.S.'s inconsistent messages and actions hurt Peru's effort—Peru continued to look upon the U.S. as the principal foreign power likely to lobby on its behalf against Chile and its British supporters.[8] Several Peruvian presidents sought to negotiate the lease of Peru's northern port Chimbote to the U.S. in return for U.S. diplomatic support in Peru's border conflicts; after the Panama Canal site had been established, though, the U.S. was not interested.

For Peru, the economic consequences of the War of the Pacific were catastrophic. Not only had it lost most of its guano and nitrate reserves to Chile, but it was also deeply indebted. Peru's creditors, predominantly Englishmen, would not make new loans to Peru without major concessions from the country—but without new loans, Peru fell farther behind on its debt service.

Into this impasse stepped Michael P. Grace, brother of U.S. entrepreneur William R. Grace. Michael Grace, hoping himself to manage the repair and extension of Peru's railroads, negotiated intensively with both bondholders based in London and the Andres Avelino Cáceres government in Lima. Finally, in 1888, the agreement that became known as the Grace Contract was signed: Peru was relieved of responsibility for its foreign debts, but in return Peru's bondholders gained 769 miles of state railways for sixty-six years plus guano export rights and other concessions. The agreement enabled the Cáceres government to begin Peru's reconstruction, but the conditions were harsh and widely criticized in Peru.

Although the Grace Contract opened the way for a dramatic increase in British capital in Peru, this increase did not happen. The British were primarily interested in Peru's silver, and the world silver price began to fall in the 1890s at the same time that the Peruvian government appeared more unstable. By far the most important event eroding British influence in Peru (and Latin America in general), however, was World War I (1914–1918). First, as a result of security risks from hostile submarines and raiders, high freight rates, and a shortage of commercial ships, British trade with Peru was seriously disrupted. Second, the war was costly to the British, and in general weakened its economy.

At the same time that World War I weakened the British global position, it strengthened that of the United States, whose intervention allowed the Allied victory. The increase in U.S. economic influence was also greatly facilitated by the opening of the Panama Canal in 1914 and the concomitant establishment of new steamship lines between New York and South American ports. In 1916, the U.S.

had an overwhelming 60 percent share of Peruvian exports and imports.[9] The stage was set for U.S. surpassing of Great Britain as the preponderant international power in Peru.

FROM 1919 TO THE ONSET OF THE COLD WAR:
THE ESTABLISHMENT OF U.S. PREPONDERANCE

After approximately 1919, the United States became the most important international actor in Peru, as it did in most of Latin America. Amid this context of higher status and importance, the U.S. encountered sharper criticisms from Peruvians than in the past. In particular, the 1919–1930 pro-American government of Augusto B. Leguía was to provoke a nationalistic backlash. Indeed, the alternation of pro-American and nationalistic currents in Peru was to characterize Peruvian politics to the end of the twentieth century.

World War I and the Panama Canal were not the only factors in the U.S. eclipse of Great Britain as the leading international power in Peru. Also important was presidential leadership. U.S. president Woodrow Wilson (1913–1921) upheld high global ideals for peace and democracy, and these ideals were attractive to Peruvians.[10] Peruvians hoped that a U.S. administration committed to the self-determination of peoples would provide diplomatic support for Peru in its negotiations with Chile about the future of the Tacna and Arica provinces. One of the main avenues of Lima was renamed Avenida Wilson in honor of the U.S. president.

In Peru, the president during much of the first quarter of the twentieth century was Augusto Leguía, the most fervently pro-American leader in the country's history. Leguía was fluent in English as a result his education at an English school in Chile; one of his first positions was general manager for the New York Life Insurance Company of Peru, Ecuador, and Bolivia. After appointments to high-level financial positions in government, he was elected president in 1908. Among Leguía's various initiatives to associate Peru and the United States was a proposal for the U.S. acquisition of Chimbote, which—as mentioned above—did not interest the U.S. because of the development of the Panama Canal.

After Leguía was succeeded by Guillermo E. Billinghurst in 1912, friction emerged between the ex-president and the incumbent, and ultimately Leguía was exiled. While in the United States on his trip to and back from London, Leguía met with key figures in the U.S. business and diplomatic communities, and their favorable impression of the man was important to U.S. recognition of Leguía's second government when, despite his apparent election in 1919, he seized presidential power by force prior to his inauguration. Leguía's actions seemed prompted primarily by his disinclination to govern against a congress dominated by the opposition. Although Leguía sought to maintain a democratic facade to his government, it was considered a dictatorship by the vast majority of Peruvians.

Leguía's second government (1919–1930) was pro-American in numerous respects. The president appointed a large number of North Americans to high positions in key ministries. He proclaimed July 4 a public holiday partially in honor of the birthday of the United States. Also, Peru was the only Latin American nation to declare approval of the U.S. Marines' occupation of Nicaragua.

Leguía warmly welcomed U.S. capital. Numerous large U.S.-based corporations either began or expanded their operations in Peru. The biggest was Cerro de Pasco, the largest copper-mining enterprise in South America at the time and possibly the largest in the world.[11] Located in Peru's central highlands, in 1922 the company opened a new smelter at La Oroya, with double the capacity of its biggest first one. In a deal that became extremely controversial in the 1960s (see below), the International Petroleum Company (IPC), a subsidiary of Standard Oil of New Jersey, purchased the oil fields at La Brea and Pariñas in 1924. Between 1919 and 1929, IPC's production of petroleum products multiplied five times; the company's refinery at Talara was the largest on the west coast of South America.[12] The Grace Company, whose steamship and shipping business had grown dramatically during World War I, expanded its textile operations, owning more than 50 percent of the Peruvian textile sector in the late 1920s.[13] In sum, whereas U.S. direct investment in Peru was only about $6 million in 1900, by the end of the 1920s it had increased more than thirty times, to $200 million, surpassing considerably the British investment figure of $125 million in 1925.[14]

As U.S. businesses expanded in Peru, coming to dominate or even monopolize their respective sectors, they were resented by more Peruvians. The primary problem was that these companies (Cerro de Pasco and IPC in particular) were enclave enterprises, extracting nonrenewable resources from their host countries without concern for the impact of their operations on the people around them, as well as sending their profits abroad. The U.S. companies sought to maintain their privileges via the provision of moneys or other resources desired by Peruvian authorities. Moreover, most U.S. managers were contemptuous not only of Peru's indigenous peoples, but also of Peruvians in general; at IPC on Peru's north coast in the 1920s and 1930s, dining rooms for Peruvians and Americans were separate, and a visiting Colombian leader commented after a tour that "It's a wonderful, progressive place, but I didn't meet any Peruvians."[15]

Leguía welcomed not only U.S. investment capital but also U.S. loans, and domestic criticism of the government's borrowing policy was similarly intense by the end of the decade. Between 1920 and 1929, the Leguía government borrowed more than $100 million from U.S. private firms and banks.[16] At first, the loans were used primarily for an ambitious set of infrastructure, school, and irrigation projects that was enthusiastically greeted by Peruvians, but large loans in 1927 and 1928 were for debt service on the previous loans. These loans were criticized in Peru because of high profits for U.S. creditors, concessions by Leguía to foreign companies to secure the loans, and exorbitant commissions for Peruvian negotiators (including almost $500,000 to President Leguía's son).

A policy priority for Leguía was the resolution of Peru's various border disputes. Leguía hoped that his friendship with the United States would prompt U.S. support for Peru in these negotiations, and that the result might be the return of both Tacna and Arica to Peru.[17] The plebiscite that had been posited for Arica and Tacna within ten years of the signing of the Treaty of Ancón in 1883 had not been held. The Leguía government said that the people of Tacna and Arica had been subject to intense Chilean propaganda and intimidation, and accordingly a plebiscite could not be fair; U.S.-led arbitration was the viable approach to a resolution of the conflict. The Chilean government argued to the contrary that a plebiscite was viable. Successive U.S. administrations became deeply engaged in the negotiations and gradually came to support the Peruvian position. With U.S. mediation, the Tacna and Arica Treaty and Additional Protocol, signed in June 1929, divided the two disputed provinces: Peru gained Tacna and Chile held Arica. Although this compromise appeared to most experts to be as favorable as Peru could expect, many Peruvians had hoped for more concessions; to mollify these criticisms, Leguía exaggerated the U.S. role in the development of the accord. Not suprisingly, Leguía's tactic increased anti-Americanism among Peruvians. This was especially the case given that the 1922 Salomón-Lozano Treaty between the Leguía government and Colombia had favored Colombia (in particular, sacrificing some sixty miles of Amazon jungle, including the small port of Leticia) and had indeed been the result of U.S. pressure.[18]

In August 1930, Leguía's authoritarian regime was overthrown. Not only was popular discontent over the border treaties considerable, but the free-market economic model was shattering. The U.S. stock market had crashed in 1929, and the global depression had hit. For Peru, as for most of Latin America, the depression signified the collapse of the prices of key exports, a crisis in the balance of payments, and ultimately default on the large foreign debt accumulated in the 1920s.

Because the upshot of Leguía's cooperation with the United States was widely perceived to have been catastrophic, Peruvians' attitudes toward the U.S. became cooler. In the 1931 election campaign, there were two leading candidates: Luis Sánchez Cerro, a mestizo army commander who had led the overthrow of Leguía, and Víctor Raúl Haya de la Torre, the founder of the political party American Popular Revolutionary Alliance (APRA). Both Sánchez Cerro and Haya de la Torre articulated nationalistic views on foreign policy issues. However, Haya de la Torre, who was arguably the most significant and most controversial political actor of the twentieth century in Peru, and APRA, which was arguably Peru's only political party to achieve institutionalization during the century, were more militant, expressing a clear doctrine of anti-imperialism as well as social reform. The 1931 election was won by Sánchez Cerro (although this result was disputed by APRA).

Sánchez Cerro soon confronted serious external economic and geopolitical challenges. At the forefront of the U.S.-Peru bilateral economic agenda was Peru's default on its foreign debt. In 1931 Dr. Edwin Walter Kemmerer, the U.S. economist widely dubbed "the money doctor," traveled to Peru and provided a variety of recommendations to the government that were designed to restore Peru's standing in international credit circles and its capacity to service its debt. However, international banking institutions did not offer Peru new loans—nor did Peru pay its arrears on the previous ones. Indeed, Peru remained in default until 1946.

In 1932, to Sánchez Cerro's surprise, Peruvian agitators seized Leticia, the Amazonian town that had been ceded to Colombia according to the treaty of the previous decade. Strongly supported by Peruvian public opinion, the agitators occupied the town. The U.S. government opposed the Peruvian occupation, emphasizing that the use of force in these circumstances was a bad precedent that could provoke global chaos. Soon, in 1933, the Colombian military recaptured several outposts and prepared to recapture Leticia; then the League of Nations began to mediate. About a year later, a final settlement was reached that restored Colombia's sovereignty over the area but authorized greater rights for Peru in navigation, customs, and the like. Although Peru had suffered a diplomatic defeat, it had avoided war, and the agreement was welcomed by the large majority of Peruvians.

In 1933, Sánchez Cerro was assassinated by a member of the APRA party; the commander in chief of the armed forces, General Oscar Benavides, was named his successor by the Peruvian congress. Benavides had served in various military and diplomatic posts in Europe, and he was friendly toward Italy in particular. In part as a result of Benavides's interest in cooperation with Italy, his government was cool toward the United States. This was the case despite the 1933 inauguration of President Franklin D. Roosevelt and his launching of the "New Deal" at home and the "Good Neighbor" policy for Latin America. Whereas most Latin American nations' trade with both the U.S. and Great Britain increased considerably between 1930 and 1940, Peru's did not.[19] Even several years after the end of Benavides's administration, the amount of U.S. capital in Peru was only half the 1929 figure.[20] The United States was aloof from Peru's border-dispute negotiations, encouraging the League of Nations to play the mediation role.

As the fears of another European war intensified during the late 1930s, the U.S. government was worried about Benavides's international stance. In 1939, however, new elections were held, and the winner was Manuel Prado, a leader who was supportive of the Allies in general and the United States in particular. When the U.S. entered World War II in 1941, Prado broke diplomatic relations with the Axis powers and cooperated militarily, politically, and economically with Washington. Peru also participated enthusiastically in the U.S. program for the deportation of Japanese Latin Americans to internment camps in the United States.

World War II was an era of strong U.S.-Peruvian partnership for various reasons. Most fundamentally, Peruvians favored the democratic ideals of the Allies and rejected fascism. Haya de la Torre and the APRA party as well as Peru's nascent Communist groups, following Moscow's direction, collaborated with the Prado government. Also, as the U.S. economy expanded in wartime, U.S. demand for Peruvian exports increased, and the Peruvian economy rebounded. Very important too, in 1941 the Peruvian military defeated Ecuador in a dispute at the Amazonian border, and Peru's ownership over most of the contested region was affirmed at subsequent peace negotiations in Rio de Janeiro in 1942. Peruvians were pleased by the role played by the international mediators to the conflict, including the United States as well as Argentina, Brazil, and Chile. Finally, under the leadership of Nelson Rockefeller, the U.S. promoted public health and cultural exchange programs.

At the end of World War II, U.S. influence was at an apex in Peru (as in most Latin American nations). U.S. power was confirmed by the signing of the Inter-American Treaty of Reciprocal Assistance for mutual defense in 1947 and by the founding of the Organization of American States (OAS) in 1948. For the first time, U.S. power in Peru extended from the political, economic, and cultural dimensions to the military; whereas previously the Peruvian military had looked largely to France for military training and equipment, it now turned to the United States.[21]

In July 1945, new elections were held in Peru, and hopes were high for a positive, democratic outcome and a continued U.S.-Peruvian partnership. The stage appeared to be set: Haya de la Torre maintained the moderate, pro-American position to which he had shifted during the war, and APRA was incorporated into a new political alliance, the Frente Democrático Nacional (FDN). The tiny Communist party also supported the FDN. The FDN's presidential candidate was a distinguished legal scholar and diplomat, José Luis Bustamante y Rivero. In a relatively open and fair contest, APRA achieved a plurality in both houses of congress and Bustamante won the presidency. The electoral result pleased the U.S. government, which had encouraged the Prado administration to accommodate Haya de la Torre and APRA.

The Cold War: An Escalation of Tensions

The high hopes for democracy, reform, and bilateral cooperation at the end of World War II were dashed amid the onset of the Cold War. The dynamic within Peru was similar to that in much of the region. As Peruvians became better educated and more aware of the inequalities in their country, and as Marxist alternatives grew to appear viable, more Peruvians were attracted to leftist causes. In particular, Peruvians became more skeptical about U.S. companies' role in Peru. Fighting the Cold War, in which of course the rival superpower was Communist, the U.S. government overreacted to leftist movements and nationalist trends. In turn, the U.S. overreaction provoked more leftist and nationalist attitudes in Peru, as in other Latin American nations.

1945–1963: Peru's High Expectations—Unmet by the United States

Inaugurated in 1945, the Bustamante government survived only a little more than three years. With strong support from the APRA party in the legislature, the Bustamante government adopted new economic policies that favored labor: Tariffs were raised, import and exchange controls introduced, workers' wages and benefits were increased, and public-works projects were expanded. While these policies were not sufficiently radical to satisfy the militant wing of the APRA party, they outraged Peru's oligarchical families. Politically inexperienced, Bustamante was unable to negotiate effectively with either APRA or the oligarchy. After APRA militants assassinated the editor of an oligarchical family's major newspaper, Bustamante sought to marginalize APRA, but his attempt was considered irresolute by the oligarchy. Amid political polarization and economic deterioration and with strong oligarchical support, General Manuel Odría (a hero of Peru's 1941 war with Ecuador) led a successful coup in October 1948.

The Bustamante government had hoped to secure economic and diplomatic support from the Truman administration (1945–1953).[22] The Bustamante government had sought to please the United States with agreements for Peru's service of its long-standing debt and for the IPC's exploration for oil in Sechura in northern Peru. The Bustamante government hoped that it would be rewarded with some $30 million in U.S. loans. However, primarily due to criticisms of these agreements by Peru's oligarchical families—criticisms that were opportunistic, made in the apparent hope that the Bustamante government would fall—these agreements were not implemented, and U.S. loans were not forthcoming. It did not help Bustamante's case with the Truman administration that, together with Chile and Ecuador, Peru rejected the U.S. position that a nation had jurisdiction to only twelve miles of the waters off its coast, arguing instead for jurisdiction to two hundred miles.

Why did the Truman administration fail to support the Bustamante government?[23] Whereas Franklin D. Roosevelt had considered U.S. cooperation with Latin America vital for success in World War II and was not adverse to changes in U.S. policies to achieve the goal of cooperation, the Truman administration's approach was more traditional. The Truman administration was not committed to the promotion of democracy in Latin America or to the provision of U.S. aid for the region. Also, the Truman administration's focus was on Europe, where the "Iron Curtain" was falling, and on China, where the Communist party was winning power.

The Odría government (1948–1956) forged a highly cooperative relationship with the United States. A staunch anti-Communist who had trained at U.S. army schools, Odría was awarded the highest U.S. honor for foreign personages, a Legion of Merit, by President Eisenhower (1953–1961).

Cooperation was evident in the military sphere. Under a Military Assistance Program (MAP) signed in 1952, U.S. military aid to Peru increased from $100,000 in 1952 to $9.1 million in 1956.[24] The number of Peruvian officers training at U.S. bases also jumped: between 1949 and 1964, more than eight hundred Peruvian officers trained at the U.S. Army's School of the Americas in the Panama Canal Zone or at its Special Warfare Center and School at Fort Bragg, North Carolina.[25]

Odría's economic policies were warmly welcomed in U.S. government and business circles. Odría ended the import-substitution industrialization policies of his predecessor and reestablished orthodox liberal economic policies. For the first time since 1930, Peru resumed service of its foreign debt, enabling it to secure international loans. Odría issued new legal codes for the mining and petroleum sectors that were designed to promote investment. In particular, taxes were greatly reduced.

Fortuitously for Odría, these new policies were almost simultaneous with the outbreak of the Korean War in 1950. Not only was international demand for Peru's traditional agricultural exports strong, but international interest in Peru's metals increased dramatically. Three U.S.-based companies—Cerro de Pasco Corporation, Southern Peru Copper Corporation (SPCC), and Marcona Mining—expanded their mining operations in Peru. Overall, the value of U.S. investment in Peru jumped from $145 million in 1950 to $304 million in 1955.[26] In the context of this export and investment boom, the Odría government enjoyed considerable resources for public works as well as for services in the squatter settlements that were emerging on the outskirts of Lima.

The cooperation between the Odría government and the Eisenhower administration was not qualified by U.S. criticism of the Odría government's authoritarianism. The key tenet of the Eisenhower administration's policy toward Latin America was anti-Communism; it did not matter if Peru's Odría, Cuba's Fulgencio Batista, Venezuela's Marcos Pérez Jiménez, Paraguay's Alfredo Stroessner, or other Latin American dictators were ruthless and corrupt.[27] It did matter, however, to Peruvians. Many Peruvians were dismayed by Odría's authoritarianism when he took office; at that time, Odría banned APRA and the Communist party and held some four thousand political prisoners.[28] In "elections" in 1950, not even a retired general was allowed to compete. When the Korean War ended in 1953 and Peru's export boom did as well, dismay mounted. Increasingly, Odría appeared not only authoritarian but also incompetent and decadent; Peru's oligarchy and military withdrew their support of the government.

Ultimately, Odría had little choice but to hold the elections that were scheduled for 1956. These elections were won by former president Manuel Prado, in good part because he secured the support of the APRA party (which had been illegal for the duration of Odría's term). Like his first administration, Prado's second was considered democratic by the standards of the era; he restored political freedoms, including the legalization of APRA, and even worked with APRA on various key issues. However, Prado's roots were in Peru's oligarchy, and economic and social policies were for the most part orthodox.

During the first years of the Prado government, it became evident that nationalist and leftist tides were swelling in Peru. There were various reasons. First, in general, the Odría model of authoritarian politics, free-market economics, and pro-Americanism—a combination that had not characterized any Peruvian government since Leguía—had provoked a backlash. This backlash was intensified by the awareness of Fidel Castro's challenge to a similar political model in Cuba under Batista. Second, because of both Odría's economic mismanagement and a recession in the United States, Peru's economy was in crisis. In this context, there were more intense demands for U.S. recognition of two hundred miles of fishing rights and also for changes in the status of the U.S. company IPC (see below). Third, the U.S. recession led the Eisenhower administration to consider tariffs and quotas damaging lead, zinc, and sugar enterprises in Peru. The dramatic shift in political attitudes was evident in militant student protests at the University of San Marcos against Vice President Richard Nixon when he visited Lima in May 1958 on his tour of Latin America. Just as elsewhere in the region, students hissed, shouted, and threw stones.

After Prado's first two years in office, however, the Peru-U.S. relationship improved. In the wake of Latin Americans' rebuke of Nixon and Fidel Castro's victory in Cuba, the United States reassessed its policies toward Latin America; in March 1961, only two months after his inauguration, U.S. president John F. Kennedy announced the Alliance for Progress. While U.S. military aid to Peru was substantial throughout Prado's term—$70 million from 1956 to 1962, one of the highest figures in Latin America—economic aid increased as well.[29] Also, amid a general recovery of the U.S. and Peruvian economies, Washington transferred part of Cuba's sugar quota to Peru. For his part, Prado was critical of Fidel Castro and supported Washington's efforts to isolate the new Cuban government in the hemisphere.

The improvement in U.S.-Peruvian relations was short lived. The 1962 elections in Peru were inconclusive. While a plurality was gained by APRA's Haya de la Torre, his 32.9 percent tally was below the 33.3 percent threshold necessary to avoid the selection of the president by Peru's congress. Also, Haya's share was less than 1 percent more than that of the second-place candidate, Acción Popular's Fernando Belaúnde Terry; because Peru's voting rolls were in disarray, this margin was insufficient to yield a result that would be accepted by all parties. Further exacerbating electoral tensions was enduring opposition to APRA among significant sectors of Peru's military; when Haya and his archrival Odría began to negotiate an unseemly alliance that would have culminated in an Odría presidency, the military's dismay mounted. In July 1962, as political fevers were raging in the country, the military staged a coup.

The coup was denounced by the Kennedy administration. For almost a month, the new regime was not recognized by the Kennedy administration; economic aid was suspended for two months, and military aid for three. The Kennedy administration's policy was in accord with democratic principles, which had recently been reaffirmed in the Alliance for Progress. However, the policy was also in part a result of U.S. support for Haya de la Torre, and it was removed from the realities of politics in Peru.[30] The coup was not carried out by a caudillo seeking to govern indefinitely, but by a quartet of officers who represented the military institution as a whole and who immediately scheduled new elections for June 1963.[31] The coup was welcomed by many Peruvians—most obviously supporters of Belaúnde's Acción Popular—and was not strongly opposed even by APRA. The interim government was quickly recognized by most Latin American and European nations.

The Kennedy administration's policy angered Peruvians in general and Peruvian military officers in particular. The interim government criticized the policy as intervention in Peru's internal affairs, and declared that its foreign policy would become more independent.[32]

1963–1968: The United States and the First Belaúnde Government

When Acción Popular's Belaúnde was elected in June 1963 with 36.2 percent of the vote, expectations were high for a constructive relationship between Peru and the United States. The principles of democracy and social reform, in particular agrarian reform, were central to both the Acción Popular platform and to the Alliance for Progress. A brilliant orator and an accomplished architect, Belaúnde was from an aristocratic family and had studied at the University of Texas. President Kennedy's attitude toward the Belaúnde government was very positive; upon Belaúnde's inauguration in July 1963, Kennedy's coordinator for the Alliance for Progress, Teodoro Moscoso, visited Lima and promised a considerable increase in U.S. aid.[33]

However, the expectations for Peruvian-U.S. collaboration were not met. Conflict erupted immediately over the future of IPC (as mentioned above, a subsidiary of Standard Oil of New Jersey) and—unfortunately—persisted for five years. A second serious conflict erupted in 1967 when Peru's request to purchase supersonic jet fighters from the United States was rejected by the U.S. Congress and the Belaúnde government turned to France for the military equipment.

As a result of these conflicts, U.S. economic aid to Peru from 1963 to 1968 was much lower than what would have been expected to a Latin American nation that might have been a showcase for the Alliance for Progress. Pedro-Pablo Kuczynski calculated that, from July 1963 to June 1968, the U.S. Agency for International Development committed $90 million to Peru—versus more than $1 billion to Brazil, $353 million for Colombia, and $346 million for Chile.[34] In per-capita terms, Chile received five times as much as Peru, Colombia almost triple, and Brazil almost double.[35] U.S. economic and military aid to Peru between 1963 and 1968 was only about 5 percent of the total to Latin America during this period (see Table II.1).

The scant amount of U.S. aid to Peru was important because at this time U.S. aid was the main source of external finance for Latin America, greatly exceeding the funds available from international banks.[36] It was also important because Belaúnde was very eager to promote infrastructure (especially roads) and education in Peru, and support for these goals was expected from the Alliance for Progress. The Belaúnde government increased government spending for these projects; in 1967, Peru's budget deficit grew and the balance of payments deteriorated. Finally, the Belaúnde government devalued, exacerbating widespread perceptions of economic crisis. Subsequently, Belaúnde blamed the overthrow of his government on U.S. "financial blackmail."[37]

TABLE II.1

U.S. AID TO PERU, 1962–1990

	Current Dollars (in millions)	As a Percentage of Total U.S. Aid to Latin America and the Caribbean
Annual Averages		
1962–1968	44	5
1969–1973	21	4
1974–1975	35	7
1976–1977	49	10
1978–1979	70	15
Annual Allocations		
1980	57	11
1981	85	13
1982	60	6
1983	100	8
1984	175	11
1985	88	4
1986	59	3
1987	64	3
1988	71	5
1989	68	4
1990	93	4

Sources: U.S. Agency for International Development, *U.S. Overseas Loans and Grants and Assistance from International Organizations, July 1, 1945-September 30, 1998* (Washington, D.C.), as well as previous editions, and U.S. Agency for International Development, *U.S. Overseas Loans and Grants: Series of Yearly Data, FY 1946-FY 1985, Vol. II Latin America and the Caribbean* (Washington, D.C.).

It is not entirely clear why, during the Alliance for Progress, the U.S. government's concern was focused so much on the future of one company and so little on the future of democracy in Peru. Perhaps the reason was that, although IPC was a small company, it was a subsidiary of Standard Oil of New Jersey (now called Exxon), a large and important company that enjoyed the favor of the 1964–1966 U.S. assistant secretary of state for inter-American affairs.[38] Perhaps, although the legal issues surrounding the controversy were complex and the company's situation could have been argued to be unique, Standard Oil and the U.S. government feared the precedent of a U.S. company paying "delinquent back taxes."[39] Alternatively, perhaps there was no real reason, but merely an unfortunate confluence of personalities, passions, and mistakes.[40]

By the 1960s, IPC was one of the most important companies in Peru. With a payroll of eighteen thousand workers, it was the country's largest private employer, and its book value was the third largest in the country.[41] The company produced about three-quarters of Peru's oil and also set the prices for the oil, which of course was vital to Peru's economy and its defense.[42] The company's power provoked nationalist sentiments in Peru.

The crux of the dispute, however, was legal: Did a private party have the right to own subsoil resources in Peru and, concomitantly, to enjoy a uniquely favorable tax regime?[43] Whereas for the most part the law in the country both before and after independence stipulated that subsoil resources were owned by the state and only concessions for their exploitation could be granted, in 1824 the tar pits at La Brea were sold to a Peruvian citizen. Later, these pits, plus the adjacent hacienda of Pariñas, were resold. In the late 1800s, the owner of La Brea and Pariñas achieved a very favorable tax regime for the property. In 1922 these terms were confirmed by an international arbitration tribunal, and in 1924 La Brea and Pariñas was acquired by IPC.

In the 1960s, many informed Peruvians denounced IPC's arrangement as illegal. They argued that, even if the original title to the tar pits at La Brea were valid, it did not extend to the oil. They pointed out that, when IPC became interested in the purchase of La Brea and Pariñas under the advantageous terms, it gave President Leguía $1 million toward this end.[44] They charged further that the company had paid less than 5 percent of the taxes for which it was responsible, and that the company owed Peru between $50 million and $1 billion. (In 1968, the taxes due were calculated at $144 million by the Belaúnde government.[45])

At the time of Belaúnde's election in 1963, nationalist views were prevalent in Peru, as they were elsewhere in Latin America. Critics of IPC included not only members of the APRA and leftist political parties but also *El Comercio*, Peru's premier newspaper, which was considered to lean toward the political right. In Belaúnde's campaign, he struck nationalist chords with his slogans "The conquest of Peru by the Peruvians" and "Peru as doctrine"; the members of the political parties that comprised Belaúnde's governing coalition were for the most part critical of IPC.

In Belaúnde's inaugural address in July 1963, he promised a definitive solution to the IPC question within ninety days. Negotiations began. In October, Belaúnde proposed that IPC yield its subsoil rights at La Brea and Pariñas in exchange for an operating contract—a proposal that IPC for the most part accepted—but also that IPC pay $50 million in back taxes and accept a tax regime that the company claimed would exceed 100 percent of its profits. The government's proposal was adamantly and publicly rejected by IPC; the proposal also sparked criticism by the U.S. embassy and State Department officials in Washington.[46]

A month later, after John F. Kennedy's assassination, President Lyndon B. Johnson appointed Thomas C. Mann to the post of assistant secretary of state for inter-American affairs. A Texan, Mann had long-standing relationships with Texas oil interests.[47] Under Mann, it was quickly decided that U.S. aid to Peru would not be disbursed until an agreement was reached with IPC. However, this decision was not communicated to the Belaúnde government; rather, U.S. officials said that U.S. aid was mired in red tape and bureaucracy. Possibly as a result, at first President Belaúnde may not have understood the U.S. position on the issue and might not have placed sufficient importance on an accommodation.[48]

The U.S. decision to condition aid upon an agreement ultimately may have hardened the positions of both IPC and the Peruvian government.[49] IPC executives may have believed that the company had a trump card in the negotiations. Among Peruvians, as they became aware of the U.S. policy, they became angry about it and more nationalistic. In general, the more the IPC case was debated, the more passionate both sides' positions became. IPC executives insisted that their original agreement with Peru was valid and there was no reason for the payment of "back taxes"; they emphasized that IPC had made major positive contributions to Peru's development. In contrast, many Peruvians—including most political leaders in both APRA and Acción Popular—became persuaded that nationalization was the best option.

As indicated above, the result of the continuation of the conflict was the loss of considerable U.S. economic assistance. Although U.S. aid for Peru was allocated, it was not disbursed between approximately late 1963 and early 1966. By one estimate, the loss to Peru during this period was some $150 million.[50]

Early in 1966, Mann was succeeded as assistant secretary of state for inter-American affairs by Lincoln Gordon. Gordon was more tolerant of Peru's position on IPC than Mann, and U.S. aid to Peru resumed. However, by this time the health of the Peruvian economy was declining; also, aid flows were interrupted subsequently when Gordon in turn was replaced and when new conflicts erupted.

In the mid-1960s, several Latin American governments sought to purchase supersonic aircraft from the United States. Citing its fears of an arms race in Latin America, the U.S. government was skeptical. As a result, in early 1967 Chile—

Peru's traditional rival—turned to Great Britain for the purchase of twenty Hunter attack fighters.[51] Accordingly, Peru asked to buy Northrup F5A Freedom Fighters from the United States. When Peru's request was denied by the U.S. Congress, the Belaúnde government began negotiations for the purchase of supersonic aircraft from France. The U.S. Department of State sought to reverse the U.S. position and allow the sale of the U.S. aircraft. Angry at the position of the U.S. Congress, however, the Peruvian military pressured the Belaúnde government to finalize the purchase from France. In mid-1967, Peru bought twelve Mirage V fighters—arguably the most sophisticated military aircraft in Latin America at the time.[52] The relationship between the U.S. and Peruvian militaries soured.

The IPC controversy was pivotal not only during the course of the Belaúnde government but also to its demise. By 1968, elections were due the following year, and both IPC and the government were increasingly eager for an accommodation. For its part, IPC was aware that nationalistic attitudes toward the company were widespread and that, if an agreement with Belaúnde was not reached, the company was likely to be expropriated by his successor.[53] For its part, the Belaúnde government was desperately trying to increase U.S. and international assistance for Peru.[54]

After several weeks of intense negotiations, President Belaúnde signed the Act of Talara in August 1968. Belaúnde proclaimed the agreement a triumph for Peru: IPC yielded not only its title to the subsoil resources at La Brea and Pariñas but also its ownership of the surface installations there. However, there was a major concession by the Belaúnde government: No "back taxes" were mandated. Also, IPC gained an operating contract under which Peru's state oil company would sell 80 percent of the crude oil that it extracted from La Brea and Pariñas to IPC, and IPC would have the right to refine and distribute petroleum in Peru for forty years.

The most difficult point in the negotiations was the price that Peru's state oil company would receive for the crude oil. As the terms of the contract became known, critics charged that the price was too low. In September, the head of Peru's state oil company, Carlos Loret de Mola, alleged that the contract shortchanged Peru. Specifically, he claimed that he had signed a final page to the agreement—a "page 11"—that stipulated a minimum dollar price for Peru's crude oil; he added that this page was now missing. Although these charges were not proven, they were credible, and proved devastating in the context of Peruvians' scant support for an agreement with IPC.[55] A military coup followed within a month.

1968–1980: The U.S. and Peru's Leftist Military Government

The military coup was led by General Juan Velasco Alvarado, whose government is widely considered the most leftist military regime to come to power in twentieth-century Latin America. Indeed, it can be argued, on the basis of the

Velasco government's close relationship with the Soviet military and its initial policy toward IPC, that it was more threatening to U.S. interests than was the government of Salvador Allende in Chile (1970–1973).[56] Not surprisingly, therefore, the relationship between the United States and the Peruvian military government was tense. However, the U.S. did not try to overthrow the Velasco government—probably in part because the Velasco government did not embrace a clear socialist agenda and in part because, as a military government, it would have been difficult to oust. Also, some sectors of the U.S. government during the Johnson and Nixon administrations tended toward positive views of Latin American military governments.[57] Gradually, support for the Velasco government eroded within Peru; in a palace coup in 1975, Velasco was replaced by a moderate, General Francisco Morales Bermúdez.

Why did the Peruvian military develop these reformist inclinations? To an unusual degree among Latin American nations, Peru's officers were drawn from lower-middle-class, mestizo, and provincial backgrounds; also to an unusual degree, they became well educated. Whereas in some Latin American nations the military was closely tied to landowning elites, this was not the case in Peru. Rather, the Peruvian military's primary concern was external war. Deeply affected by its loss to the Chileans in the War of the Pacific (see above), the Peruvian military envied the level of national integration achieved by Chile and doubted that Peru could win a second war against Chile if Peru's peasants did not become more committed to the nation. Also, during the early 1960s, highlands peasants had been attracted to incipient revolutionary movements, and the military feared renewed insurgencies. The military came to believe that agrarian reform would satisfy peasants' demands and enhance the country's social integration.

Also, as suggested above, the conflicts between Peru and the United States during the Belaúnde government had increased nationalism among Peruvians, including (as would be expected) Peruvian military officers. The IPC case in particular infuriated many officers. President Velasco himself had been angry for many years at what he considered the company's disrespect for Peru. As a child growing up in the department of Piura on Peru's north coast, where IPC was based, Velasco apparently perceived the company as arrogant. Then, in 1941, just as the war between Peru and Ecuador was about to break out, Captain Velasco sought IPC vehicles to move his troops to the border; his request was not granted for some twenty-four hours, and Velasco's resentment deepened.

The relationship between the Velasco government and the United States was especially acrimonious during the Velasco government's initial years. Not surprisingly, the first confrontation was about IPC. Within a week of the coup, the Peruvian military government expropriated IPC on the grounds that the company's initial contract was invalid. The company demanded $120 million in compensation; while recognizing IPC assets in amount of $71 million, the Peruvian government argued that IPC owed Peru $690 million in unpaid back taxes on the petroleum that it had illegally extracted over the years.[58]

At this time, a series of U.S. congressional amendments to U.S. foreign aid bills—among which the best known was the Hickenlooper Amendment—required the suspension of U.S. economic aid for any government that did not provide adequate compensation for an expropriated U.S. company. Although none of these amendments was formally invoked against the Velasco government, the result was much the same: U.S. economic aid was meager (see Table II.1). Also, in part because of U.S. pressure and in part because of the attitudes toward uncompensated expropriations within the international financial community, loans from the World Bank and the Inter-American Development Bank (IDB) were also scant.[59] For example, between 1969 and 1973, the World Bank provided Peru less than one-third the sum that it had over the previous five years.[60]

Neither the Peruvian nor the U.S. government wanted a complete rupture of economic ties, however.[61] In its negotiations with the Nixon administration, the Velasco government emphasized that IPC was one particular U.S. company with one particular history, and that Peru would work with other U.S. companies for the purpose of mutually beneficial investment agreements. In contrast to the positions of the Allende government or socialist movements in Latin America, the Velasco government proclaimed that foreign capital was necessary for Latin American development, and that its policy toward foreign capital would be pragmatic. For their part, especially by the early 1970s, the United States and the international financial community did not favor severe sanctions against Peru; a world shortage of oil and other key minerals was becoming apparent, and reserves of these resources were believed to be abundant in Peru.

Overall, the Velasco government's stance toward U.S. foreign investment was much more restrictive than in the past. By 1975, the amount of foreign capital in Peru was down approximately 40 percent from its levels during the Belaúnde government.[62] For varying reasons, the government expropriated W. R. Grace and Company, which owned sugar haciendas; the Cerro de Pasco Corporation; the Peruvian Corporation and Conchán oil refinery; some fishing enterprises; and, in the context of agreements that were satisfactory to the companies, International Telephone and Telegraph and Chase Manhattan Bank. Also, the government drove hard bargains with the Southern Peru Copper Corporation for its development of the mammoth open-pit Cuajone copper mine and with Occidental Petroleum for the rights to oil exploration in the Peruvian jungle. Finally, toward the end of the Velasco government (and perhaps hastening its demise) came the expropriation of Marcona Mining Company, an iron-ore enterprise that was tied to the Utah Construction Company and that enjoyed a favorable reputation in Peru.

The tension between the Velasco and U.S. governments over the question of compensation for IPC was finally resolved in February 1974. Pressure for an agreement mounted because an Export-Import Bank credit that was necessary for

Southern Peru Copper Corporation's development of the Cuajone mine was frozen by the IPC dispute. A New York banker, James Greene, was appointed a special emissary of the U.S. government, and a creative agreement was achieved. The Peruvian government would provide $76 million in compensation to a list of U.S. companies that had lost assets; IPC was not identified as one of these companies, but in an appendix to the agreement the U.S. government was given the right to pay firms not on the list, and the U.S. government did provide funds for IPC.

The status of U.S. companies in Peru was not the only source of conflict between the Velasco government and the Nixon administration. The law of the sea—specifically, Peru's claim to sovereignty extending two hundred miles from its coast—was an increasingly contentious issue. In February 1969, these tensions were exacerbated by what was called the "Tuna War."

The "Tuna War" referred to Peru's seizure of two U.S. tuna boats, using gunfire, for fishing in what Peru argued to be its waters. Responding in part to the anger of the U.S. fishing industry, the Nixon administration invoked the Pelly Amendment, which required the suspension of U.S. military aid to any country that illegally seized U.S. fishing boats. Furious, Velasco ordered the expulsion of the U.S. military mission from Peru. Although tensions were eased by the two countries' diplomats over the next few months, the number of U.S. military personnel in Peru declined from forty-one to six.[63]

It was in this context of tensions on economic issues and the law of the sea that, in 1973, the Velasco government became the second in the hemisphere to purchase Soviet armaments.[64] First, the government bought medium-sized tanks, tank transporters, anti-aircraft guns, rocket launchers, and helicopters. Then, in 1976, the succeeding military government initiated the purchase of more sophisticated equipment, including Sukhoi Su-22 fighter bombers and AN-26 F Antonov airplanes. It is estimated that, between 1968 and 1980, the Peruvian military acquired more than $1.6 billion worth of Soviet military equipment.[65] During this period, approximately one hundred Soviet technical advisers were stationed in Peru for the purposes of maintaining the equipment and training Peruvians in its use. Also, from the mid-1970s to the late 1980s, more than eight hundred Peruvian military personnel traveled to the Soviet Union for military training.

Why did the Peruvian military government turn toward this relationship with the Soviet Union? The Peruvian government emphasized that the decision was practical, not ideological. Most obviously, the U.S. Congress had denied the sale of U.S. weapons to Peru in 1967, and in mid-1973 Washington refused to respond to a Peruvian request for weapons.[66] Also, the terms of the Soviet sale were relatively generous; prices and interest rates were low, and grace periods long.[67]

Still, the Peruvian government's decision to purchase Soviet weapons was in a context of considerable ideological distance between Peru and the United States.

The Velasco government was active in initiatives that promoted the cooperation of Latin American and Third World nations, often against the interests of the U.S. In 1969, Peru was pivotal to the establishment of the Andean Pact, and it also became a leader in the "Group of 77," the common name at the time for the movement of nonaligned Third World countries. For the first time, Peru established diplomatic relations with the Soviet Union in February 1969, and trade and cultural ties increased considerably.

Gradually, however, Velasco lost support within the Peruvian military. Whereas most of his government's initial reforms had been broadly acclaimed, his subsequent reforms divided the military into ideological factions, sparking concern among top officers for the coherence of the institution. Also, Velasco's behavior became increasingly erratic; the problem was widely attributed to the abdominal aneurysm and amputation of a leg that he had suffered in 1973. A third factor was that, as payments on Peru's debt (most of which had been contracted from private international banks on terms much more stringent than those of the World Bank and the IDB) jumped, Peru's economy weakened.

Amid these concerns, Velasco was deposed in a bloodless coup by General Morales Bermúdez. The grandson of a former president with experience as finance minister for both Belaúnde and Velasco, Morales Bermúdez was Velasco's logical successor: At the time of the coup, he was the senior active-duty general and prime minister. Although the U.S. government played no apparent role, it was aware that Morales Bermúdez's position on economic issues was much more orthodox than Velasco's, and was presumably pleased by his accession.[68] Gradually, Morales Bermúdez shifted the government toward the political center, and the U.S.-Peruvian relationship improved. Especially after July 1977, by which time Jimmy Carter had become the U.S. president and Morales Bermúdez had announced a transition to democratic government, U.S. aid to Peru increased considerably (see Table II.1).

Without the resources to meet staggering debt-service obligations, the Morales Bermúdez government decided not to default but to reach an accommodation with the international financial community.[69] In early 1976, the government announced a preliminary agreement for the compensation of Marcona Mining Company (which had been expropriated by Velasco in July 1975). This step facilitated an agreement between Morales Bermúdez and a consortium of international private banks for a $400 million loan package for Peru, contingent upon Peru's implementation of an economic-stabilization program. The government imposed drastic austerity measures, including devaluation of the currency, the reduction of subsidies on food staples and gasoline, and other budget cuts. After these measures provoked protest within Peru, the government did not fully comply with the program stipulated by the international private banks. Finally, as the payments due on Peru's debt reached 55 percent of export revenues, Peru and the International Monetary Fund (IMF) negotiated an even more stringent and detailed stabilization plan.[70]

One of the reasons for the difficulties in the achievement of economic stabilization was a large military buildup, initiated by Velasco in 1973 and continued under Morales Bermúdez. Between 1973 and 1978, the value of Peru's arms imports was estimated at more than $1.2 billion, versus $410 million for Chile's arms imports and $425 million for Ecuador's.[71] Peru's military buildup coincided with heightened geopolitical tensions. An underlying factor was that 1979 would mark the one-hundredth anniversary of the outbreak of the War of the Pacific, and both Peru and Chile worried about renewed hostilities. Also, in 1975, negotiations for a Bolivian outlet to the sea had been reinvigorated, only to break down amid acrimony among Bolivia, Peru, and Chile. Peru might have contemplated the possibility of an alliance with Bolivia and Argentina (which was at odds with Chile over the Beagle Channel) against Chile, especially because the Pinochet government had become relatively isolated internationally.[72] At the same time, Peru's relations with Ecuador, its geopolitical rival to the north, were deteriorating.[73] Peru was aware that its military purchases would disturb the U.S. government and international financial agencies, and it had been in part for this reason that in 1976 it had sought an agreement with the private banks rather than the IMF and had also kept the purchase secret for as long as possible.[74]

By the middle of 1977, however, the stage was set for a rapprochement in U.S.-Peruvian relations. Negotiations with the IMF were ongoing; additional military purchases were not planned; and President Morales Bermúdez was deciding to preside over Peru's return to democratic government. There were various reasons for Morales Bermúdez's decision. First, spearheaded by Peru's vigorous political left, protests against the government were escalating; in July 1977, the nation was virtually shut down by the first general strike since 1919 and the largest in the nation's history. Among the protesters' demands were not only an end to austerity policies but also a return to democratic government. Second, after more than a decade in power, the military was demoralized, and charges of corruption were rampant. A third factor was that Morales Bermúdez's own political views were pro-democratic—he was to be a presidential candidate in 1985—and his views were reinforced by the Carter administration (1977–1981). Of course, during the Carter years, human rights and democracy became an official concern of the U.S. Department of State, and the administration encouraged Peru's democratic opening.[75]

After Morales Bermúdez's announcement of a transition to democracy on July 28, 1977, cooperation between the United States and Peru grew. Although protests against the stabilization program continued, the government appointed a highly professional economic team, headed by Javier Silva Ruete, which won the confidence of the international financial community. Peru was meeting IMF targets, its external debt was rescheduled, and in 1979 economic growth resumed. Geopolitical tensions abated. Constituent Assembly elections were held in Peru in 1978, a new constitution was signed in 1979, and new elections—freer and fairer than any in the country's history—were held in May 1980. These developments were welcomed by the Carter administration, which hoped that Peru's economic prudence and democratic transition would set positive examples in the region.[76]

The U.S. and the Elected Governments of the 1980s

The U.S.-Peruvian cooperation of the late 1970s was not sustained in the 1980s. Although Presidents Fernando Belaúnde (1980–1985) and Alan García (1985–1990) were freely and fairly elected, both were for the most part at odds with the U.S. government. This section focuses primarily on the U.S. and the 1980–1985 Belaúnde government; the relationship between the U.S. and 1985–1990 García government on key items of the bilateral agenda is described in subsequent chapters as a prelude to the 1990s. The erosion of cooperation was indicated by the decline in U.S. aid to the 1980–1985 Belaúnde government and then by the virtual halt in U.S. aid to the 1985–90 García government (see Table II.1).

At the core of the bilateral tensions of the 1980s was the ideological divergence in the two countries during the decade. From 1981 to 1989, the U.S. government was led by President Ronald Reagan, who hailed from the conservative wing of the Republican party. The hard-line Cold War views that prevailed in the U.S. government were rejected by most Peruvians. Although the leftist military regime had ended, among its legacies was the strongest pro-Marxist electoral coalition in Latin America, the Izquierda Unida (United Left). Peru's center-right party, the Partido Popular Cristiano (PPC, Popular Christian party), won only about 10 percent of the presidential and legislative votes in 1980 and was arguably even weaker by 1985.[77] In this context, it is not surprising that both the Belaúnde and García governments were at odds with the Reagan administration on the key hemispheric issue of the 1980s, the Central American conflicts. Both the Belaúnde and García governments were more sympathetic to Nicaragua's Frente Sandinista de Liberación Nacional (FSLN) and more eager for a negotiated solution to the conflicts than the Reagan administration could countenance.[78]

In 1980, Fernando Belaúnde was reelected to Peru's presidency. As in 1963, a positive bilateral relationship was expected, but not achieved. On the one hand, despite the bilateral conflicts during President Belaúnde's 1963–1968 government, Belaúnde's personal views were favorable to the United States; indeed, after 1968 he had spent most of his years in exile teaching at U.S. universities.

Also, Belaúnde appointed numerous ministers who enjoyed the respect of the international financial community, including in particular his first prime minister and economics minister, Manuel Ulloa, and his first minister of energy and mines, Pedro-Pablo Kuczynski. To a certain extent as in his first government, however, President Belaúnde tended to try to straddle the positions of the right and the left, with a result that satisfied neither. Also, perhaps to an even greater degree than in his first government, he did not assert civilian authority over the military; issues of geopolitics and military purchases continued to plague the bilateral relationship, and the issue of the military's human-rights violations was added to the bilateral agenda. In off-the-record interviews, most U.S. officials were critical of Belaúnde's leadership; they considered him "fixated on the 1960s," "out of touch with Peruvian realities," "unable to get things done," and "unwilling to make tough decisions."

As in the past, the top item on the bilateral agenda during 1980–1985 was economic policy. At first, the Belaúnde government's free-market reforms, including the reduction of tariffs and more favorable rules for foreign investment, heartened the international financial community. As a result, Belaúnde—who it should be recalled was an architect committed to the building of Peru's infrastructure—was able to secure large loans from the international development banks for superscale irrigation, energy, and highway projects.

However, in 1982, Mexico announced that it could not meet its debt-service obligations, and what was called Latin America's debt crisis began. At this time, amid a global recession, the prices of key exports plummeted, interest rates jumped, and new international loans were not available—in Peru just as in most of the region. Unfortunately, the Belaúnde government continued to spend; Peru's budget deficit skyrocketed to 8.8 percent of gross domestic product (GDP) in 1982 and 11.9 percent in 1983.[79] These negative trends were exacerbated in Peru by an exceptionally severe 1982–1983 El Niño (a periodic reversal of ocean currents) that devastated agriculture and fishing. GDP declined about 13 percent in 1983—the worst single-year decline of the post-World War II era.[80]

After the 1983 economic disaster, the Belaúnde government's economic policy floundered. Especially given that the rhetoric of the president and his economic team was neoliberal (even though policy was not continuing to shift in free-market directions), citizens tended to blame the economic catastrophe on neoliberalism, and they increasingly looked to the political left for solutions. In municipal elections in November 1983, Izquierda Unida won the municipality of Lima and APRA's Alan García became the odds-on favorite to win the 1985 presidential elections. The U.S. government was also worried about the likely outcome of the upcoming elections, and somewhat belatedly in 1984 sought to bolster the Belaúnde government with considerable economic assistance (see Table II.1).

In this political context, the government was at a loss for an effective economic policy. Belaúnde was under pressure even from Acción Popular for economic reactivation prior to the elections. Although an agreement with the IMF was signed in August 1984, the Belaúnde government failed to comply. Indeed, quietly, the government suspended interest payments on the debt. The government seemed unable to find solutions to problems that did not appear especially complex, such as a dispute with Eastern Airlines over carrier routes and landing rights that disrupted travel between the United States and Peru for more than a year. By the end of Belaúnde's second term, as real wages declined and unemployment increased, per-capita income was about 12 percent below the 1980 figure—yet the international financial community was not pleased, and direct foreign investment was minimal.[81]

Geopolitical tensions were also marked during the second Belaúnde government. In January 1981, a border clash erupted between Peru and Ecuador; at an estimated toll of two hundred casualties, the five-day clash was the most serious between the two countries since 1941.[82] The dispute was won by Peru, and President Belaúnde's nationalistic tones in his celebration of the triumph strengthened his relationship with the Peruvian military but not with the U.S. government. President Belaúnde also took a strong stand in the April 1982 war between Argentina and Great Britain over the Falkland/Malvinas Islands. After Belaúnde's attempt at mediation between the two countries failed, Peru became one of Latin America's most fervent supporters of Argentina. Peru provided considerable military assistance to Argentina, reportedly including the loan of fourteen Mirage jets.[83] Needless to say, the Belaúnde government's position did not please the Reagan administration, which of course was allied with Great Britain.

In part as a result of Peru's involvement in these geopolitical conflicts, the Belaúnde government reinitiated weapons purchases. Just as during the mid-1960s, a Peruvian request for the purchase of U.S. jet fighters was denied by Washington, and in December 1983 the Belaúnde government announced a plan to buy twenty-six highly sophisticated Mirage-2000 jets from France. The potential cost of these twenty-six jets, sold at high interest rates, might have exceeded $1 billion.[84] At the same time, Peru continued to buy military equipment from the Soviet Union—approximately $390 million worth between 1980 and 1985, more than the value of transfers from the Soviet Union to Nicaragua during this period.[85] Peru's arms purchases during the 1980–1985 Belaúnde government totaled about $1.5 billion, only about 25 percent less than the purchases between 1975 and 1979 under the military government.[86] Peru's purchases were considerably larger than Chile's or Ecuador's.[87] As would be expected, the Reagan administration considered these purchases destabilizing and exorbitant. The Reagan administration was also dismayed that one-hundred-odd Soviet military advisers were in Peru, primarily to train Peruvians in the use and maintenance of the equipment.

Not surprisingly, in the context of this relationship between the Peruvian and Soviet militaries, the relationship between the Peruvian and U.S. security forces was cool. Although the Shining Path guerrillas were expanding dramatically in Peru in the early 1980s (see Chapter IV), the Central Intelligence Agency (CIA) was either unable or unwilling to provide significant intelligence information to Peruvian officials.[88]

Although the importance of the "war against drugs" was rising on the bilateral agenda between 1980 and 1985, it was not a top priority.[89] The U.S. and Peruvian positions on the war against drugs between 1980 and 1985 are discussed in Chapter VI. President Belaúnde agreed with the Reagan administration that drugs were a scourge; projects for coca eradication were advanced. The results of these projects were minimal, but the failure did not provoke significant bilateral tension, because the war against drugs was in its initial stages.

Another issue on the bilateral agenda between 1980 and 1985 was democracy and human rights. For the most part, there was consensus between the Reagan administration and the Belaúnde government on these issues. The Reagan administration tended to define *democracy* as reasonably free and fair elections—without much consideration of a country's human-rights record. During the Belaúnde government, elections were held regularly and met international standards; in general also, constitutional principles were upheld. However, as the Shining Path expanded, the Peruvian military committed serious human-rights violations (see Chapter VII). U.S.-based human-rights groups and U.S. human-rights officials became increasingly critical of the failure of the Belaúnde government to control these violations. Still, these concerns were far from the top of the bilateral agenda.

In 1985, Alan García of the APRA party was elected president. President García's leftist positions were reinforced rather than restrained by Peru's congress; while APRA enjoyed a majority in the congress, the second largest party was the pro-Marxist Izquierda Unida.[90]

As the data in Table II.1 suggest, U.S.-Peruvian relations descended to a nadir during 1985–1990. President García was an outspoken champion of Third World causes who frequently denounced imperialism and rejected capitalism. In his inaugural address, he referred to the United States as "the richest and most imperialist country on Earth."[91] At least in the eyes of U.S. officials, García insulted first Secretary of the Treasury James Baker during García's 1985 inauguration ceremonies and then Secretary of State George Shultz during the 1985 UN General Assembly meeting.[92] For several years, Peru was at the forefront of Latin American nations resisting the international financial community's strategies for the amelioration of the debt crisis.

In off-the-record interviews, U.S. insiders described Washington's reaction to García's positions as "furious." Said one U.S. insider: "On Washington's hate list, Peru is after Nicaragua." Some U.S. officials praised García's brilliance, but most also considered him "immature," "unstable," "inexperienced," and "power-hungry."

In the context of the heated confrontation between the U.S. and García governments on economic issues, it is noteworthy that the bilateral relationship did not collapse altogether. As subsequent chapters indicate, U.S. and Peruvian officials collaborated to a degree on noneconomic issues, in particular narcotics control, and cited this collaboration in an effort to reduce tensions. There was also recognition among U.S. officials, in particular Ambassador Alexander Watson, that García had been freely and fairly elected and that democracy and human-rights concerns had ascended higher on the U.S. agenda.[93]

CHAPTER III

BILATERAL POLICY MAKING DURING THE 1990s: TRENDS AND ACTORS

THE TRENDS IN THE MAKING OF U.S. AND PERUVIAN FOREIGN policies in the 1990s were sharply divergent. Overall, U.S. interest in Peru declined, as did U.S. interest in the hemisphere in general (with the exception of Mexico). President Clinton's role in policy making toward Peru was limited, and became more limited during the course of his two administrations. If Clinton had been engaged in U.S. policy making toward Peru in 1999 and 2000, it is possible that the U.S. policy of the handshake for the Fujimori government would have been challenged. Without major input from Clinton or another top official authorized to pose questions about overarching, long-term U.S. interests and priorities and their application to Peru, however, officials' major goal was to do their job. Although these officials were located across a spectrum of agencies—the Treasury Department, the Department of Defense, the Central Intelligence Agency (CIA), the Office of National Drug Control Policy, and the Department of State—they were in overall agreement until June 2000 that they were being helped to do their jobs by the Fujimori government and that this cooperation was important. Accordingly, bureaucratic conflict was not as intense as might have been expected.

In contrast, the Fujimori government was very interested in the U.S. government and considered U.S. support important to its overall power. Also by contrast, President Fujimori and his key advisers were pivotal actors in the making of Peru's foreign policy. At the start of Fujimori's government, his advisers included not only Vladimiro Montesinos (who in 1990 was merely Fujimori's "personal legal adviser") but also politically independent policy experts. By the end of the decade, however, these experts had been sidelined and power was exercised almost exclusively by Fujimori and Montesinos. Although Fujimori and Montesinos misjudged the U.S. government more than once, their overall capacity to manage the bilateral relationship to their advantage is evident from their having broken international democratic rules twice—with the 1992 autogolpe and the 2000 rigged elections—and yet maintaining the U.S. handshake.

The implications of these distinct patterns were considerable. On the one hand, in the context of the numerous actors in the making of U.S. policy and its ad hoc character, the process must have appeared uncertain to the Fujimori government. Among the objectives articulated by the U.S. government for Peru, which was "really" most important? How much abuse of democratic standards would the Clinton administration tolerate? No one in the Peruvian government or opposition could be sure.

For the Clinton administration, Peru's authoritarian policy making had important implications as well. Especially by the late 1990s, President Fujimori and Vladimiro Montesinos were the only actors who could make anything happen. If the Clinton administration wanted to get things done in Peru, it had to deal with these men. If U.S. officials were critical of the government's authoritarian proclivities, they feared that the Fujimori government would end its cooperation on key issues on the bilateral agenda.

At the same time, policy making by both the United States and Peru was increasingly affected by other nations and especially by transnational actors. Due in large part to Fujimori's Japanese heritage, Japan became an important actor in Peruvian politics; Japan was sympathetic to the Fujimori government. The role of the Organization of American States (OAS) was significant with respect to issues of democracy and human rights. Amid globalization, Peruvians became much more aware of international patterns and trends, in part through cable television and the Internet and in part through increased personal interaction. The number of transnational organizations, in particular transnational human-rights organizations, multiplied. These transnational actors are outside the immediate purview of this book, however, and accordingly their roles are described as they become relevant in subsequent chapters.

This chapter describes first the Clinton adminstration's policy making toward Peru and then the Fujimori government's policy making toward the United States. We must, however, caution readers that there is much about these topics that cannot be known at this time. Although we interviewed scores of former U.S. and Peruvian officials, most official U.S. documents remain classified; answers to numerous key issues about Peru's policies are available only from Alberto Fujimori and Vladimiro Montesinos, and are unlikely to be forthcoming.

THE CLINTON ADMINISTRATION'S POLICY MAKING TOWARD PERU

During the 1990s, two trends were evident in U.S. policy making toward Latin America. First was a decrease in U.S. interest in Latin America. The decrease was a result of the end of the Cold War and the concomitant termination of U.S. concern about the expansion of Communism in the region.[1] It was also the result of President Clinton's own apparent disinterest in the region and U.S. political dynamics during his eight-year administration. A corollary of the White House's disinterest that has been widely criticized by scholarly analysts was failure to reconcile the policy preferences of different Washington bureaucracies; the problem was called "bureaucratic balkanization" by Peter H. Smith and "ad hoc-racy" by Richard N. Haass.[2] As noted above, however, the key corollary with respect to U.S. policy toward Peru was the absence of a powerful voice challenging the wisdom of a policy advantageous to the spectrum of bureaucracies at the time.

A second important trend was that, to the extent that clear priorities were evident in the Clinton administration's agenda, economic issues—trade, finance, and investment—moved to the top.[3] Clinton administration officials for Latin America often began their speeches by highlighting the dramatic increase in U.S. exports to the region and the potential for further U.S. commercial gains.[4] Samuel P. Huntington wrote: "In case after case, country after country, the dictates of commercialism have prevailed over other purposes, including human rights, democracy, alliance relationships, and other strategic and political considerations described by one administration official as 'statocrap and globaloney.'"[5] In 2000, a foreign policy analyst identified the Clinton legacy as an "Economic Engine for Foreign Policy."[6] It was important to the United States that Latin American nations open their markets to U.S exports, welcome foreign investment, service their international debts, and maintain stable national currencies. As the importance of economic issues rose on the U.S. agenda, the power of the U.S. Treasury and Commerce Departments increased vis-à-vis other U.S. bureaucracies.

As free-market reform moved to the top of the U.S. agenda, the Clinton administration proclaimed an overarching goal for its foreign policy: "enlargement of the world's free community of market democracies."[7] The administration was emphatic that it was committed to democracy promotion, but also proclaimed that free-market reform and democracy were mutually reinforcing.[8] There was a spoken and unspoken view within the Clinton administration—as arguably there has been in most U.S. administrations—that a market economy is the foundation for economic growth and that economic growth in turn is the foundation for democracy. Clinton himself regularly argued that "the spread of American-style capitalism would eventually help spread American-style democracy."[9] Accordingly, for the most part, when U.S. officials believed that free-market goals were at odds in the short run with the democracy goal, they could opt for free-market goals with the explanation that democracy would gain over the longer run.

At its top levels, the Clinton administration had much less to say about security and narcotics-control issues than it did about free-market reform and democracy. At first, President Clinton appeared interested in various dimensions of reform in U.S. security and narcotics-control practices, but ultimately—for whatever set of reasons—he opted not to pursue reform. In the case of Peru, over the course of the Clinton administration there were arguably more problems and opportunities that commanded the attention of U.S. security and narcotics-control personnel than in any other Latin American nation. By 2000, having closely collaborated with the Fujimori government on any number of issues over almost a decade, U.S. security and narcotics-control personnel were likely to have been at the forefront of U.S. policy making toward Peru.

The U.S. President and His Advisers

President Clinton's predecessor, President George Bush (1989–1993)—a former director of the CIA and a resident of the border state of Texas—was very interested in Latin America. As the Cold War ended, hopes were high for peace and democracy in the world, and Bush trumpeted the arrival of a "New World Order." The North American Free Trade Agreement (NAFTA) was initiated under President Bush; it was Bush's original concept that NAFTA embrace not only Mexico but also most or all Latin American nations. The problem of the flow of narcotics from Latin America to the United States was accorded much more attention and funding by the Bush administration. Also, in the context of the development of rationales for the U.S. role in Central America during the 1980s, considerable emphasis was given to the goal of democracy promotion in Latin America. In 1991, the General Assembly of the OAS adopted the Santiago Commitment to Democracy (Resolution 1080), mandating an OAS response to the interruption of a constitutional or democratic government.

By contrast, there was nothing in President William J. Clinton's personal or professional background that had sparked an interest in Latin America. As the governor of a small southern state, Clinton had not developed significant foreign policy expertise, and his 1992 campaign platform emphasized that presidential attention should be upon domestic issues. His campaign mantra was, "It's the economy, stupid"; Clinton was signaling that he would shift U.S. attention from foreign policy to the nation's economy.

There is a broad consensus that Clinton fulfilled his campaign promise. Even during his first term, his interest in foreign policy was limited and uneven. He was the first U.S. president in several decades not to travel to Latin America (with the exception of a few hours in Haiti). In a reference to previous perceptions that President George Bush lacked strategic vision ("the vision thing"), Jorge Domínguez said wryly, "I long for Bush's 'vision'!"[10] In a "report card" on the first three years of Clinton's foreign policy, one pundit gave Clinton a C, commenting that "Mr. Clinton gets along well with others but needs to pay attention in class and study for the final exam."[11]

Clinton's major achievements were in international economics. Despite sharp criticism from important constituencies within the Democratic party, he worked to secure passage of NAFTA by the U.S. Congress in November 1993. In December 1994, the Miami Summit of the Americas produced a pledge to work for a

Free Trade Area of the Americas by 2005. The same month, Mexico confronted a severe financial crisis, and the Clinton administration lobbied to raise more than $40 billion for a rescue package for the Mexican peso. Also in 1994, after considerable indecision, Clinton became the first U.S. president to approve a military invasion of a Western Hemisphere nation primarily on the grounds of democracy and human rights. The imminent invasion—which had secured the approval of the United Nations—persuaded Haiti's ruling military junta to leave the country and allow the return of ousted president Jean-Bertrand Aristide.

During Clinton's second term, his interest in Latin America eroded further. Although he did travel to the region four times during his second term, only one of the four trips was to South America (Venezuela, Argentina, and Brazil in 1997); his journeys in Africa, Asia, and the Middle East were more extensive. Of course, during Clinton's second term, the 1998 Monica Lewinsky scandal, the president's 1999 impeachment, and finally the 2000 elections absorbed much of the president's attention. Commented Richard Haass:

> [We must note] the extraordinarily low status that Clinton accorded international affairs. . . . It is instructive to look at how the president chose to use the bully pulpit during his term in office. Of some 300 Saturday morning radio addresses he has delivered, perhaps 35—less than 12 percent—were devoted to matters of foreign policy and national security.[12]

Even the Clinton administration's pursuit of a free-market agenda lagged during his second term. Despite his promise of a Free Trade Area of the Americas by 2005 at the Miami Summit, he did not move quickly and vigorously to secure fast-track authority from the U.S. Congress for this purpose. Ultimately, in November 1997, Clinton was denied fast-track authority to negotiate trade agreements by the U.S. Congress, becoming the first president since 1974 to be denied this authority. In Clinton's defense, the U.S. public had not been enthusiastic about NAFTA before Mexico's financial crisis, and it had become less so afterward; this was even more the case for core constituencies in the Democratic party. It is dubious that Clinton would have won fast-track authority even if he had launched an all-out effort. Without such authority, the opportunity for action in the area of greatest interest to Clinton was lost. Still, the administration was awarded some good marks for its support for Brazil during its 1998–1999 financial crisis.

Other Clinton initiatives were blocked by the Republicans' achievement of majorities in the U.S. Senate and House of Representatives after the November 1994 midterm election. For example, as mentioned above, the CIA's role in Peru was very important during the 1990s, and changes at the CIA's top ranks might have led to changes in its role in Peru. At the beginning of his second term, Clinton nominated Anthony Lake, his first-term national security adviser, to direct the CIA, which at the time was confronting widespread demands for reform. A former professor at Mount Holyoke College and former head of the Carter administration's policy planning staff at the State Department, widely considered a liberal Democrat, Lake was expected to pursue greater accountability and transparency at the CIA. However, led by Jesse Helms, congressional Republicans challenged Lake, and he was not confirmed. Clinton appeared to yield to Republicans' pressure; in July 1997, George Tenet, then CIA deputy director, became director, and CIA reform was put on the back burner.[13] Overall during this period, Clinton appeared wary of the CIA, but disinclined to confront it.[14]

With respect to U.S. goals in Peru, Clinton is not known to have advanced any particular views.[15] He was not engaged in policy making about Peru's 2000 elections. He was, however, interested in the plight of Lori Berenson, a U.S. citizen hailing from New York City who was at a minimum sympathetic to the cause of the Movimiento Revolucionario Túpac Amaru (MRTA) and who was convicted of treason in Lima in January 1996 by a faceless military tribunal (see Chapter VII).

As has often been the case, the National Security Council (NSC) was more influential than any other entity in the making of U.S. foreign policy. The size of the NSC increased dramatically under Clinton, and the NSC, not the State Department, was routinely called for information by journalists.[16] During Clinton's first term, the head of the NSC was the aforementioned Anthony Lake. Even during Clinton's first term, however, his closest foreign policy adviser may have been Samuel R. (Sandy) Berger. Berger became a friend to Clinton during George McGovern's presidential campaign and a foreign policy adviser to him in the mid-1980s. Upon Clinton's election, Berger was offered the position as head of the NSC, but declined in favor of the more seasoned Lake. Still, Berger became Lake's deputy and gained the head position in Clinton's second term. In contrast to the backgrounds of most national security advisers in government or academia, Berger had been a trade lawyer at a premier Washington law firm, with a special interest in China. Berger's foreign policy prism was widely considered "cautious" and "realpolitik-minded," and accordingly "just right for the President's concept of foreign policy."[17] However, among the sharp criticisms were: "You can't expect a trade lawyer to be a global strategist" and "Sandy's a carpenter, not an architect."[18] Berger was widely considered the most influential national security adviser since Henry A. Kissinger.[19]

Within the NSC, the first senior director for Western Hemisphere affairs was Richard Feinberg, whose background was in academia. For some months in 1993, Feinberg was the only administration official working on Latin American issues, as other officials had to be confirmed by the U.S. Senate; Feinberg's role in policy making toward Peru in the tense period after the autogolpe was considerable.[20] From June 1999 through 2000, the senior director for Western Hemisphere affairs was Arturo Valenzuela, whose background was also in academia; Valenzuela was an active participant in policy making toward Peru during this period.[21]

For much of Clinton's eight years in office, however, his most important adviser on Latin American issues was a southern businessman: Thomas "Mack" McLarty. A "Friend of Bill" since kindergarten in Arkansas, McLarty enjoyed exceptional access to Clinton. As Clinton's first chief of staff, he was key to the orchestration of the passage of NAFTA in 1993; he remains an outspoken advocate of free trade in the Americas.[22] Then, as White House special envoy for Latin America, he was pivotal to the convening of the Miami Summit in 1994 and the Santiago Summit in April 1998. Latin Americans, especially Latin American business leaders, perceived the gregarious, courteous McLarty as a good listener who effectively conveyed their concerns to Clinton.[23] McLarty was among the U.S. officials who espoused the view that free markets and democracy are "two sides of the same coin," and seems unlikely to have expressed criticism of the Fujimori government to the president.[24] In mid-1998, McLarty resigned; his successor, former Florida governor Kenneth "Buddy" MacKay, did not enjoy any particular access to Clinton, and Latin America slipped lower on the U.S. foreign policy agenda.

Agencies of the Executive Branch

For many analysts, the most powerful U.S. foreign-policy-making agency during the Clinton administration was the Treasury Department.[25] The Treasury Department vigorously promoted its proposals for the solution of financial crises, both at the White House and at the International Monetary Fund (IMF) and the World Bank. As Jacob Weisberg commented in the *New York Times Magazine:* "For Administration insiders today, something as recondite as a currency intervention can bring about the political drama—and the sleepless nights—once reserved for decisions about whether to stick with a third-world anti-Communist dictator."[26]

The Treasury Department's role expanded in part because of the capabilities of Robert E. Rubin, who served as secretary from 1995 to 1999. After Clinton's election in 1992, the former head of Goldman, Sachs was appointed chair of the National Economic Council, a panel created by Clinton to be on a par with the National Security Council, and then in early 1995 to the treasury position. Rubin "redefined [the treasury] post from discreet adviser and signatory of our currency to a sort of global emissary and projection of American geopolitical clout as it is expressed now—not in warheads or throw weights but in loan guarantees and bailout packages."[27] Rubin was often judged the most important member of the Clinton administration after the president himself.[28]

After Rubin's resignation in May 1999, he was succeeded by Lawrence H. Summers, who at the time was deputy secretary of the treasury and had also previously served as undersecretary of the treasury for international affairs. The youngest tenured professor in the history of Harvard University (and also chosen in 2001 for the presidency of Harvard), Summers was by all accounts brilliant. It had long been Summers's, rather than Rubin's, role to work with Latin American governments for economic stabilization and free-market reform. The 1992–1999 Peruvian ambassador to the United States, Ricardo Luna, praised Summers as "one of the architects of Peru's reinsertion."[29] It is likely that, after Summers was promoted to the top position at treasury, he maintained a voice on U.S. policy toward Peru.

Arguably, although the Treasury Department increased its influence during the Clinton administration and became the most important actor for numerous Latin American nations, the most powerful U.S. agencies with respect to Peru were those whose primary goal was security—namely, the CIA and the U.S. Southern Command (SOUTHCOM, the joint-service command of the U.S. Department of Defense for Latin America). According to various reports, the CIA was the dominant influence in the U.S. embassy in Peru from approximately 1992 to 1995.[30] At U.S. interagency meetings about U.S. policy toward Peru in the late 1990s and 2000, the CIA was the agency that spoke most forcefully on behalf of the maintenance of the U.S. relationship with Vladimiro Montesinos, and its position prevailed through approximately June 2000.[31] It also appears that, as SOUTHCOM became increasingly active in Peru, its September 1997-September 2000 commander in chief, General Charles E. Wilhelm of the U.S. Marine Corps, met regularly with Montesinos and Peruvian military officers and came to value their cooperation.[32]

The CIA and SOUTHCOM were supportive of the Fujimori government in part because U.S. security officials cooperated effectively with Montesinos and other Peruvian officials for many years on numerous issues. As Chapter IV describes, in the early 1990s the Shining Path (Sendero Luminoso) guerrillas were a major threat to the Peruvian government, and the CIA provided significant support to the Fujimori government's intelligence capabilities. In January 1995, a border war erupted between Peru and Ecuador, and U.S. military personnel joined other Latin American military forces to separate Peruvian and Ecuadorian soldiers in the conflict area and to establish a demilitarized zone (see Chapter IV). In December 1996, the MRTA seized the Japanese ambassador's residence and held seventy-two powerful persons hostage; U.S. security personnel helped train the Peruvian commandos who rescued the hostages and also facilitated intelligence gathering (see Chapter IV). In the late 1990s and into 2000, the CIA and SOUTHCOM worked with Montesinos to advance Plan Colombia (see Chapter IV).

The capacity of the CIA and SOUTHCOM to advocate cooperation with the Fujimori government was increased by their roles in narcotics control. Although the primary mission of both CIA and SOUTHCOM is security, both were deeply involved in narcotics-control activities in Peru (see Chapter VI). Indeed, in the Andean nations in the 1990s, counterterrorism and counternarcotics activities often converged. It seems possible that, while overall the CIA valued Montesinos first and foremost because of his cooperation on intelligence problems, the agency publicly justified its relationship with him on the grounds of U.S. narcotics-control objectives.[33]

Of course, narcotics control per se was a key U.S. goal in Peru. In January 1996, after General Barry R. McCaffrey became the director of the White House's Office of National Drug Control Policy, he became a salient U.S. actor in Peru as well.[34] Considered at this time a hero of the Gulf War, McCaffrey had previously served as the commander in chief of SOUTHCOM, and in that position had coordinated the U.S. military's antinarcotics effort. McCaffrey's appointment was to reinvigorate the Clinton administration's war against drugs, which had languished under his predecessor, New York City police commissioner Lee Brown.

Perceived to be more interested in the public spotlight than in policy making, McCaffrey did not enjoy broad respect among Clinton administration officials.[35] However, he was important to the administration's claims to U.S. successes in the war against drugs. McCaffrey regularly traveled to Peru and regularly applauded the Fujimori government's narcotics-control programs (see Chapter VI). Although McCaffrey was dismayed by Montesinos's public revelation of one of their meetings, he continued to tout the Fujimori government's narcotics-control successes. It seems likely that he would have been an advocate of the Fujimori government in interagency meetings and that other officials would not have wanted to challenge him.

In most analysts' views, in the 1990s the power of the Treasury Department, the Department of Defense, and the CIA were eclipsing the U.S. Department of State, which of course is traditionally the U.S. agency primarily responsible for U.S. foreign policy. The eclipse was caused in part by the lack of rapport between President Clinton and his two secretaries of state, Warren M. Christopher and Madeleine K. Albright.[36] It was also caused in part by the decline in the budget of the U.S. Department of State mandated by the Republican majority in the U.S. Congress.[37] In the case of Peru, however, it is not clear that the decline in State Department power affected policy outcomes. Although there were probably more officials within the Department of State than within other U.S. agencies who were deeply concerned about democracy promotion in Peru, for the most part these voices did not prevail within the department.

Neither of Clinton's two secretaries of state was particularly interested in Latin America. His first was the reserved lawyer Warren M. Christopher; during his four years, Christopher visited the Middle East fifteen times, but spent a mere twenty-four working hours in Latin America.[38] During Clinton's second term, the U.S. Department of State was headed by Madeleine K. Albright. Although Albright took a greater interest in Latin America than Christopher and traveled to the region nine times, she was widely perceived as primarily interested in U.S. policy toward Eastern Europe and the Middle East.[39] Commented a *New York Times* journalist: "Madeleine K. Albright was increasingly playing the role of secretary of state for the Middle East and Eastern Europe; she ceded swaths of the world to Mr. Rubin, Mr. Summers and other officials."[40] Until about mid-2000, she did not appear to take an interest in Peru or advance any policy preferences for the country.[41]

Without leadership on Latin American issues from the secretary of state, it is likely to have fallen to the assistant secretary of state for inter-American affairs to advance the department's positions with respect to the region. The Clinton administration's first assistant secretary for the region, career foreign-service officer Alexander Watson, did express concern about democracy and human rights in Peru, and in particular about Montesinos's increasing power, to other U.S. officials. However, he indicated that Montesinos enjoyed support among other U.S. agencies and implied that his views had not prevailed.[42]

There is no available indication that subsequent assistant secretaries for the region expressed serious concern. Career foreign-service officer Jeffrey Davidow served from August 1996 to July 1998, when he became the U.S. ambassador to Mexico. In the course of his career, Davidow does not appear to have taken strong stands favoring democracy and human rights.[43]

After Davidow's posting to Mexico, Peter F. Romero, a career foreign-service officer who had been the U.S. ambassador to Ecuador, was nominated to succeed him. Romero reported to the author that, although he was concerned throughout 2000 about the U.S. relationship with Vladimiro Montesinos, his influence on policy making toward Peru was limited for various reasons.[44] First, as the U.S. ambassador to Ecuador during the Ecuador-Peru border conflict, Romero had been charged by the Fujimori government of a tilt toward Ecuador; accordingly, it behooved him to be cautious in his criticism of the Peruvian government. Also, primarily because of his activities in the Colombian peace process, Romero was unable to secure confirmation from the U.S. Congress and accordingly served as acting assistant secretary.

At least in public, Romero was disinclined to discuss U.S. policy toward Peru. For example, in testimony on "current issues" to the Western Hemisphere Subcommittee of the U.S. House of Representatives in 1999, Romero discussed issues relating to Colombia, Cuba, Panama, Nicaragua, Venezuela, and Haiti, but not Peru.[45] In his presentation on political parties in Latin America at the Inter-American Dialogue on November 2, 1999, the Peruvian experience was not described. The acting assistant secretary declined an invitation to speak at the conference "Peace and Democratization in Peru: Advances, Setbacks, and Reflections on the 2000 Elections," held on January 27, 2000 at George Washington University. Although there are many possible reasons for Romero's reticence, it seems likely that he was conflicted by his cooperation with the Fujimori government, especially on behalf of U.S. business interests, and his knowledge of the regime's authoritarian proclivities. In early 2001, Romero retired from the U.S. Department of State for a position with Violy, Byorum, and Partners, a New York-based firm that specializes in mergers and acquisitions. He also became a paid consultant to Newmont Mining, a U.S.-based company whose interests he had advocated in a legal dispute in Peru in 1998 (see Chapter V).[46]

Through the 1990s, four successive career foreign-service officers were posted as the U.S. ambassador to Peru: Anthony Quainton (1989–1992); Alvin Adams (1993–1996); Dennis Jett (1996–1999); and John Hamilton (1999-). In a 1999 poll of Peruvian elites about power in the country, the U.S. ambassador to Peru was judged the second most influential foreigner in the country's course of events; Federal Reserve chairman Alan Greenspan topped the list.[47] Both Jett and Hamilton were controversial, high-profile ambassadors, whose roles are elaborated in Chapter VII.

Ambassador Jett was an outspoken critic of the Fujimori government's record on democracy and human rights. Not surprisingly, his criticism alienated the Fujimori government. The distance between Ambassador Jett on the one hand and President Fujimori and his top officials on the other was considered counter-productive by Davidow and Jett's other superiors in Washington.[48] Jett was dismayed; after his tour in Peru, he retired from the foreign service.

It was widely reported that, when Ambassador Hamilton was posted to Peru, he was asked by his superiors to reestablish a constructive relationship with the Peruvian government. He did so with gusto. For example, he took long-distance runs with Fujimori's daughter, Keiko, as she prepared for the New York Marathon in October 2000.[49] As Chapter VII describes, Hamilton became sympathetic to the Fujimori government's perspective. His analyses of Peruvian politics were influential in Washington; they were carefully considered, for example, by Arturo Valenzuela at the NSC.[50]

A senior U.S. diplomat whose influence was also significant was Luigi Einaudi. Einaudi was the U.S. special envoy for the Ecuador-Peru peace process from its inception in 1995 to its conclusion in 1998; also, after nominations by Peru, Ecuador, Bolivia, and the United States, he was elected assistant secretary general of the OAS in June 2000. Beginning in 1974, Einaudi was at the U.S. Department of State for twenty-four years, including twelve years as director of policy planning for the Bureau of Inter-American Affairs (1977–1989) and four years as U.S. ambassador to the OAS (1989–1993). Peru was a nation in which Einaudi had a strong interest. As a political scientist with the Rand Corporation between 1964 and 1974, Einaudi carried out studies of the Peruvian military; for example, he testified on the topic to the Subcommittee on Western Hemisphere Affairs of the U.S. Senate in 1969. During this period, Einaudi met Vladimiro Montesinos (see next section). In the poll cited above, Einaudi was ranked as the eighth most influential foreigner in Peru's course of events.[51]

The U.S. Congress

During the 1990s, a role in the making of U.S. policy toward Peru was played by the U.S. Congress. The U.S. Congress was especially mindful of human-rights violations in Peru, and its stance toward the country was by and large more critical than the Clinton administration's. This was especially the case during the period before and after Peru's rigged 2000 elections, when U.S. officials were debating the appropriate U.S. policy response. Congressional criticism was in part a reflection of lobby efforts by human-rights groups and the Peruvian opposition. (However, the power of both opposition and government Peruvian lobby groups paled in comparison to the most powerful Latin American lobbies, such as the Mexican.)

In the November 1994 midterm elections, the Republicans won a majority in the U.S. Congress, and Jesse Helms, U.S. senator from North Carolina, became the chairman of the U.S. Senate Foreign Relations Committee. In this position, of course, Helms wielded tremendous power over budgets, nominations, and treaties. Helms was skeptical of the Fujimori government. One reason for the animosity was that a U.S. crewman who died in 1992 when Peruvian fighter jets shot down a U.S. Air Force Hercules C-130 was from North Carolina (see Chapter VI). Indeed, Republicans' distrust of the Peruvian military was long standing; recall from Chapter II that the Peruvian military's ties to the Soviet Union had annoyed Republican legislators in particular from the 1960s through the 1980s.

In 1997, the Fujimori government revoked Baruch Ivcher's Peruvian citizenship and denied his right to own a Peruvian media organization (see Chapter VII); Ivcher fled to the United States and initiated a lobbying effort against the violations of media freedom in Peru. Ivcher's cause was taken up by Elliott Abrams, assistant secretary of state for Latin America under President Reagan, who was in close contact with Helms. Abrams galvanized Helms to take the lead on various congressional resolutions critical of the Fujimori government's record on the media and democracy. At the same time, human-rights groups, in particular the Washington Office on Latin America, lobbied congressional Democrats on the issue.

The plight of Lori Berenson, which was mentioned above for its interest to President Clinton, was also a concern for numerous Democrats in the U.S. Congress. Human-rights groups argued that Berenson should have the right to a fair trial and that her case showed the continuing lack of due process in Peru.

U.S. Public Opinion

The Clinton administration's scant attention to Latin America and the U.S. Congress's scant resources for it were in good part a reflection of limited interest in the region among the U.S. public. Ironically, despite globalization and worldwide integration of markets and knowledge, most U.S. citizens are disinterested in Latin America. In public-opinion polls in the late 1990s, majorities of 55 to 66 percent said that what happens in Western Europe, Asia, Mexico, and Canada had little or no impact on their lives, and of course the percent with this view about what happens in Peru would be much greater.[52]

In a vicious circle of public disinterest and media disinterest, coverage of foreign events in the U.S. media plummeted.[53] For example, in the first two months of 2000 (near the height of Peru's electoral campaign), the *Washington Post* published no articles on Peru; in contrast, during the same two months during Peru's 1980, 1985, and 1990 elections, the newspaper published nine articles each year (and four during the same two months for the 1995 elections).[54]

The Clinton administration's priorities in Peru were also to a degree a reflection of the U.S. public's priorities. In a survey by the Chicago Council on Foreign Relations in late 1998, more than 80 percent of the U.S. public ranked "stopping the flow of illegal drugs into the United States" as a "very important" foreign policy goal.[55] About 40 percent ranked "defending our allies' security" as very important. In contrast, only about 35 percent judged "protecting and defending human rights in other countries" as very important, and less than 30 percent believed that "helping bring a democratic form of government to other nations" was very important. Unlike Clinton administration officials, however, the U.S. public was not particularly enthusiastic about the goal of "promoting market economies abroad"; only about 30 percent considered it very important.

Accordingly, although U.S. scholars were skeptical of the Clinton administration's foreign policy performance, the public was enthusiastic. In 1998, according to the same Chicago Council on Foreign Relations polls cited above, the public's consensus was that Clinton's foreign policy performance was "outstanding."[56] His foreign policy performance was ranked the best of all post-World War II U.S. presidents.[57]

THE FUJIMORI GOVERNMENT'S POLICY MAKING TOWARD THE UNITED STATES

Whereas President Clinton was minimally engaged in U.S. policy making toward Peru and numerous agencies played a role in policy making toward the country, in Peru policy-making power was concentrated in President Alberto Fujimori and his national security adviser, Vladimiro Montesinos. Fujimori was a key actor for all policies on the U.S.-Peruvian bilateral agenda. Montesinos played a central role in all policies—security, narcotics control, and democracy and human rights—except free-market reform.

A crucial question is the nature of the relationship between Fujimori and Montesinos, but its precise nature remains unclear. For the most part, U.S. government officials respected Fujimori and believed, virtually until his resignation in November 2000, that he would be an effective Peruvian president without

Montesinos at his side.[58] Peruvians' assessments of Fujimori were much less favorable. In the mid-to-late 1990s, Peruvians tended to see Fujimori as the weaker of the two men, beguiled and gradually controlled by Montesinos; Montesinos was most commonly dubbed "Fujimori's Rasputin." Most Peruvians doubted that Fujimori could remain in power very long without Montesinos to protect and/or advise him. Toward the end of the regime and after its downfall, Peruvians' evaluations were harsher: the two were considered partners in crime. After Fujimori and Montesinos dressed virtually identically for a television interview in 1999, they were often called "the Siamese twins"—joined together in the flesh.

Although Fujimori and Montesinos were the most important makers of Peruvian foreign policy, other actors played key roles during particular periods. For some six years—between approximately 1993 and 1998—the commander in chief of the armed forces, General Nicolás de Barí Hermoza, was pivotal to various policies; indeed, during this period Fujimori, Montesinos, and Hermoza were dubbed the power "triumvirate" or "troika." Also, in the first years of the Fujimori government, independent technocrats were influential in the establishment of free-market reform and in the defense of the government's autogolpe; subsequently, at the foreign ministry, they were also influential in the negotiations for a Peru-Ecuador border accord and in democracy controversies.

Fujimori's Cultural Identity and Decision-Making Style

Long before President Fujimori's faxing of his resignation from Japan, questions about his cultural identity were common. Many analysts doubted his patriotism and questioned whether or not it was his unusually international background that led him to closer collaboration with the United States than any other Peruvian president since Leguía. For their part, some U.S. officials may have wondered how Fujimori's successor could possibly be as international in his background as Fujimori.

Alberto Fujimori was the son of Naoichi and Mutsue Fujimori, who had emigrated from Japan to Peru in 1934. According to the available documents, Alberto was born in Peru in 1938 on July 28 (Peru's independence day). However, the place and date of his birth were doubted; there were suspicious corrections on his birth certificate and on the registry of the boat from which his parents disembarked in Peru.[59] The question was important because, if Fujimori had not been born in Peru, he would not have been eligible for the country's presidency. After Fujimori's flight to Japan in 2000, the question appeared settled by the Japanese government's announcement that Fujimori's parents had registered his birth in the Japanese consulate in Lima.

The events of Fujimori's youth were unlikely to have endeared Peru to him.[60] In contrast to many first-generation Japanese immigrants (called "nisseis" in Peru), Fujimori's parents struggled economically. Although his father moved up from his first job in Peru as a farmhand to become a small businessman, he lost a cotton farm, a tire-repair shop, a hardware store, and a flower shop before establishing a small poultry farm. During World War II, anti-Japanese sentiments were intense in Peru; more than fifteen hundred prominent Japanese men were detained during the war. Like most nisseis in Peru, Fujimori's parents feared arrest. The language in the Fujimori home was Japanese, and Alberto did not begin to study Spanish until he was almost eight years old.

Alberto's gift was mathematics. Having excelled in mathematics on an entrance examination, Alberto was admitted to an outstanding public secondary school. Smart and diligent, he graduated at the top of his class. Aspiring to a profession as an agricultural economist, he went on to Peru's Agrarian University, called La Molina; he graduated in 1961, again at the top of his class. However, during his high school and university years, Fujimori was a loner; he had few if any friends, and—perhaps most tellingly—he did not participate in political activities.

Fujimori's academic abilities earned him scholarships abroad. In 1964, he was able to study in France; then, in 1970–1972, he studied for a master of science degree in the United States at the University of Wisconsin. Fujimori's experience in the United States was very positive. He noted that it was "one of the most gratifying experiences of my life. This was especially so because it allowed me to go deeper into mathematics with a rigor that tempered my mind and spirit . . . my logic was enriched with the mathematical premise that every problem has a scientific and practical solution."[61] However, at Wisconsin, Fujimori also seemed to make more friends and enjoy more social activities than at any previous time in his life.[62] A pre-university academy founded by Fujimori and his wife was named Wisconsin in honor of this U.S. university.

In 1972, Fujimori returned to Peru and resumed teaching mathematics at La Molina. Two years later, he married Susana Higuchi, who was also the child of Japanese emigrants to Peru (but who had been more successful than Fujimori's parents). The Fujimoris' four children were all given Japanese first names and Spanish middle names. In the 1990s, Fujimori's eldest son, Hiro Alberto, worked in Japan. His other three children studied in the United States; his eldest daughter (and, after his divorce, his first lady), Keiko Sofía, graduated from Boston University. In part to see his children, President Fujimori visited the United States frequently (see below).

Fujimori was also fond of Japan. After his 1990 electoral triumph, one of the first countries that he visited was Japan, and he returned frequently. During a failed attempt at a "countercoup" in November 1992 (see Chapter VII), Fujimori sought refuge in the Japanese ambassador's residence. Fujimori's affection for Japan was reciprocated. On his visits to the country, he was warmly welcomed, often by huge crowds. Japan was the first country in the "Support Group" that was committed to what was called Peru's reinsertion in the international financial community (see Chapter V). Japan was generous with aid and donations. How-

ever, Japanese investment in Peru did not increase significantly. Japanese investment in Peru was only $42 million between 1990 and 1997 (of a total of about $7
billion); Japan's share of foreign capital was a mere 0.7 percent, ranking it four-
teenth among country investors in Peru.[63]

In general, Fujimori was an extremely frequent traveler. Between July 1990
and September 1998, he logged a hundred trips to forty-seven countries; in contrast, between 1980 and 1985 President Belaúnde logged six trips abroad, and
between 1985 and 1990 President García logged thirteen.[64] During the eight
years, Fujimori's most frequent destinations were the United States (fifteen visits), Bolivia (twelve), Japan (nine), and Brazil (eight). The cost of these trips was
estimated at $11,492,346. In 1995, by confidential decree, Fujimori approved the
purchase of a Boeing 737–500 jet for his exclusive use.[65] The reasons for Fujimori's extensive travels were controversial. The president said that, given the
deficiencies of Peru's foreign ministry, presidential diplomacy was necessary; the
trips brought Peru investment, markets, and goodwill.[66] Critics retorted that,
given Fujimori had spent an entire year out of the country during his eight years
in office, the benefits from his travels were insufficient. It is now clear that Fujimori was able to travel frequently because he delegated many responsibilities to
Montesinos. Also, the possibility that Fujimori traveled in order to move money
out of Peru has been raised.

Fujimori's family background as well as his mathematical orientation were
factors in his decision-making style. This style was commonly described by his
supporters as "pragmatic" and by his critics as "calculating."[67] In general, Fujimori made decisions with one or two advisers; uncomfortable with others and
disliking negotiation, decisions were taken first and explained later. But Fujimori
was also focused. As Ecuadorian president Jamil Mahuad said after the Ecuador-
Peru accords were concluded:

> [It is true that Fujimori is] reserved, calculating, cold, introverted, [but he is
> also] a man who takes decisions, with whom you can converse with ab-
> solute frankness and one who made the effort to understand what was
> going on in Ecuador. . . ."[68]

During Fujimori's ten years in office, his circle of advisers narrowed. During
his first eighteen months in office, Fujimori was considered to have three sets of
advisers.[69] Arguably the set that appeared most powerful at this time were family
members, in particular his younger brother Santiago. A lawyer with extensive
ties to Japanese Peruvians, Santiago was considered chief of staff and "shadow
foreign affairs minister"; he oversaw foreign investment projects, coordinated
Fujimori's trips, and helped the president in numerous other ways.[70] Other family members, including Fujimori's wife Susana, his brother Pedro, his sister Rosa,
and her husband Víctor Aritomi were also influential. Gradually, however, Fuji-

mori and his key family members became estranged. Just before the autogolpe, Susana accused her husband's brother and sister of corruption, and she was ousted from the presidential palace. As Montesinos's power increased, Santiago's declined; after 1995, he was rarely at the presidential palace. By 2000, the only family members at Fujimori's side were his children, in particular his daughter Keiko.

A second circle of advisers was commonly referred to as "independent technocrats." These advisers were "independent" in the sense that they were not members of political parties. Usually, of course, presidents (including Belaúnde and García in Peru in the 1980s) recruit their top advisers on policy issues from party ranks. However, Fujimori had assembled Cambio 90, his political vehicle for the 1990 elections, quickly; he had not even met many of its members. A considerable number of Cambio 90 members were evangelical Christians without professional stature; not surprisingly, the president sought expertise outside the party. Among the most important independent technocrats were Hernando de Soto, Carlos Boloña, and Francisco Tudela. Even in the late 1990s—as the Peruvian political arena polarized between "government" and "opposition," allegations of corruption mounted, and the applicability of the label "independent technocrats" became questionable—the Fujimori government was able to recruit some respected professionals to its ranks.

A businessman who combined the characteristics of "family member" and "independent technocrat"—Jaime Yoshiyama—was influential in the early and mid-1990s. The Yoshiyama and Aritomi families were both originally based in the mountain city of Huancayo and knew each other well; Víctor Aritomi recruited Jaime to head a state company. Fujimori and Yoshiyama had a great deal in common: Both were descendants of Japanese immigrants, both had studied in the United States, and both had considerable background in science and mathematics. The rapport between the two was strong.[71] Yoshiyama became minister for transport and communications and then minister for energy and mines. Heading the government's political coalition in the 1992 elections, Yoshiyama presided over the Constituent Assembly. Gradually, Yoshiyama, who had studied at Harvard University and enjoyed considerable prestige in international circles, came to be considered a likely successor to Fujimori and was widely dubbed his "dauphin." However, in 1995, Yoshiyama ran as the government's candidate for the mayoralty of Lima and was defeated by another businessman, Alberto Andrade. In the wake of this defeat, signaling that Yoshiyama was unlikely to win in 2000, the relationship between Yoshiyama and Fujimori cooled. In September 1996—within weeks of the congress's passing of the law that permitted Fujimori to run for a third consecutive term—Yoshiyama abruptly resigned.[72] The departure of Yoshiyama was probably a pivotal Fujimori turn away from advisers who were relatives or friends and toward Montesinos.

The third "circle" of "advisers" was Montesinos. While not unimportant to Fujimori during his presidential campaign and the first eighteen months of his presidency, Montesinos's power increased dramatically after the 1992 autogolpe. His institutional base of power in the Servicio de Inteligencia Nacional (National Intelligence Service, SIN) expanded concomitantly. At the same time, however, after the 1992 autogolpe, the military also became a critical base of power for the regime, and a complex relationship emerged between Montesinos and the commander in chief of Peru's armed forces, General Hermoza. It was only in 1998 that Montesinos achieved the goal he appeared to have sought for several years— the status not as Fujimori's most important adviser, but his only "adviser."

The changes in Fujimori's circles of advisers is indicated by the annual Apoyo surveys among elite Peruvians about power in Peru.[73] From 1991 through 1995, the power of Santiago Fujimori was ranked either fifth, sixth, or seventh; thereafter, his ranking fell out of the top ten. Independent technocrats Hernando de Soto and Carlos Boloña were among the top six in 1991–1992, but by 1994 their rankings were out of the top twenty. After 1994, the only independent technocrats among the top ten were Francisco Tudela (number nine in 1997) and Fernando de Trazegnies (number nine in 1999). From 1993 through 1996, Jaime Yoshiyama was ranked fourth; thereafter, he was not among the top thirty. From a number twelve ranking in 1991 and a number four ranking in 1992, Vladimiro Montesinos rose to number two in 1993, a ranking he held through 1999—except for the year 1997, when he tied with Fujimori as the most powerful person in Peru. For five of the six years from 1993 through 1998, General Nicolás de Bari Hermoza was ranked third, directly after Fujimori and Montesinos.[74]

Vladimiro Montesinos, Nicolás de Bari Hermoza, and Peru's Security Forces

How did Vladimiro Montesinos overcome a past in which he had been cashiered from the army and had been a lawyer for drug traffickers to become virtually copresident of Peru? Or, in the most common epithet, Fujimori's Rasputin? How did he outmaneuver even General Hermoza, who, as the commander in chief of the armed forces and the commander of the army from 1991 through 1998, had appeared to control what was arguably Peru's most important institution during the increasingly authoritarian Fujimori government?

Although we do not have the complete answer to this question, Montesinos's guile was clearly very important. Montesinos was extraordinarily cunning and had no moral scruples. He appeared to possess virtually infinite amounts of intelligence on important actors—especially within the military and judiciary. Montesinos's and Fujimori's political styles were similar: Both were chess players who sought to control events and space to maximize their opportunity for maneuver and to exclude and defeat opponents.[75]

Montesinos was "Mr. Fix-It" not only for Fujimori but also for the U.S. government. Both Fujimori and Montesinos believed that the U.S. government was a key base of support, and Montesinos—primarily because of his relationship with the CIA and U.S. narcotics-control units—was essential to the maintenance of this support.

It should also be mentioned—in part because it often is not—that Montesinos was intelligent, well read, and could be very charming; all these traits very probably were important to his relationship with both Peruvian and U.S. officials. At the same time, it is possible that, especially by the late 1990s, Montesinos was blackmailing his colleagues, including Fujimori. For many years, it was hypothesized (incorrectly) that Montesinos had documents showing Fujimori's birthplace to be not Peru but Japan. Probably each had material that compromised the other. At the same time too, Montesinos was arrogant; arrogance was apparently important to his various political miscalculations in 2000 (see Chapter VII).

In the early 1970s, Montesinos was an army captain working for various powerful government ministers, and by virtually all accounts at that time he became a spy for the CIA.[76] Montesinos was keenly interested in geopolitics and security issues, and his knowledge of these issues was impressive to his superiors. In 1973, General Edgardo Mercado Jarrín became prime minister, defense minister, and commander in chief of the army in the Velasco government, and Montesinos became one of his assistants. From that position, Montesinos had access to classified information, which he was soon suspected of selling to the CIA. Some of this information was about Peru's acquisition of Soviet armaments. Montesinos also made the acquaintance of Luigi Einaudi, who was at this time a political scientist researching the Peruvian military for the Rand Corporation (an institution with close links to the U.S. government) and would later become a high-level official in the U.S. Department of State.[77]

By 1976, not only had the Velasco government fallen, but suspicions that Montesinos was a spy mounted. In September, the captain who had enjoyed access to the highest levels of power was suddenly posted to a small garrison in a desolate part of Peru. The most carefully researched report of subsequent events is by Gustavo Gorriti, who wrote that "[within days of Montesinos's posting], he requested sick leave, returned to Lima, stole a blank army travel form, falsified it, and went to the U.S. Embassy. There he received an official invitation to the U.S., which had either been on hold or was instantly arranged. . . . Once in Washington . . . he met with Luigi Einaudi, then at the Policy Planning Staff of the State Department, and CIA Office of Current Intelligence Officer, Robert Hawkins."[78] According to other accounts, he participated in conferences at the Pentagon and the CIA.[79] However, at the Inter-American Defense College, Montesinos was recognized by a Peruvian general who immediately cabled Lima. On Montesinos's return to Peru, he was arrested and charged with high treason, "falsehood," and "dereliction of duty." Ultimately, the charge of treason was dropped, but Montesinos was convicted of the two latter charges, dishonorably discharged from the army, and sentenced to one year in jail.

It is not clear exactly how or when Montesinos's relationship with the CIA was renewed. During the 1980s, his primary work was as a lawyer for drug traffickers. According to Gorriti, however, his services "went far beyond the practice of law. He rented homes for Colombian traffickers, advised accessories of traffickers when to go into hiding, managed the disappearance of files of fugitive Colombian traffickers to prevent extradition requests, and in at least one case, produced falsified documents to buttress his defense of a cocaine dealer. . . . He also maintained contacts in the army."[80] It is possible that Montesinos's information was of interest to the CIA at this time.[81]

Montesinos and Fujimori met just after the first round of the 1990 elections. President García, who was siding with Fujimori in the runoff, directed the SIN (at that time a small agency) to help Fujimori. Fujimori and his wife were confronting allegations of underpayment of taxes on their real-estate business and falsifications in the purchase of a farm. At the time a lawyer working for Peru's attorney general and also collaborating with the SIN, Montesinos was introduced to Fujimori. Montesinos promised Fujimori that he could "fix anything"—words that as noted above became his mantra. Apparently, at their first meeting, Montesinos repeated to Fujimori: "Forget the problem! It's already taken care of."[82] Indeed, Peru's public prosecutor issued a judgment favorable to Fujimori. Fujimori appointed Montesinos his legal adviser, and Montesinos and Fujimori began to meet almost every night at 11:00 p.m.[83]

After Fujimori's election, Montesinos sought an institutional base, which was to be the SIN. In early 1991, Montesinos achieved the appointment of a nonentity to the formal leadership of the SIN so that he himself could be the real power at the agency. In contrast to most political actors in Peru, Montesinos preferred to exercise power behind the scenes. The likely reason was that, without an official post, Montesinos could not be interrogated by legislators or journalists—or, indeed, by anyone. He was accountable only to Fujimori. Montesinos's behind-the-scenes position apparently pleased Fujimori, who as a result did not fear that Montesinos would steal his spotlight.

Montesinos also sought to increase his and Fujimori's power by intervention in the norms for promotion and retirement within the military. As a 1970s army captain, Montesinos was familiar with most of the officers who had now achieved high military ranks. He counseled Fujimori to retire various officers who were advocates of a professional, nonpoliticized military institution. Then, in November 1991, with the encouragement of Montesinos and the use of special-power executive provisions, Fujimori introduced dramatic changes in the regulations for the military institution. Traditionally, military promotions were made annually, according to seniority, professional reputation, and the meeting of educational requirements. Also, the high command was renewed annually. Under the new law, the president gained the power to appoint the commander in chief from among the highest-ranking officers and to retire any officer at will. Also, annual rotation and mandatory retirement provisions were ended; now a commander in chief could stay in power indefinitely.

The immediate beneficiary of this law was General Nicolás de Barí Hermoza, who became army commander and commander in chief of the armed forces in December 1991. An undistinguished, second-rank officer, Hermoza apparently achieved his promotion through a pledge of compliance with key decisions made by Montesinos and Fujimori—including support for the autogolpe, which was already being planned.[84]

Also, in 1990–1992, Montesinos's relationship with the CIA became closer. As Montesinos's reports about the new government's policies and personnel proved accurate, he became "a prized and protected asset of the CIA."[85] According to an anonymous U.S. diplomat interviewed by Gorriti, the CIA station chief in Lima was "bamboozled by Montesinos."[86] In 1991, a counternarcotics unit was established in the SIN and Montesinos emerged as Peru's lead actor in antidrug initiatives; in part due to his relationship with the CIA, the CIA's role in the antidrug war in Peru was strengthened against the Drug Enforcement Agency's. Needless to say, given Montesinos's background, some officials in DEA and the Narcotics Assistance Unit of the State Department were angry, but their opposition was ineffective.[87] Collaboration between Montesinos and the CIA station chief in Lima reinforced their increasing political power.

After the 1992 autogolpe, the power of the SIN greatly increased.[88] The SIN gained control over the intelligence arm of each sector of the armed forces. It achieved ministerial rank, directly responsible to the president. It was not subject to oversight by the Peruvian congress or any other institution. Although the SIN's formal responsibilities were the combat of terrorism and drugs, in practice the SIN became a political police, dedicated to the elimination of opposition to the Fujimori government. By the late 1990s, with a staff of some 1,500 employees—plus about 13,500 agents in branches of the armed forces and police—the SIN and Montesinos investigated, bribed, intimidated, and harassed Peruvian media magnates and journalists, judges, election officials, candidates, and many other members of opposition groups or potential opposition groups.[89]

The power of General Hermoza also increased after the autogolpe. Although Hermoza's greater power did not appear to have been anticipated by Fujimori or Montesinos, it was not surprising. Most obviously, it was now more important to Fujimori and Montesinos that the commander in chief be willing to order the troops into the streets in a political crisis—and Hermoza was willing to do so. It was not clear how many of Peru's ranking officers would be so inclined. After the capture of Abimael Guzmán in September 1992 and the concomitant eclipse of the insurgency, many top officers became more concerned about the authoritarian proclivities of the regime and intensifying politicization of the military institution. In November 1992, some of these officers plotted a countercoup against the Fujimori government and, in April 1993, others charged Montesinos and Hermoza with responsibility for the human-rights violations at La Cantuta University.[90] On both occasions, Hermoza ordered his troops into the streets.

Gradually, just as Fujimori and Montesinos had co-opted Hermoza, the general was able to co-opt his own allies within the military and accordingly secure a network of support that provided the general his own power base and, accordingly, a degree of autonomy.[91] Also, Hermoza was able to enhance his power within the military by positioning himself as an advocate of its strength and capabilities, during both the Peru-Ecuador border conflict and the rescue of the hostages at the Japanese ambassador's residence.[92]

In 1997–1998, however, the tensions within the troika mounted. Competition over credit for the hostage rescue was intense (see Chapter IV). Also, Hermoza tended to favor renewed military action against Ecuador rather than the negotiated settlement that was to be reached in October 1998.[93] In the context of these tensions, Montesinos maneuvered to place officers loyal to him rather than Hermoza in key commands. Montesinos's maneuvers were facilitated by the fact that seniority remained a factor in promotions and the class of 1966, which had been Montesinos's class, was now positioned to secure top ranks.[94] In August 1998, at a meeting of the high command in the presidential palace, Fujimori took not only Peruvians but also Hermoza by surprise: He announced the replacement of Hermoza by Peru's defense minister, General César Saucedo.

With the dismissal of Hermoza, Montesinos had achieved the goal that he had apparently sought for several years: sole partner to Fujimori. He was careful that no new rivals would emerge. For example, in 2000, twelve of the seventeen divisions of the army were from Montesinos's 1966 army class; the commander for the key Lima military region was his brother-in-law.[95]

Montesinos's partnership with Fujimori (and also with the CIA) was apparently not affected by the indications of Montesinos's corruption, which became more ample in the government's second term. In 1996, the notorious jailed Peruvian drug lord Demetrio Chávez Peñaherrera (dubbed "El Vaticano") testified in court that he paid Montesinos $50,000 a month for information on antidrug raids in 1991–1992. In 1997, it was reported that Montesinos had earned a 1995 income of about $700,000—an amount that was impossible to be earned legally by a Peruvian government official.[96] In 1999, it was revealed that his annual income had risen above $2 million.[97] After the Fujimori government's downfall, Montesinos was charged with illicit enrichment from government arms purchases, drug trafficking, and human-rights abuses (among other crimes).

The Role of "Independent Technocrats"

Especially at the start of Fujimori's government, when he was the surprise winner of the elections without a conventional political party behind him, the president recruited "independent technocrats"—well-educated, prestigious policy experts who were not affiliated with any political party. These technocrats were influential primarily in the areas of free-market reform and diplomacy.

Within hours of Fujimori's victory in the June 1990 runoff, the president-elect called Hernando de Soto.[98] Although Fujimori had campaigned on a center-left platform, he had decided that de Soto could be helpful. De Soto was able and respected in pro-free-market circles. In the 1970s, de Soto had earned a graduate degree in international economics and law at the Institut Universitaire des Hautes Etudes in Geneva and had then become a managing director of a Swiss consulting firm. Returning to Peru, he founded the Institute for Liberty and Democracy, which was funded by the U.S. Agency for International Development and the U.S. Chamber of Commerce, among other donors. In 1986, de Soto's book, *The Other Path*, was published; the text criticizes Latin American states for their establishment of endless webs of red tape that stifled the entrepreneurial spirit of the region's majorities and ultimately served the interest of oligopolies. The book was the subject of an article by Mario Vargas Llosa in *New York Times Sunday Magazine* and topped best-seller lists in numerous Latin American countries.

Although de Soto was not enthralled by Fujimori, he was ambitious and interested in the promotion of his free-market ideas. Indeed, despite the relatively leftist policies of the García government, de Soto advised it on the delivery of property titles. Soon after de Soto's initial meeting with Fujimori, de Soto became key to the development of Fujimori's economic program, in particular what Peruvians called Peru's "reinsertion" into the international financial community (see Chapter V). He also provided important input on the government's antinarcotics program and on its position about democracy. However, although de Soto was playing the role of prime minister, he eschewed any formal title in the government.

De Soto's Institute for Democracy and Liberty became a source for various top officials. In February 1991, it was decided that Fujimori's first economics minister, Juan Carlos Hurtado Miller, who had been the 1983–1985 agriculture minister in the second Belaúnde government, did not have sufficient free-market convictions or technical knowledge for his position; as his successor, de Soto recommended Carlos Boloña. Boloña, who had an M.A. in economics from the

University of Iowa and a Ph.D. in economics from Oxford University, was firmly committed to a comprehensive, profound free-market reform that would gain the confidence of the World Bank and the IMF (see Chapter V).

In January 1992, de Soto left Fujimori's side. De Soto had been working with Peru's coca growers to persuade them to plant other crops, and he charged that his work was being compromised by corrupt officials in the coca-growing areas and that the government's antinarcotics effort was insufficient. He was also concerned about Fujimori's authoritarian proclivities; in particular, de Soto espoused "Democratization of Decisions"—a proposal for the prepublication of legislation so that it could be debated by the public—but the proposal was rejected by Fujimori.

After the hostile international reaction to Fujimori's autogolpe (see Chapter VII), however, de Soto agreed to advise the government again. He persuaded Fujimori to travel to the Bahamas meeting of the OAS that would decide the organization's response to the autogolpe. De Soto was also the primary author of Fujimori's persuasive speech for the meeting; this speech argued that the goal of the autogolpe was "true democracy" rather than the previous "party-ocracy" (domination by entrenched political parties). When Fujimori ultimately did not deliver on most of the proposals in de Soto's speech, however, their relationship ended.

Still, for the most part the independent technocrats responsible for free-market reform remained in the Fujimori government for at least some months after the autogolpe. Boloña served as economics minister through the end of 1992. Another independent technocrat, Manuel Estela, became the director of the Superintendencia Nacional de Administración Tributaria (SUNAT, National Tax Administration Superintendency).[99] Hailing from the Universidad Católica del Perú (Catholic University of Peru) and a former head of economic research at Peru's central bank, Estela was an able and respected professional who, from early 1991 until December 1992, coordinated a thorough reform of personnel and programs at SUNAT (see Chapter V).

Gradually, the Fujimori government became more authoritarian and its capacity to attract independent technocrats declined. The term *independent technocrats* became less appropriate. Still, there were various key officials to whom the label was often applied; most of these officials were brought into Peru's foreign ministry from Peru's Catholic University or from Lima think tanks.

Probably the most important of these was Francisco Tudela, at one time a director of the Catholic University's Instituto de Estudios Internacionales (IDEI, Institute of International Studies). Holding an M.A. degree in international public law from the London School of Economics and Political Science, Tudela was one of the most respected foreign ministers of the Fujimori government, serving from 1995 until mid-1997. Although he resigned in protest of the government's treatment of media magnate Baruch Ivcher (see Chapter VII), he was Perú 2000's first vice presidential candidate and then first vice president in 2000.

After Tudela's resignation, the Fujimori government continued to recruit lawyers who were considered independent technocrats to the position of foreign minister. The 1997–1998 foreign minister, Eduardo Ferrero Costa, had completed graduate studies at the University of Wisconsin (as had Fujimori) and had established Peru's only respected foreign policy think tank.[100] Fujimori's final foreign minister, Fernando de Trazegnies, had earned a doctorate in law from the University of Paris and had been dean of the law faculty at the Catholic University.

Peru's Foreign Ministry

As Fujimori increased presidential power in foreign policy making, he concomitantly reduced the power of Peru's foreign ministry. Although professional diplomats as well as independent technocrats were important to the government's efforts to restore Peru's democratic credentials after the autogolpe and also to the resolution of the Peru-Ecuador border conflict, overall they were slighted under the Fujimori government.

Traditionally, Peru's foreign ministry was recognized as one of the most professional, with the most important policy-making role, in the region. The foreign ministry was located in a colonial-style building called the Palace of Torre Tagle. Diplomats were among the distinguished members of Peruvian society. In 1955, a diplomatic academy was established as a center for high studies and professional development. The principal diplomatic doctrines were nonintervention in a state's internal affairs and the search for independence from potentially hegemonic powers.

During the 1970s, leftist international ideological currents entered the foreign ministry. Spearheaded by the diplomat Carlos García Bedoya, the foreign ministry was active in the solidarity movements of Latin American and Third World countries. This stance intensified during the presidency of Alan García. During this period, Peru's foreign ministry sought to rally Latin American nations behind Peru's debt-service policy. Also, the García government supported the Contadora countries' efforts for negotiated settlements to the conflicts in Central America and temporarily recalled the Peruvian ambassador to the United States to protest the U.S. invasion of Panama in December 1989.

President Fujimori sought to excise leftist ideology from the making of Peru's foreign policy. The government's watchword was *pragmatism*.

Toward this end, the government signaled to diplomats that they served at the pleasure of the president; all foreign ministers except Fujimori's first were recruited from nondiplomatic backgrounds, and their tenures were brief. There

were four foreign ministers between Fujimori's inauguration and the days immediately after the autogolpe. The foreign ministers during the government's two
terms and their professional backgrounds were:[101]

Luis Marchand Stein	1990–1991	Diplomacy
Vice Admiral Raúl Sánchez Sotomayor	1991	Navy
Carlos Torres y Torres Lara	1991	Law
Augusto Blacker Miller	1991–1992	Economy
Oscar de la Puente Raygara	1992–1993	Law
Efraín Goldenberg	1993–1995	Business
Francisco Tudela	1995–1997	International law
Eduardo Ferrero Costa	1997–1998	International law
Fernando de Trazegnies	1998–2000	Law

Also, after the autogolpe, the foreign ministry's power was reduced. Whereas
under the previous law "the Ministry conducts the foreign affairs of the Republic," under the post-autogolpe law "the President of the Republic conducts the
international relations of Perú. The Foreign Ministry is the organ responsible for
executing the directives as dictated by the Chief of State. . . ."[102] Simultaneously,
the Fujimori government began one of the largest purges of foreign ministry
officials in Peru's history. As many as 117 diplomats were accused of homosexu-
ality and/or incompetence and fired.[103] Further, the 20 percent ceiling on the
number of ambassadors that a president could appoint was eliminated.[104] Fujimori began to name friends and relatives to key foreign policy posts: His high
school classmate Oscar de la Puente became the 1992–1993 foreign minister, and
his brother-in-law Víctor Aritomi became Peru's ambassador to Japan.

Fujimori also established a new institution, PROMPERÚ (Commission for the
Promotion of Peru), for the purpose of Peru's public relations. The idea was to
counter the negative image of Peru as the country of the autogolpe, human-
rights violations, and drug trafficking with a positive image of a "new Peru" that
had not only a rich cultural history but was also politically stable and economically dynamic.[105] With such major cultural expositions as the "Lord of Sipán,"
and the "Ice Queen" in the United States and elsewhere, PROMPERÚ proved effective and to a certain extent displaced Peru's embassies in their traditional
public-relations role.[106]

There were some exceptions to this pattern of deprofessionalizing the foreign
ministry, however. In December 1992, the Fujimori government appointed a
distinguished diplomat, Ricardo Luna, to the critical position of Peruvian ambassador to the United States. With a B.A. from Princeton University, and an M.A.
from Columbia University, and a fellowship position at Harvard University as
well as a degree from Peru's diplomatic academy, Luna was well educated and sophisticated. As a career diplomat, he had served in eight different Peruvian

embassies and was Peru's ambassador to the United Nations from 1989 through 1992. Especially during 1993 and 1994, Luna's intelligent, energetic diplomacy was invaluable to the restoration of a positive relationship between Peru and the United States.[107]

As the tensions of the autogolpe ended and the relationship between Peru and the United States began to warm, the emphasis of Peru's foreign ministry shifted. In 1993, when official attention was centered on the promotion of investment and commerce, President Fujimori appointed as foreign minister Efraín Goldenberg, a businessman with no diplomatic or political experience. After the 1995 outbreak of hostilities between Peru and Ecuador, however, the ministry's attention turned quickly toward the resolution of the border conflict.[108] Goldenberg was replaced by Francisco Tudela, an international lawyer whose distinguished credentials were cited above; Tudela was succeeded by Eduardo Ferrero, whose foreign policy expertise was also outstanding. Both Tudela and Ferrero were Peru's lead actors in the negotiations with Ecuador.[109] In August 1998, however, as the negotiations were in their final stage, Fujimori himself assumed primary responsibility for the outcome; Fujimori assented to a concession that Ferrero considered unnecessary, and Ferrero resigned in protest (see Chapter IV).

In the final year of the Fujimori government, just as in 1992–1993, the primary mandate of Peru's foreign ministry was to defend the government's human-rights and democracy record. In particular, the foreign ministry sought to discourage U.S. criticism of the 2000 elections.

The foreign ministry's fulfillment of its charge was impeded by the transfer to Lima of the Peruvian ambassador to the United States, Ricardo Luna. On February 5, 1999, Fujimori arrived in Washington to celebrate the peace accord between Peru and Ecuador. Fujimori was not happy with his visit. On the day of his arrival, the accord was praised but Fujimori's democracy record was criticized in an editorial in the *Washington Post*. Fujimori was also annoyed that his agenda was not as full as Ecuadorian president Mahuad's and that he did not attend a Capitol Hill prayer breakfast in which Mahuad enjoyed the opportunity to meet President Clinton. Fujimori did not attend the prayer meeting because of miscommunications among Peruvian officials, for which Fujimori blamed Luna and transferred him back to Peru. Given Luna's almost seven years of experience as ambassador and his outstanding reputation in the capital, he would almost certainly have helped the Fujimori government make its case.

Arriving in Washington only in the fall of 1999, the incoming Peruvian ambassador, Alfonso Rivero, was not able to gain the confidence of U.S. officials. The Peruvian ambassador to the OAS from the mid- to late 1990s through 2000, Beatriz Ramacciotti, was articulate and capable, but did not have Luna's stature. Desperate, the Fujimori government contracted the lobbying services of the Patton Boggs law firm and the Shepardson, Stern, and Kaminsky public relations

company in October 1999.[110] Not very familiar with Peru, however, these lobby-
ists were relatively useless.[111]

The Peruvian Congress

The capacity of Peru's congress to affect foreign policy was very limited. One
reason was that the only foreign policy power given to the congress in the 1993
constitution was the power to approve or reject international treaties. A second
reason was that, given the government's congressional majority throughout the
decade, the congress's Foreign Relations Commission chose not to question or investigate policies but to defend them. In the face of the government's majority in
the congress, opposition political parties were for the most part at a loss. Almost
all the initiatives of the Commission on Foreign Relations were on issues of secondary importance, such as the promotion of the study of tourism in high schools
and the labor rights of Peruvian shepherds on American ranches.

At only two junctures during the decade was congressional action on a foreign
policy issue significant. The first, in 1993, was its decision not to approve agreements for the implementation of the 1929 treaty with Chile about the future of
Arica. The Peruvian and Chilean foreign ministers had signed agreements that
would grant Peru access to Chile's port facilities in Arica and establish various
initiatives for cross-border integration. However, public-opinion specialists
determined that the people in Arica were overwhelmingly opposed to the
agreement. As a result, the Commission on Foreign Relations of the Congreso
Constituyente Democrático (CCD, the Democratic Constituent Congress) decided not to approve the agreement—although it was not rejected, but merely
transmitted back to the ministry with the specialists' comments.[112]

A second important congressional role was played in the resolution of the
Peru-Ecuador border conflict. Fearing that the actual terms of the agreement
would be rejected by their respective congresses, both Fujimori and Mahuad
asked these bodies to authorize the guarantors of the Rio Protocol to arbitrate the
definitive demarcation of the border. In October 1998, after only days of debate,
the Peruvian congress did make the authorization, with eighty-seven votes in
favor and twenty-six against.

For the most part, the role of the Peruvian congress was to defend Fujimori's
foreign policy. First, the congress obstructed attempts to oversee the executive.
Investigations of mismanagement or corruption relating to foreign policy were
systematically blocked. Among the allegations that were not investigated were
the purchase of defective police uniforms from South Korea; arms trafficking
from Argentina to Ecuador; opaque debt negotiations by Jorge Camet with the
Russian Federation; and bribery in the acquisition of armaments from Italy.

Also, the congress sought to shield the Fujimori government against external
criticism. For example, when U.S. ambassador Dennis Jett became critical of the

Fujimori government's human-rights record, the president of the Commission on Foreign Relations, Oswaldo Sandoval, held that Jett's statements were an unacceptable intrusion into Peru's internal affairs.

Peruvian Public Opinion

In general in the 1990s, Peruvians were aware that global power relations had changed considerably after the end of the Cold War. However, their attitudes toward this change were not entirely clear.

As this book shows, the overall trend under the Fujimori government was toward collaboration with the United States and other important global powers— but this policy was not strongly endorsed by Peruvians. In a September 1998 survey, the government's "foreign policy" found approval among only 30 percent of respondents, versus disapproval among 47 percent.[113] The reasons for the high disapproval rate are not clear; the meaning of the term *foreign policy* was not specified.[114]

By the late 1990s, Peruvians were supportive of international human-rights and democratic norms. In March 1999, a U.S. Department of State's Human Rights Report that was critical of Peru found approval from 65 percent of respondents versus disapproval from 28 percent.[115] Most respondents said that these reports contributed to the improvement of human-rights conditions in Peru.[116] On the other hand, during the autogolpe in particular, Peruvians tended to oppose the application of economic sanctions by the U.S. government.

Peruvians' attitudes toward the United States were mixed. The U.S. topped the list of nations in the world most admired by Peruvians.[117] Also, the percentage of Peruvians naming the United States as the most admired nation in the world increased somewhat during the 1990s. Still, in 1999, this figure was 39 percent—a figure that many might deem surprisingly low. Japan was the nation most admired by 14 percent, and one of fourteen other nations was most admired by 1 percent or slightly more.

CHAPTER IV

THE BILATERAL AGENDA FROM THE 1980s TO 2000: NATIONAL SECURITY

THE TERM "NATIONAL SECURITY" IS COMMONLY DEFINED AS THE state's concern for its territorial integrity.[1] During the Cold War, the U.S. government's primary concern was the security threat posed by the Soviet Union, and the U.S. government viewed internal and external conflict in Latin America through the lens of its rivalry with the Soviet Union and its fear of Communism. Especially when the U.S. government perceived a security threat from a Latin American government shifting to the left or from a Latin American government threatened by the left, the Central Intelligence Agency (CIA) and the U.S. military were key U.S. actors. As Chapter II described, for the most part during the Cold War this U.S. perspective on national security was not shared by the Peruvian government, and security collaboration between the two countries during the Cold War was scant.

As Chapter III described, when the Cold War ended, anti-Communism was no longer the overarching principle for U.S. policy in Latin America; the importance of free-market reform and other issues rose on the bilateral agenda. At the same time, however, security problems and opportunities gained importance in Peru. The major Sendero Luminoso (Shining Path) insurgency threatened the Peruvian state in the early 1990s. A second insurgency, the Movimiento Revolucionario Túpac Amaru (MRTA, Túpac Amaru Revolutionary Movement), held seventy-two military officers, businessmen, diplomats, and others hostage for four months at the Japanese ambassador's residence in 1996–1997. Not only internal but also external enemies were threatening Peru's security; in January 1995, war broke out between Peru and Ecuador.

In part as a result of these intense security problems, the Peruvian government sought U.S. support. While Chapter II described the tensions between the U.S. and Peruvian governments on security issues during the Cold War, this chapter indicates the close collaboration of the 1990s. U.S. intelligence support was important to the capture of the Shining Path leadership in 1992 and to the military raid that rescued seventy-one of the seventy-two MRTA-held hostages in 1997. Also, as Chapter II indicated, prior to the Cold War Peru had frequently sought U.S. support in the mediation of border conflicts; after the outbreak of war between Peru and Ecuador in 1995, both governments sought international assistance to resolve the dispute. U.S. government officials played an important role in reestablishing peace and in negotiating a 1998 peace agreement. Finally, at the end of the 1990s and through 2000, as the U.S. government became increasingly concerned about escalating political violence and drug trafficking in Colombia, U.S. security personnel and the Fujimori government also cooperated on this problem.

Although security collaboration between Peru and the United States increased during the 1990s, it held serious costs. First, much of the collaboration was covert, facilitating the manipulation of facts and fiction by the Fujimori government for its own purposes. Probably most seriously, however, the collaboration on various security threats appeared to be not as much between two countries, or even two governments, as it was between CIA agents and Montesinos. As some dimensions of the relationship between the CIA and Montesinos were revealed, dismayed publics in both the United States and Peru demanded to know why the U.S. agency had maintained a relationship with a monster. Could security objectives truly be met through a deal with a devil?

The Resolution of Internal Conflict: U.S.-Peruvian Cooperation Against Peru's Insurgencies

Peru's security was intensely threatened by guerrilla movements during the mid-1980s through the mid-1990s. During this period, the only Latin American nation that was facing as significant a revolutionary challenge as Peru was El Salvador. (The challenges in Colombia intensified at the end of the 1990s.)

The primary internal threat to the Peruvian government between 1980 and 1992 was mounted by the Shining Path.[2] The Shining Path was a savage, disciplined Maoist insurgency that was more akin to Cambodia's Khmer Rouge than to other Latin American revolutionary movements. Sendero Luminoso was created and led by one man: Abimael Guzmán, regarded as a deity by his followers, who themselves behaved like disciples. The movement started in Peru's remote southern highlands, advanced in the mid-1980s to the coca-producing areas and the central highlands, and finally expanded in the late 1980s to most of the country, including Lima. The Shining Path enjoyed ample financial resources, in the range of $100 million per year, gained primarily by its activities in the drug-producing areas (charging Colombian drug traffickers for use of airstrips that Sendero controlled, for example). As of 1990, more than twenty-five thousand Senderistas were prepared to undertake at least elementary military tasks. The

Shining Path was supported by approximately 15 percent of Peruvian citizens and controlled about 25 percent of the country's municipalities.

The Túpac Amaru Revolutionary Movement was a secondary insurgency, never posing a threat to the survival of the Peruvian state.[3] However, as the MRTA's dramatic seizure of the Japanese ambassador's residence on December 17, 1996, showed, the movement did represent significant challenges. The MRTA's ideology—like that of numerous Latin American revolutionary movements—was influenced by the Cuban *foco* model: Its emphasis was on the popular attack that commands great publicity and—accordingly without the need for a coherent revolutionary organization—gains popular support. In Peru during this period, when elected governments were not despotic but ineffectual and undisciplined, only relatively small numbers of Peruvians were attracted to a revolutionary opposition that also appeared undisciplined. Numbering approximately one thousand militants at its apex and based primarily in Lima, Huancayo, and the coca-producing San Martín department, in the late 1980s the MRTA was responsible for about 10 percent of all political attacks and roughly 5 percent of all deaths from political violence (in comparison to Sendero's approximately 75 percent and 50 percent).

In the late 1980s and early 1990s, the Shining Path's expansion was provoking panic among large numbers of Peruvians.[4] The number of deaths from political violence between 1989 and 1992 was more than three thousand per year.[5] Although most analysts had doubted that an authoritarian, rigid movement like Sendero could penetrate Lima, a politically organized and culturally sophisticated capital, it did. Controlling many shantytowns on Lima's outskirts, Sendero detonated about eight car bombs a month; by mid-1992, the car bombs became truck bombs. In July 1992, in the worst terrorist incident of the war, a truck bomb killed 22 people and injured 250 on the small street of Tarata in Miraflores, a neighborhood that was the center of middle-class Lima life. The Tarata bomb was the start of a weeklong wave of terror—daily attacks against police stations, factories, schools, and businesses—that culminated in a two-day armed strike paralyzing Lima and cutting the capital's road and rail links to the nation's interior. Among both soldiers and officers in the Peruvian military, rates of desertion were very high. Businessmen, doctors, and many other members of Peru's middle class were trying to leave the country. Warned experts on the conflict: ". . . the state is on the verge of defeat. The armed forces could tumble down at any moment," and "If they [the Shining Path] continue this way, they will be able to beat the Peruvian state."[6]

Security Cooperation Between the U.S. and García Governments[7]

As indicated previously, the overall relationship between the U.S. and García governments was tense. Security cooperation between the two governments was

minimal, although in the second half of the García government some steps toward a renewal of cooperation were taken. Under García, the Peruvian military
continued the friendly relationship with its Soviet counterpart that had begun in
the late 1960s; in August 1987, however, for the first time in decades, military ex-
ercises between U.S. and Peruvian forces were conducted.[8] Also under García, the
Peruvian government continued to maintain official distance from the CIA; still,
official contact between Peruvian government officials and the CIA was made on
narcotics-control issues in approximately 1986 and on counterinsurgency issues
in approximately 1989.[9]

In this context, U.S. concern for Peruvian security was not as intense as it
often was during the Cold War. Not only was the U.S. government distant from
the Peruvian government, but the Shining Path was a Maoist insurgency that did
not receive support from either the Soviet Union or post-Mao China and accordingly did not threaten U.S. global security interests in the way that most Latin
American insurgencies did. Also, the focus of the Reagan administration was on
Central America, not South America.

Still, there was a degree of concern on the part of both the Reagan and Bush
administrations about the expansion of the Shining Path and MRTA in Peru. In
1985, the Reagan administration proposed a doubling of U.S. military aid, primarily for Peru's counterinsurgency effort, and regularly sought increases in
U.S. military aid for Peru.[10] However, these increases were rejected by the U.S.
Congress for various reasons (and in any case were not sought by the García government).[11] During much of this period, the Brooke-Alexander Amendment
prohibited U.S. military aid to countries that were in arrears on their official debt
service to the U.S. government, as Peru was. Also, military aid was opposed by
Republicans, who were usually concerned about the García government's foreign
policy, as well as by Democrats, usually concerned about the Peruvian military's
human-rights record. These legislators were persuaded by human-rights groups'
arguments that the Peruvian military was engaged in a consistent pattern of
gross violations of internationally recognized human rights and that U.S. aid to
the Peruvian military would thus violate U.S. law and signal toleration of the violations (see Chapter VII). Accordingly, U.S. aid to the Peruvian military—or at
least aid to the Peruvian military that was not classified as antinarcotics aid—declined to virtually nothing in 1986–1988 (see Table I.2).

In 1989, under the Bush administration, increases in U.S. aid to the Peruvian
security forces were again proposed. At this time, the stipulated purpose was narcotics control, and the U.S. Congress approved the increases. In 1987–1989,
antinarcotics aid to Peru increased to about $9 million annually (see Table I.2).
However, the Bush administration also promoted a massive $35.9 million aid
package for the Peruvian military—classified as aid for the control of narcotics
but probably expected to be advantageous for counterinsurgency (see Chapter

VI). This proposal was rejected by the García government in April 1990 for various reasons that are more fully described in Chapter VI. In general, however, Peruvians desired only economic aid—which, in the context of the García government's economic policy, the United States did not want to provide. As one political leader said, "What we need in this country are greenbacks, not Green Berets."[12]

At the same time, however, both the U.S. and Peruvian leaderships began to consider new kinds of U.S. support for counterinsurgency. Since President García's inauguration, he had emphasized that his top counterinsurgency priorities were the enhancement of intelligence on Sendero in general and the capture of Guzmán in particular. Working with his close friend Agustín Mantilla at the interior ministry, García augmented the resources and staff of the antiterrorist police, subsequently called Dirección Nacional Contra El Terrorismo (DINCOTE). In the late 1980s, primarily under Mantilla's auspices, the contours of a working relationship between Peruvian security personnel and the CIA were explored by the two governments.[13] In approximately early 1990, Assistant Secretary of State Bernard Aronson asked the CIA to support Peruvian intelligence efforts.[14] Finally, between March and June 1990, the CIA did support the establishment of a small, elite unit named the Grupo Especial de Inteligencia (GEIN)—whose single objective was the capture of Guzmán—within DINCOTE.[15]

Security Cooperation Between the U.S. and Fujimori Governments Against the Shining Path

After the inauguration of Fujimori and the Peruvian government's overall shift toward a closer relationship with the United States, the ties between the CIA and Peruvian security personnel increased significantly. The CIA was helpful to the GEIN in its effort to capture Guzmán—an effort that, led by police colonel Benedicto Jiménez, succeeded in September 1992 and proved the turning point in the conflict. After the capture of Guzmán, it is also possible the CIA worked with the Servicio de Inteligencia Nacional (SIN) to capture other militants and also to develop an anti-Sendero media campaign. However, in other initiatives important to the decimation of the Shining Path—in particular the military's establishment of peasants' *rondas* (self-defense patrols) and judicial changes—U.S. actors appeared to play no role.[16]

Whereas the primary strategy of other Peruvian counterinsurgency groups was repression, the GEIN's approach was to track high-ranking Senderistas and gain the intelligence that would lead to Guzmán.[17] By 1991, the CIA's support for the GEIN was major and multifaceted.[18] The CIA provided the GEIN with sophisticated cameras, video recorders, listening devices, night-vision goggles, as well as instruction in their use. The CIA also furnished an interrogation room, and trained the GEIN's detectives; for example, possibly with an expert from Britain's Scotland Yard, CIA agents instructed GEIN personnel on the conduction of surveillance in disguise (such as how to act and dress as sanitation workers when they examined the trash at possible Guzmán safe houses). The CIA also provided cash, probably in the range of $5,000 per month, for such expenses as meals for GEIN's underpaid, overworked detectives.

The relationship between the SIN and the GEIN was tense. At first, it appears probable that Montesinos helped secure resources from the CIA for the GEIN.[19] Soon, however, the SIN and the GEIN were battling over strategy and turf. The SIN was constantly prodding the GEIN for more "results," more quickly, and seeking to bring the GEIN as well as DINCOTE as a whole under its control.[20] Apparently, Montesinos infiltrated his own agents into the GEIN—but these agents' loyalties were discovered, and contact between the GEIN and the SIN was discontinued.[21] To their fury, neither Montesinos nor Fujimori was alerted that the capture was imminent, and neither was present at the event to bask in the media glory. Fujimori, whose favored intelligence unit was of course the SIN, expressed his resentment by summarily transferring most of the top officials at DINCOTE and the GEIN to relatively unimportant positions soon after the capture. Also after the capture, the relationship between Ketín Vidal, the head of DINCOTE, and the head of the GEIN, Benedicto Jiménez, became strained; Vidal secured primary credit for the capture until Jiménez's public disclosures in 2000.[22]

During this period, it does not appear that Montesinos's SIN could claim any particular counterinsurgency success. To the contrary, Montesinos was the presumed mastermind of a death squad, called the Grupo Colina (Colina Group), which belonged to the army intelligence unit and worked with the SIN. The Grupo Colina was generally considered to have been responsible for the massacre of seventeen people at a chicken barbecue in the Barrios Altos section of Lima in November 1991 and also the disappearance of nine students and a professor from La Cantuta University in Lima in July 1992 (see Chapter VII). These crimes disgusted many Peruvians, including some military officers, who began to leak information about the death squad in 1992.[23] Information about Montesinos's role in the death squad was offered to the CIA; the CIA knew of this likely role but was not sufficiently troubled either to investigate further or to sever its ties to the spymaster.[24]

After the capture of Guzmán, the Fujimori government turned its focus to the decimation of the movement's cadres. To date, information about the actors—either Peruvian or U.S.—in post-September 1992 initiatives is scant. Overall, however, the results were positive: Although the Grupo Colina death squad endured and repression was considerable in some parts of the country,[25] Sendero was defeated with less bloodshed than most other Latin American guerrilla movements. Toward this end, a media campaign mocking Guzmán was very effective. Also, intelligence units capably used information about Sendero cadres obtained at Guzmán's safe house.

While most scholars have credited Sendero's defeat to numerous individuals and institutions in Peru, as well as to the Peruvian people in general, it would appear that the CIA primarily credited Montesinos. Despite scant public evidence of any particularly significant contribution to the defeat by Montesinos—and some evidence of a negative role—the CIA seemed to consider him the mastermind of counterinsurgency in Peru. This assessment of Montesinos as knowledgeable about counterinsurgency and capable of the coordination of complex operations became the basis for much of the CIA's subsequent collaboration with him.[26]

Security Cooperation Between the U.S. and Fujimori Governments Against the MRTA

The dramatic strengthening of security collaboration between the United States and Peru was especially evident during the 1996–1997 hostage crisis at the Japanese ambassador's residence. Although detailed information is not available, it would appear that, in the hostage-rescue effort, the U.S.-Peruvian cooperation that had previously developed between the two countries' intelligence agencies emerged between the two countries' militaries as well.

On December 17, 1996, fourteen MRTA rebels took over the Japanese ambassador's residence during a party. Although warnings of an imminent major MRTA operation had been made,[27] police officers and bodyguards had let an ambulance carrying the armed guerrillas pass through a cordon toward the residence. Most of the six-hundred-odd partygoers were quickly released, but seventy-two military officers, businessmen, and diplomats—including Peru's foreign minister Francisco Tudela, the Japanese ambassador, the Bolivian ambassador, and Fujimori's brother—remained captive.

The Fujimori government opened negotiations with the MRTA rebels, who were led by Néstor Cerpa Cartolini. The government offered the rebels safe passage to Cuba and ransom. Cerpa responded derisively that, if he had wanted to leave Peru, he could have found an easier way than seizing an embassy. The MRTA's key demand was the release of more than four hundred of their imprisoned comrades. The release of such a large number of MRTA prisoners was opposed by more than 80 percent of Peruvians, and Fujimori was categorically against meeting this demand.

Subsequent negotiations, led by Archbishop Juan Luis Cipriani, brought the two sides' positions somewhat closer. The government considered offering parole to some MRTA prisoners who had not committed violent crimes and improved prison conditions for the others. For his part, Cerpa reduced the number of

MRTA prisoners whose release he demanded; in the last negotiations on April 14–15 the number was twenty-one, including his wife, Nancy. Fujimori accepted the release of six—who were youths, elderly, or very low ranking in the MRTA. By this time Cerpa was ready to yield, and would have done so if his wife were released with the other six prisoners, but his proposal was rejected by his MRTA colleagues.[28] The viewpoints of the MRTA leaders were known to the Fujimori government through listening devices.

Virtually from the start, the government also pursued a military alternative, and in the planning and executing of this alternative U.S. actors were important. The plan was called Chavín de Huantar, in honor of a pre-Incan architectural tunnel complex. Early in January, expert miners began to build five illuminated, air-conditioned tunnels to different parts of the residence. In February, the best commandos from various branches of Peru's armed forces were selected and then provided training by U.S. special forces and the antiterrorism unit of the Federal Bureau of Investigation (FBI).[29]

The pivotal U.S.-Peruvian collaboration was in the gathering of intelligence for the raid. A U.S. antinarcotics spy plane, a Schweizer RG-8A known as "the condor" or "phantom plane," which looks like a glider and is practically silent, was positioned for aerial multispectral imagery over the ambassador's residence.[30] The imagery facilitated mapping the area, detection of mines set by the rebels, and eavesdropping on conversations inside the residence. Also for the purpose of eavesdropping, one of the hostages, retired Peruvian navy admiral Luis Giampetri, who was an expert in intelligence and command operations, was provided with a tiny radio set. Sophisticated miniature microphones and video cameras were hidden in guitars, thermoses, and even a crucifix, and smuggled into various locations in the residence.[31]

The rebels detected the construction of the tunnels, but they were not aware of the other extensive intelligence gained by the government. They did not know, for example, that their propensity for an afternoon soccer game on the first floor had been detected. Also, they believed that the Fujimori government would need Japan's approval for a military raid: By international law, the residence was Japan's property; Japan was a strong supporter of the Fujimori government and was adamantly opposed to military action. (In the event, Fujimori did not seek Japan's approval.)

By April 20, more than four months after the MRTA's assault, negotiations between the government and the rebels appeared exhausted; when Cerpa abruptly refused to permit medical teams to visit the hostages, Fujimori readied the military option. In the afternoon of April 22, Giampetri notified intelligence officers through a microphone that most of the rebels were on the first floor of the residence playing soccer. Assured that other key conditions had been met as well, Montesinos telephoned Fujimori, who gave the go-ahead.

From the tunnels, roofs of neighboring buildings, and the front gates, 140 Peruvian commandos blasted into the residence. It is possible that U.S. security personnel were stationed near or even in the tunnels.[32] By conventional standards, the rescue operation was successful: Seventy-one of the seventy-two hostages and 138 of the 140 commandos survived. The reverse, however, was also true: The lives of one hostage and two soldiers were lost, as were the lives of all fourteen MRTA rebels (including adolescents, some of whom may have been forcibly recruited). The agriculture minister and several other hostages would probably have died if a rebel who had entered their hideout and raised his rifle had opted to shoot.

Soon after the raid, Fujimori visited the residence and proclaimed his valor as the overseer of the raid. Neither Fujimori nor any other Peruvian leaders appeared worried by charges that some of the rebels had been killed after they had surrendered. At the time, many Peruvians were willing to set aside their traditional rejection of the death penalty and applaud the raid. After the government's demise, however, the MRTA rebels' bodies were exhumed; it was demonstrated that, indeed, they had been killed after they had surrendered. One of the current Peruvian government's charges against Fujimori is complicity in these deaths.

In the immediate aftermath of the rescue, though, the question was who would receive the credit for the raid. In October 1997, in his presentation of his book about Chavín de Huantar, General Hermoza portrayed himself as the head of the military dimension of the raid and Montesinos the head of the intelligence dimension; and he tipped his hat to Fujimori as well.[33] On some occasions, however, Hermoza and other military officers allocated larger shares of the credit to themselves. Fujimori—who, it will be recalled, did not receive the credit that he had sought for the capture of Guzmán—was apparently furious. On December 17, 1997, Fujimori gave an interview to the newspaper *El Comercio* in which he denied any role at all for Hermoza in the planning of the raid.[34] In Fujimori's account, only Montesinos, three army colonels working for Montesinos, and himself were responsible for the planning of the raid. Indeed, in Fujimori's account, his son Kenyi was more valuable to the raid than Hermoza; according to Fujimori, Kenyi's telescope was the instrument for surveillance of the residence.

The tensions escalated. Apparently, Fujimori and Montesinos were planning to dismiss Hermoza. However, Fujimori's account was construed not only by Hermoza but also by most other Peruvian military officers as an affront to the military institution; after all, Hermoza was the official commander for the 140 commandos who had risked their lives at the residence. On December 19, on the pretext of celebrating his birthday, Hermoza rallied his regional military commanders to his side in Lima in a show of support. Hermoza may also have developed new allies within the U.S. Southern Command (SOUTHCOM). In any case, Hermoza stayed—for awhile.

Amid the rivalry between Montesinos and Hermoza and the classified nature of U.S. support for the raid on the residence, it is not clear exactly how the Peruvians and the North Americans collaborated. Presumably, however, Montesinos and his SIN were working with U.S. intelligence agents and Hermoza and the military command with U.S. military personnel at SOUTHCOM. Also, it would appear likely that the outcome of the raid increased U.S. respect for Montesinos's counterinsurgency capabilities, and its respect for whichever Peruvian leaders were responsible for the selection of the commandos.

THE RESOLUTION OF EXTERNAL CONFLICT: THE U.S. AND THE PERU-ECUADOR BOUNDARY ACCORD[35]

The conflict between Peru and Ecuador about their border was long standing, and had provoked several of the most serious military clashes in the hemisphere. Between the 1940s and 1998, the primary focus of tension was some seventy-eight kilometers between the Condor mountain range (Cordillera del Condor) and the Cenepa River, located among eastern tributaries to the Amazon River. This territory was part of the border area between Peru and Ecuador that was claimed by both countries and remained undemarcated. Although the disputed terrain was small, inhospitable, sparsely populated, and without obvious economic potential, it was considered necessary by Ecuador for its access to the Amazon River and pivotal to its historical claim to be an "Amazonian nation."

When war broke out in this area in January 1995, it shook a conventional optimism that had emerged at the end of the Cold War about the potential for peace and economic integration in Latin America. In the context of Ecuador's relative success in this war, there was international concern that the Peruvian military would renew the fighting and, accordingly, strong international desire for an accord. Ultimately, the October 1998 agreement was judged one of the Fujimori government's most positive achievements; during the construction of the accord, collaboration increased not only between U.S. and Peruvian security institutions but also between Fujimori and international diplomats.

A History of the Border Conflict From the 1820s Through the García Government

As Chapter II indicated, tensions between Peru and its neighbors over their borders began immediately after independence. The first hostilities between Peru and Ecuador erupted in 1827. Thereafter, Peru and Ecuador both sporadically fought on the battlefield and argued the legal issues of the dispute. Fundamental to Ecuador's case was the international legal principle *uti possidetis* (signifying for Ecuador that the administrative frontiers of the Spanish Empire became the international frontiers of the newly independent countries); fundamental to Peru's position was physical possession and occupation of the territory.

After the failure of intense negotiations in the mid-1930s, border skirmishes became common. The Peruvian government, dissatisfied with other recent territorial losses, prepared for war. Between July and September 1941, well-equipped and well-led Peruvian armed forces, including an effective air force, quickly and overwhelmingly defeated vastly outnumbered Ecuadorian troops. The Peruvian military penetrated deeply into Ecuador itself, threatening even Guayaquil. The Peruvian military was not to withdraw from Ecuador until Ecuador recognized Peruvian claims in the Amazon. The victory was the most decisive in Peruvian history.

The peace treaty, titled the Protocol of Peace, Friendship, and Boundaries and commonly called the Rio Protocol, was signed by the Peruvian and Ecuadorian foreign ministers in Rio de Janeiro in January 1942. Just entering World War II, the United States was extremely concerned that the nations of the hemisphere stand together against the Axis and pressed for a rapid agreement. U.S., Brazilian, Argentine, and Chilean officials worked with the two foreign ministers and committed their respective nations to act as "guarantors" to help settle subsequent disagreements about the treaty. Peru was delighted by the role of the U.S. government in these negotiations.

Under the terms of the protocol, Ecuador renounced its claims to the disputed territory. It also ceded to Peru approximately 13,500 square kilometers that Ecuador had previously held, including navigable portions of Amazonian tributaries that were important for Ecuador's access to the river. The protocol denied Ecuador sovereign access to the Amazon, although it did grant the right to transit rivers. Virtually no civilian populations were displaced, however. The precise boundary was to be demarcated according to identified sites and physical features of the land. The treaty was approved by the congresses of both Peru and Ecuador.

Ecuador, however, was soon unhappy with the protocol, arguing that it had been imposed by force. Official Ecuadorian maps continued to depict its sovereignty over the land won by Peru, and its official publications included the inscription "Ecuador Was, Is and Shall Be an Amazonian Nation." In 1948, after markers were in place along more than 95 percent of the border, Ecuador interpreted a U.S. aerial survey to reveal inaccuracies in the geographic stipulations of the framers of the Rio Protocol. Specifically, whereas the protocol stipulated that the border should be at the separation of the waters of the rivers of the Amazon basin, and Peru argued that this watershed was in the Condor mountain range, Ecuador claimed that the U.S. aerial survey revealed a second watershed, farther to the east by the Cenepa River. Accordingly, the Ecuadorian government declared the protocol impossible to implement and halted demarcation of the border. In 1960, Ecuador declared the protocol null and void in its entirety.

In 1981, the day before the thirty-ninth anniversary of the signing of the Rio Protocol, shooting broke out in the area of the upper valley of the Cenepa River. The consensus among international analysts was that Ecuador had precipitated the hostilities to secure renewed international attention to its claims.[36] After five days of fighting and some two hundred deaths, however, Peru triumphed again. To secure the terms for a cease-fire, Ecuador humbly requested the auspices of the guarantors of the protocol that it had repudiated.

From 1981 through the García government, a conventional wisdom emerged that Peru and Ecuador were shifting toward peace and that renewed military conflict over the border was extremely unlikely.[37] The reasons were various. First, Peru's victory in the 1981 clash had been decisive; it seemed obvious that Peru enjoyed both a superior military capability and a superior legal case. Second, the value of the disputed land did not appear to warrant another risky military gamble by Ecuador. Moreover, both Peru and Ecuador were now considered democratic nations, and democratic nations are not expected to fight each other.

Finally, especially in its initial years, the García government actively sought to improve Peru's relations with its neighbors. In part reflecting the APRA party's long-standing commitment to regional solidarity, García promoted regional disarmament. Soon after García's inauguration, Foreign Minister Allan Wagner visited Ecuador. In part as a result, the development of an irrigation project called Puyango-Tumbes, which was to benefit both Ecuadorian and Peruvian land and had been halted after the 1981 conflict, was resumed. In 1989 a new mechanism for diplomatic consultation between Ecuador and Peru was established, and García became the first Peruvian president in decades to set foot on Ecuadorian soil.

The Outbreak of the 1995 Peru-Ecuador Border War

Of course, the conventional wisdom that military conflict would not be resumed was wrong. Apparently, as of approximately 1991, the Ecuadorian military command doubted that Peru would be able to counter its advances as effectively as it had in the past. The Ecuadorian military decided—largely correctly—that the Peruvian military's priority was the struggle against the guerrillas and the drug traffickers, that Peruvian military capability was suffering amid the nation's economic crisis, and that President Fujimori's politicization of promotions within the military and the foreign ministry was undermining these institutions.

Beginning in 1991, the Ecuadorian military command infiltrated military units into the disputed territory between the Condor mountain range and the Cenepa River. Border incidents ensued in mid-1991. A "gentleman's agreement" was signed between the foreign ministers of Ecuador and Peru, but was disavowed by Peru. Concerned, President Fujimori sought to reduce tensions between the two countries. In January 1992, he made the first official visit ever of a Peruvian head of state to Quito, presenting proposals for a border agreement to the Ecuadorian government. He visited subsequently as well, but none of his thirty-seven proposals was accepted by the Ecuadorian government.[38]

The Ecuadorian command continued to infiltrate military units into the disputed area. By 1993 or 1994, Ecuador had constructed three heavily fortified outposts in the higher part of the disputed territory, just east of the Condor mountain range. One of these outposts was called Tiwintza. These outposts included underground bunkers, held large numbers of weapons, and were surrounded by land mines.

Apparently, the Peruvian military was aware of Ecuador's deployment; however, amid the government's peace initiatives, it chose not to react.[39] In December 1994, however, Peruvian officers in the area (probably without authorization from Lima) warned Ecuadorian officers that they should withdraw. When they did not, the Peruvian military began to construct a helicopter landing site to the north of Ecuador's new outposts (but within the area Peru considered its own). As tensions escalated, in a phone conversation with the Ecuadorian president, President Fujimori asked Ecuador to withdraw from the disputed area, but was rebuffed.[40] To the contrary, on January 26, the Ecuadorian military command bombarded the new Peruvian helicopter landing site.

Not surprisingly, Ecuador's bombardment provoked Peruvian retaliation, and the subsequent intense fighting was called the War of the Upper Cenepa. Approximately three thousand Ecuadorian and two thousand Peruvian troops were deployed in the area, exchanging fire from mortars and rocket launchers for four weeks. Especially given its three fortified outposts in the higher ground near the Condor mountain range, Ecuador enjoyed considerable logistical and resupply advantages over Peru. In the midst of presidential and congressional elections, the Fujimori government was able to spin Peruvian media coverage so that Peru appeared victorious, but this was not the case. At the end of the fighting, Ecuador remained in control of at least two of its forward outposts, including—despite Fujimori's claims to the contrary—Tiwintza.[41] The human toll was approximately three hundred to four hundred total deaths for both sides and an economic cost up to $1 billion for the two countries.[42]

The Construction of the 1998 Peace Accord

Ironically, the war set in motion attitudinal changes among Ecuadorians, Peruvians, and the international guarantors that were positive to the eventual peace. Among Ecuadorians, their military's superior performance recouped the country's sense of self-respect, which it had lost in the 1941 war. At the same time, however, Ecuadorians knew that, if Peru were to seek revenge and actually launch a full-scale attack on Ecuador, Peru was very likely to win.[43] This was especially the case as Peru began to purchase sophisticated new weapons, including twelve Russian combat MIG-29 jets.

For Peru, the war was a painful reminder that the border conflict endured despite the Rio Protocol—that the disputed territory was not demarcated and the threat of violence was constant. Some Peruvian leaders were persuaded that concessions would be appropriate for its resolution. It is also important to note, however, that Peru's dismal performance in the war led other Peruvian military leaders—including the commander in chief of the armed forces, General Hermoza—to hope for an opportunity for revenge, including Peruvian air force attacks on Ecuadorian cities.

Another positive result of the war was intense concern by the four guarantor countries and their respective envoys. Especially pivotal to the peace process was Luigi Einaudi, the U.S. special envoy for the Ecuador-Peru peace process from its inception in 1995 to its conclusion in 1998 and a highly respected, experienced diplomat (see Chapter III). He was the only one of the envoys for whom the peace process was a full-time job; in his sixties, he was the only one who hoped that his work toward a settlement would be his signatory life achievement.[44] In recognition of his role, Einaudi was decorated by Mahuad and Fujimori in Washington in February 1999. Said one of Peru's foreign ministers: "He was very important. He helped to bring the parties together, and he advanced proposals."[45] Commented Jorge Valdéz, a vice foreign minister for Peru: "Luigi Einaudi was the only American who followed this [process] throughout. His creativity and diplomatic skills were major contributions."[46] As mentioned in Chapter III, in Apoyo's 1999 poll about the foreign actors who most influenced events in Peru, Einaudi was ranked eighth.[47]

Brazil president Fernando Henrique Cardoso (ranked as the ninth most influential foreign actor in the Apoyo poll) also played a major role. As the widely respected president of the largest guarantor country—the only one of the three Latin American nations that was not traditionally allied with either Ecuador or Peru—Cardoso wielded major political influence. At critical moments, when concessions were being resisted by Peruvian military officers or other Peruvian leaders, Cardoso stood by Fujimori and helped him carry the day.[48] Also, when U.S. support for the guarantors' peacekeeping mission was flagging, Cardoso provided additional resources.

The shift to peace began on February 17, 1995, when the Declaration of Itamaraty, signed by Ecuador, Peru, and the guarantor nations, called for a cease-fire overseen by the guarantor nations and the renewal of talks. Still, fighting continued until February 28, when representatives of all the relevant countries met for the inauguration of the president of Uruguay. Soon thereafter, the guarantors' peacekeeping mission, called the Military Observer Mission Ecuador-Peru (MOMEP), was dispatched to the disputed area; the primary initial objective was to separate the combatants. Involving military forces from all four guarantor countries, the establishment of MOMEP was complex; SOUTHCOM (headed by General Barry McCaffrey at the time) was concerned about the danger to U.S. personnel in the disputed area, and SOUTHCOM and Brazilian military leaders debated MOMEP's direction and coordination.[49] Ultimately, however, MOMEP proved very successful. By mid-May, it had largely achieved the separation of the Ecuadorian and Peruvian forces; by early August, it had established a 528-square-kilometer demilitarized zone in the disputed area.[50] However, MOMEP's success was something of a double-edged sword for the U.S. government; it feared that, without hostilities, Peru and Ecuador would not have sufficient incentive to forge an agreement, and frequently stated that U.S. financial and military support for MOMEP was conditional upon progress in the negotiations.

In 1996, meetings among the foreign ministers began, and agreement was reached on the substance and procedure for discussion. However, despite frequent meetings, by September 1997 the two countries' positions were virtually the same as they had been for decades: "Peru reaffirmed its claim to every millimeter of the territory it had always claimed, while Ecuador sought to document rights to major parts of that very same territory."[51] Peru's major goal was the demarcation of the Peru-Ecuador boundary as stipulated by the Rio Protocol, while Ecuador continued to argue that the protocol was partially inapplicable and sought sovereign access to the Amazon via the Marañon River.

A breakthrough was finally achieved in Brasilia in November 1997. Peru and Ecuador agreed that four commissions, comprised of diplomats and technical experts, would be established to study the issues in contention and propose solutions. The four issues were commerce and navigation for Ecuador on the Amazon; border economic integration; confidence-building measures; and finally, and most important, on-site border demarcation. The demarcation commission was to be composed of geographers and legal experts, and its judgment was to be issued last.

The commissions worked effectively, and areas of disagreement narrowed. In May 1998, the border-demarcation commission issued its judgment confirming the rightness of the Peruvian claim—that the demarcation stipulated in the protocol for the Condor mountain range was correct. The verdict was rejected by the outgoing Ecuadorian president, and war loomed once again.

Both Ecuador and Peru mobilized thousands of troops in the jungle, some just yards apart from each other. On August 6, Peruvian foreign minister Eduardo Ferrero accused Ecuador of infiltrating troops several kilometers into Peruvian territory. Possibly, Peru hoped to focus the attention of incoming Ecuadorian president Jamil Mahuad and of the guarantors on the problem early in the new president's term. Also, Peru—and in particular the hawkish General Hermoza—probably sought to serve notice to Mahuad that Peru really would resort to force if necessary. Since 1995, the Peruvian government had purchased approximately eighteen new MIG-29 aircraft. Ultimately, however, the two nations drew back from the brink; Peruvian and Ecuadorian forces were separated in the area in question.

Hermoza remained opposed to a settlement, and this opposition became a cogent reason for Fujimori's dismissal of the general (which Fujimori had wanted since their rival claims to the leadership of Chavín de Huantar).[52] To the extent that Hermoza had previously enjoyed international allies, it is likely that his hawkish position on the border conflict had alienated them. On August 20, 1998, having gathered other key commanders in the presidential palace and having secured their support for his decision, Fujimori called Hermoza to his office; to the general's total surprise, Fujimori announced Hermoza's retirement.

For his part, Montesinos did not play an overt role on this issue. For example, Ambassador Einaudi said that he did not meet at any time with Montesinos.[53] Subsequently, however, it has become clear from a videotape that he did not shrink from advocacy of force against Ecuador; for Montesinos, a hard line signified larger arms purchases and greater opportunity for personal enrichment.[54] At the same time Montesinos was probably aware that clear opposition to an accord would alienate his international allies.

Despite Montesinos's likely subtle opposition, progress toward a settlement accelerated dramatically. Born in a border region of Ecuador, Mahuad was especially aware of the potential benefits of a peace settlement. Mahuad and Fujimori met privately several times in different Latin American capitals (in particular at least once over a long lunch), and rapport emerged.

The primary remaining question seemed to be—given that the border was to be demarcated as Peru had sought—the kind of concession that could be given to Ecuador to make the settlement palatable for the smaller country. Discussion focused on Tiwintza, the military outpost in Peru that Ecuador had captured (and that Fujimori had inaccurately claimed to have fully recovered) during the 1995 hostilities. For many Ecuadorians, ownership of Tiwintza would be a symbol of their military strength and valor; unfortunately, of course, for many Peruvians it would be a symbol of the reverse. The expectation of a concession to Ecuador on Tiwintza sparked the resignation of Peru's foreign minister, Eduardo Ferrero, on October 2.

Mahuad and Fujimori decided to ask the legislatures of their respective countries to authorize the guarantors to arbitrate the definitive demarcation of the border. This request was in accord with protocol stipulations; whatever the decision of the guarantors was, it would be binding. It seems likely that Mahuad and Fujimori had already decided the terms of border demarcation and the fate of Tiwintza between themselves, but believed that the terms would be accepted more readily in both countries if they appeared to come from the guarantors; otherwise, the terms might be rejected by their respective congresses.[55] Both congresses voted favorably within a matter of days, and within ten days the guarantors reported their decision.

The peace agreement was signed in Brasilia on October 26, 1998. Peru achieved its major objective: Permanent frontier markers (granite obelisks called *hitos*) would finally be placed where Peru and now the technical commission had

said they should be along the seventy-eight kilometers of formerly disputed territory. On either side of the border, ecological preserves would be established
(whereas a single binational park, where the border would not be precisely
demarcated, had been favored by Ecuador). However, Ecuador was granted significant concessions. Peru ceded to Ecuador ownership over Tiwintza, identified
as a one-square-kilometer area within Peru. The concepts of ownership and
sovereignty were divided: Ecuador gained ownership but Peru would retain sovereignty. Ecuador said that it would build a memorial to its fallen soldiers at the
site.

Also, Ecuador gained free navigation along the Amazon and the right to establish two 150-hectare commercial centers with port facilities, storage facilities, and
processing plants on major waterways in the area of Iquitos, a Peruvian jungle
city near Brazil. These provisions were deeply resented by Peruvians around Iquitos, who feared Ecuadorian infiltration into Peruvian territory and considered
the commercial rights granted to Ecuador excessive. Some Iquitos residents even
interpreted the accord as a Brazilian plot for the penetration of Peru.[56]

Considerable resources for border integration were also envisaged in the
agreement. Approximately $3 billion in the next several years for joint projects
including roads, airports, health centers, schools, irrigation canals, and other river
port installations was expected from the international financial community. At
the same time, Peru and Ecuador agreed not to spend a cent on new armaments in
the next four years.

All parties hailed the agreement. Fujimori said, "There are no losers, but all
[are] winners."[57] The guarantors were delighted; "[The peace agreement is] a triumph for the entire hemisphere," said Einaudi.[58] The peoples of Peru and
Ecuador were not so enthusiastic, however. Especially in Peru, where citizens had
had little knowledge of the likely terms of the agreement, the first reaction was
dismay, and serious demonstrations against the treaty erupted in Iquitos. For
many Peruvians—who had never recognized the validity of Ecuadorian claims in
the first place and who had received scant warning that Tiwintza's fate was in
question—this concession was a humiliating shock.

At first, considerable numbers of analysts were skeptical about the prospects
for permanent peace between Peru and Ecuador. For these analysts, an unpatriotic
president had allowed the United States to impose peace terms that were against
Peru's national interest. In this interpretation Fujimori—like Leguía in 1929—
had ceded territory that was rightfully Peru's without due consultation with the
Peruvian congress or the Peruvian people. To gain the settlement, Fujimori had
dismissed both his armed forces commander and his foreign minister.

After the initial shock about Tiwintza's fate had faded, however, the prospects
for permanent peace appeared favorable. Having secured virtual control over the
Peruvian media by this time (see Chapter VII), the Fujimori government effec-

tively made its case for the accord. By the first anniversary of the agreement, a majority of Peruvians were supportive; in October 1999, 58 percent of Peruvians approved the agreement and another 26 percent disapproved, but accepted it; only 14 percent rejected it.[59] Only in the area of Iquitos did public opinion remain strongly opposed. Most Peruvians considered that Fujimori, his ministers, and the guarantors' envoys had negotiated for a long time and in good faith, and were willing to make some concessions in order to achieve border demarcation and avoid the human and economic devastation of another war. Also, most were not troubled by the guarantors' having formally made the final decision; they appeared to consider not that the guarantors had imposed peace terms on Peru, but rather that they had assumed their due responsibilities.

The 1998 accord was a breakthrough that would not have occurred without the mutual trust established not only between Fujimori and Mahuad but also between the two presidents and international actors, in particular Einaudi and Cardoso. Also, through the activities of MOMEP, SOUTHCOM's interest and knowledge of Peru were enhanced, and the successful outcome appeared to increase its respect for the Fujimori government.

The United States, Plan Colombia, and Vladimiro Montesinos

By the final years of the decade, Peru's internal and external conflicts were by and large resolved. In Colombia, however, long-standing guerrilla movements were expanding dramatically, and the U.S. government was increasingly concerned. For Plan Colombia—the U.S.-led effort to counter the Colombian guerrillas—Fujimori and Montesinos afforded security support. As of the writing of this book, however, the precise nature of Peru's support and the degree of its importance to U.S. security units are not known. In any case, in August-September 2000, amid the advancement of Plan Colombia, the charges that Montesinos had masterminded the sale of weapons to the Colombian guerrillas became a scandal that was one of the catalysts to his downfall.

During the mid- and late 1990s, political violence escalated in Colombia. The presidency of Ernesto Samper (1994–1998) was crippled almost from its inception by charges that, during the campaign, his team had accepted money from the Cali drug cartel. Samper's visa for the United States was revoked, and Colombia was twice "decertified" in the U.S. review of international cooperation in the war against drugs. At the same time, the epicenter of coca production was shifting from Peru and Bolivia to southern Colombia (see Chapter VI), and this shift increased the availability of drug-trade resources in the area. These changes were exploited by Colombia's largest guerrilla group, the Fuerzas Armadas Revolucionarias de Colombia (FARC, Revolutionary Armed Forces of Colombia) and also by a smaller guerrilla group, the Ejército de Liberación Nacional (ELN, Army of National Liberation).

In August 1998, Samper was succeeded by Andrés Pastrana, and cooperation between the U.S. and Colombian governments was resumed. Amid hopes for successful peace negotiations between the Colombian government and the FARC, President Pastrana promoted a "Plan Colombia" that would resemble the U.S. Marshall Plan of social and economic aid for Europe after World War II. At the same time, however, the U.S. government increased military cooperation between the two countries; policy proposals with a large military component emerged.

Proposals for a major increase in the U.S. military role in Colombia were controversial within both the United States and Latin America. Ultimately, Plan Colombia was to be a $1.3 billion two-year aid package for Colombia and its neighbors; 80 percent of the funds for Colombia was to be allocated for its military and police. Among most of Colombia's neighbors, there was fear that a U.S.-backed military project in southern Colombia would push the guerrillas out of Colombia—and right into their own countries.

Among Latin American governments, the Peruvian stood out for its enthusiasm for Plan Colombia. In the context of the widespread acclaim for the Fujimori government's successes against the Shining Path and the MRTA, it was politically advantageous for the U.S. government that President Fujimori endorsed military solutions for Colombia's conflict. In February 1999, for example, in a speech to the Inter-American Defense College that was primarily in celebration of the Peru-Ecuador border accord, President Fujimori belittled dialogue as a road to peace: "I repeatedly refused to accept blackmail by terror. A country of 24 million people could not be subject to a gang of criminals. The law and order issuing from the Constitution of the State was once more imposed."[60] In some analysts' views, U.S. and Peruvian officials were collaborating in the elaboration and communication of the messages about Colombia that the Peruvian government would send.[61]

The Fujimori government also supported U.S. policy in Colombia in substantive respects. To prevent the spillover of the Colombian conflict to Peru, the Fujimori government dispatched troops to the Peruvian-Colombian border.[62] Probably most important, however, was collaboration between U.S. security units and Montesinos. Unfortunately, at the time of the writing of this book, the evidence about this collaboration is not definitive. For the most part, the collaboration can only be inferred from Montesinos's statements in "Vladivideos" (tapes of his conversations broadcast after his downfall), from the pattern of U.S. policies during 2000, and from knowledgeable persons' insights into both of the above.

In the "Vladivideos," Montesinos speaks frequently of what he claims to be his role in Plan Colombia activities. It is evident that Montesinos is trumpeting his importance to the United States in order to increase Peruvians' perceptions of his power. For example, he speaks of his work with U.S. counterparts on a plan for a military invasion of Colombia as if the plan were likely, when it was probably one of numerous hypothetical contingency plans.[63]

However, there is considerable opinion that Montesinos was indeed providing intelligence about the FARC to the CIA somewhat as he claimed to be in his conversations with Peruvian actors.[64] In a conversation between Montesinos and Francisco "Pancho" Tudela (who at the time was either the vice presidential candidate for Perú 2000 or about to become the vice presidential candidate), Montesinos said to Tudela:

> So that you know, Pancho, the best intelligence network that we have in Latin America is in Colombia.
>
> In [Colombia's demilitarized zone] I have five undercover agents; the best information that Washington has about Tirofijo [the FARC's leader] is the information that I send them from there. . . . Because, as you know, satellite intelligence can't get in there. . . . And they can't send any Colombian for fear about the issue of corruption, the issue of drug trafficking. So, I have prepared five men and I have achieved their penetration into the demilitarized zone, and I have had them living there for two years now, and I have a detachment of intelligence [agents] working for me in Bogotá who can move about in different critical areas where the FARC, the ELN, and the paramilitary are. I have an average of almost 120 men in Colombia, distributed throughout the country.[65]

It seems likely that Montesinos was also important to aerial U.S. efforts to track the Colombian guerrillas and weapons shipments to them. It has been reported that the CIA planes that were gathering intelligence about drug trafficking in the Amazonian region spanning Peru and Colombia (see Chapter VI) were gathering intelligence about the FARC and the ELN as well.[66] If so, it is logical that at a minimum Montesinos's approval was necessary for this effort, and that probably he was considerably engaged in it.

If in fact Montesinos was not helping the CIA's intelligence effort about the Colombian guerrillas at this time, it is hard to understand why the CIA would have continued to support him at U.S. interagency meetings through June 2000 (see Chapter III). Although Montesinos's role in narcotics control was often judged his trump card by U.S. journalists, the facts of this role as of 2000 did not seem to warrant strong CIA support (see Chapter VI); indeed, this explanation was rejected by the National Security Council's senior director for Western Hemisphere affairs at the time, Arturo Valenzuela.[67] Another possible explanation is that Montesinos was blackmailing U.S. actors. It's possible that, just as

Montesinos had compromising information about Peruvian actors, he held similar information about U.S. actors.[68] Montesinos may have had evidence of unauthorized activities by a "rogue" sector of the U.S. security apparatus.[69] Or he may have threatened to reveal the identities of covert U.S. agents in Peru. Although at this time none of these possible explanations can be rejected, the opinion among the most informed analysts is that Montesinos was continuing to provide valuable intelligence information to the CIA as of the late 1990s and 2000.[70]

It was amid the international salience of Colombia's crisis that allegations about Montesinos's masterminding of arms sales to the FARC became a scandal. Although to date Montesinos maintains his innocence—and has identified two CIA agents whom he claims can vouch for him—the scandal was pivotal to his downfall.[71]

The scandal originated in the December 1998 purchase of fifty thousand AK-47 assault rifles by Peruvian military officials from the Jordanian government. The purchase was arranged through Sarkis Soghanalian, a Lebanese arms broker with connections to the CIA who as of 2000 was awaiting trial on various charges in the United States. Before the Jordanian officials made the transaction, they contacted the CIA, which apparently assumed that the weapons were for Peru's armed forces and approved the sale. Then, from March through August 1999, some ten thousand AK-47 rifles were dropped by parachute over Colombia into territory controlled by the FARC. Soghanalian said that he had become suspicious about the arms deal and aborted it at about this time. In any case, the rifles were seized by Colombian authorities and—probably by July 1999 and no later than March 2000—were traced by the CIA to the Jordan-Peru transaction.[72]

Months later—on August 21, 2000—Montesinos and Fujimori made a dramatic announcement on Peruvian television: The SIN had uncovered a Peruvian smuggling ring that had air-dropped weapons to the FARC. Although the CIA had contacted the nominal head of the SIN about the weapons shipment earlier in August, it remains unclear why Montesinos and Fujimori chose to make this announcement. Presumably, if Montesinos were involved in the smuggling ring, he would not have called attention to it. However, Montesinos's self-confidence was immense, and he may have believed he could manipulate media and judicial investigations of the ring. Alternatively, Montesinos may just not have been thinking rationally.

In any case, the announcement of the smuggling ring quickly backfired on Montesinos. The more the arms drop was investigated by Peruvian and U.S. journalists, the stronger became the suspicion that Montesinos was implicated. Montesinos's account of events was disputed by officials in Jordan and Colombia. Both the arms broker, Soghanalian, and the retired Peruvian army lieutenant who had purchased the rifles, José Luis Aybar, identified Montesinos as the mastermind behind the purchase.

Perhaps most importantly, the scandal caught the attention of U.S. authorities. Although U.S. officials did not appear persuaded of Montesinos's guilt, the scandal put the CIA and the U.S. Department of State at odds.[73] Officials at the State Department charged that the CIA had not provided timely information about the problem and were also increasingly convinced that, at a minimum, the U.S. relationship with Montesinos was embarrassing. For their part, CIA officials denied the charges. Probably, both this scandal and the fraudulent 2000 election were factors in the September 8 communication of concern about Montesinos to Fujimori by the NSC's Berger and Secretary of State Albright in New York (see Chapter VII).

It is unlikely, though not impossible, that the arms scandal led to the second—the leaking of a videotape showing Montesinos bribing a congressman to defect to the governing coalition—which was the critical event in Montesinos's downfall (see Chapter VII). At this time, neither the identity nor the motives of the person (or persons) who leaked the videotape is known. However, the responsible party is presumed to have been an insider who could secure access to the three-thousand-odd videotapes stored at SIN headquarters. It is thought likely that the party was from the navy (the most disgruntled service), and that, although the payment for the tape was one motive, there were other motives as well. Preliminary accounts attributing the leak to Admiral Humberto Rozas, the nominal head of the SIN at the time, out of dismay about Montesinos's double-dealing, are now largely discounted.[74]

It appears unlikely that the CIA played a role in the leaking of the videotape. Although this possibility was mentioned in several reports, the primary author of these reports was interviewed in Lima in July 2001, and at this time he was quite uncertain about the CIA's role.[75] Moreover, it does not appear logical that, in mid-September, the CIA would doom Montesinos by assisting in the leak of the videotape—and then some two weeks later help him flee Peru for Panama (see Chapter VII, footnote 127).

CONCLUSION

Enhanced U.S.-Peruvian collaboration was fundamental to Peru's dramatic security achievements during the 1990s. U.S. support efforts for the police unit that captured Guzmán and for the military rescue of the hostages at the Japanese ambassador's residence were significant to the Fujimori government's defeat of challenges by internal enemies. U.S. actors, in particular Luigi Einaudi, were pivotal to the 1998 Peru-Ecuador peace agreement that resolved the two countries' border dispute and thereby probably ended the threat of external war.

However, the costs of this collaboration were very high. First, the role of the CIA and other U.S. security units was covert, and accordingly it was not known to most Peruvian political analysts, let alone the Peruvian public. As a result, the Fujimori government was able to elaborate the myth of Fujimori and Montesinos as Supermen who virtually single-handedly saved Peru from terrorism. Even years after the insurgencies had been decimated, the Fujimori government's control of the media facilitated its continued emphasis on its past counterinsurgency successes. Peruvians' concomitant approval of these successes was pivotal to the support that Fujimori retained among many Peruvians. In short, the silence of the U.S. security apparatus was—indirectly—a factor in Fujimori's capacity to claim that he had won the 2000 elections.

Second, by the late 1990s and 2000, collaboration between U.S. security units and the Fujimori government had apparently become largely collaboration between the CIA and Montesinos. Gradually, as the dimensions of Montesinos's corruption and political abuses became clear, informed citizens in both the United States and Peru were dismayed. The CIA was caught in the classical trap when a deal is maintained with a devil: Only two explanations were possible, and the CIA's decision was deplorable no matter which was valid. One explanation was that the CIA had not known of Montesinos's depravity—in which case its performance as an intelligence agency was shockingly inept. The second—much more likely—explanation was that it did know but did not care. In this case, a decade after the end of the Cold War, one of the lead agencies of the U.S. government was disinterested in democracy and human rights in Latin America.

It would appear that, from the 1990s through 2000, an opportunity for sustained security collaboration between the United States and Peru may have been lost. If U.S. security units' role had been revealed in the early or mid-1990s, it would probably have been supported by Peruvians, and this support might have proven a foundation for sustained bilateral security collaboration. Instead, however, for the most part the Peruvian security units that collaborated with their U.S. counterparts are now tainted. It seems likely that the top intelligence and military officials appointed by the Toledo government will be cautious in their relationships with U.S. security networks. Still, the Cold War tensions between Peru and the United States have eroded, and overall the U.S.-Peruvian security relationship should remain friendlier than it was during the twenty-five years prior to 1990.

THE BILATERAL AGENDA FROM THE 1980s TO 2000: FREE-MARKET REFORM

CHAPTER V

B Y 1990, A SINE QUA NON FOR COLLABORATION BETWEEN THE United States and a Latin American nation was free-market reform. To immense U.S. relief, whereas the government of Alan García had attempted to lead a regional challenge to U.S. policies on debt service and free-market reform, the Fujimori government endorsed the economic policies favored by the international financial community. Through most of the 1990s, the transformation of the Peruvian economy from statist to free market was hailed by the international financial community as one of the most dramatic in Latin America. The relationship between the Fujimori government and the international financial community was close.

In the final years of the decade, however, economic growth slowed, living standards declined, and the free-market model was questioned by a growing number of Peruvians. At the same time, President Fujimori was seeking a third term; for various reasons, he was unable to reactivate Peru's economy. The government's economic policy making was increasingly erratic, and indications of duplicity and corruption were ample. Although these problems concerned some analysts in the international financial community, the large majority continued to consider Fujimori a welcome guarantee of the continuation of the free-market model in Peru and maintained a warm handshake.

THE GARCÍA GOVERNMENT'S CHALLENGE TO ECONOMIC "ORTHODOXY"[1]

As Chapter II indicated, President García challenged the international financial community's principles, which in Peru at the time were called economic "orthodoxy." In García's inaugural address, the new president referred to the United States as "the richest and most imperialist country on Earth" and announced that

Peru would devote only 10 percent of the total value of its exports to the service of the foreign debt. Although the preceding Belaúnde government had also been paying only a small fraction of its debt obligations, it was quiet about its minimal payments. In contrast, in his inaugural address President García threw down the gauntlet. For example, indicating when Peru's policy toward debt service would change, he called for the time

> when the richest countries respect a just level of exchange and the value of our work, when our silver, our copper, our fishmeal and non-traditional products recover their comparative value in relation to industrialized technological products, when the interest on capital doesn't increase just to solve the national deficit of the big creditors, when there are not attempts to limit the productive volume of our raw materials, when markets are not closed to our production. . . .[2]

García sought to rally as many Latin American nations as he could around his proposal for unilateral limitations on debt service and subsequent relaxation of debt-service terms by the international financial community. Not only did García want to be a recognized international leader, but he also knew that Peru's position was likely to prosper only if Latin American nations joined together to support it.

The García government also challenged international corporations operating in Peru. In particular, the government canceled 1982 oil exploration contracts with three U.S.-based firms, charging that tax rebates in the contracts were excessive. Two of the firms renegotiated their contracts, but Belco Petroleum—the second largest international oil firm in Peru—refused to do so. The García government's response was to expropriate Belco's offshore oil fields and transfer them to a new state enterprise, called Petromar.

Leftist political tides were flowing strongly in Peru at this time, and García's "heterodox" policy (as it was dubbed) was popular. Not surprisingly, however, the policy infuriated the U.S. government and the international financial community. Said a U.S. official: "The Treasury Department hates Peru because of its position on the debt."[3] In October 1985, the U.S. government declared Peru's debt "value impaired," which required that private banks increase the capital behind their loans to Peru, drastically reducing the likelihood of new private loans to the country. As Peru's arrears mounted, in August 1986 the International Monetary Fund (IMF) declared Peru "ineligible" for new loans. With this declaration, Peru—along with such countries as Vietnam, Zambia, Somalia, Guyana, Sudan, and Liberia—became a virtual international economic pariah. In early 1987 the World Bank suspended the disbursement of loans, and in early 1989 the Inter-American Development Bank (IDB) followed suit. Foreign investors shunned Peru.

The García government failed to achieve support for its debt-service proposals from other Latin American nations. In October 1985, the Reagan administration launched the Baker Plan, which would increase international banks' loans to debtor nations and entice them to the debt-renegotiation table. Most Latin American nations were gradually beginning to shift toward free-market principles, and the García government was increasingly isolated in the hemisphere.

Although economic growth was strong during he first two years of García's administration, it was based on unsustainable increases in public spending and the depletion of international reserves. The government was hoping that its expansionary policies would stimulate investment by Peru's own biggest business interests, but this possibility—remote in any case—was ended in July 1987 when García made a surprise announcement of his intention to nationalize private banks; this plan provoked widespread protest and was ultimately abandoned. By the end of 1987, Peru's reserves ran out, and the government had no choice but to abandon its expansionary policies. The García government reinitiated contacts with international financial institutions and implemented successive austerity packages in the hope of new international loans, but ultimately García was unwilling to implement the rigorous, comprehensive free-market program that the international financial community required.

The upshot of the García government's policies was "one of the worst economic performances in modern history."[4] By the end of the García administration, real per-capita gross domestic product (GDP) was estimated to be less than in 1960, and accumulated inflation over the five years was more than 2 million percent.[5] In 1989, the real minimum wage was a scant 23 percent of its 1980 figure, and its dollar value was a paltry $35 per month.[6] Hunger spread.

Despite the debacle, Peruvians were wary of the prospect of drastic free-market reform. In the 1990 elections, the front-runner was the renowned novelist Mario Vargas Llosa, but his emphasis upon the need for an economic "shock" frightened Peruvians, and they began to look for an alternative candidate. This candidate appeared in the person of Fujimori, who clearly opposed Vargas Llosa's "shock" and promised that he would restore economic prosperity through "gradual" changes.

The Initiation of Peru's Free-Market Reforms, 1990–1992[7]

Despite Fujimori's campaign promise of "gradual" economic reform, he was not knowledgeable about economics and was not sure of his economic policy course upon his election in June 1990. While his primary economic advisers at the time were center-leftists, he was also seeking advice from Hernando de Soto, a respected figure in U.S. foreign policy circles who was decidedly pro-market (see Chapter III).

De Soto persuaded Fujimori to travel to the United States, where his brother Alvaro de Soto, a top UN official, worked closely with Javier Pérez de Cuéllar, secretary-general of the United Nations at the time. The de Soto brothers and the secretary-general arranged meetings in Washington for Fujimori with IMF director-general Michel Camdessus, IDB president Enrique Iglesias, and World Bank president Barber Conable at the World Bank. Next, Fujimori traveled to Tokyo. In both cities, the message to Fujimori was clear: Implement an immediate, all-out liberalization program.

By the time of his inauguration on July 28, 1990, Fujimori had decided to heed the Washington-Tokyo message and pursue what Peruvians called the country's "reinsertion" into the international financial community. On August 8, economics minister Juan Carlos Hurtado Miller announced the measures that were to be dubbed the "Fujishock." Price controls and virtually all government subsidies were eliminated; the prices of gasoline, electricity, medicines, and basic foodstuffs skyrocketed overnight. Debt-service payments to multilateral creditors—about $60 million a month—were resumed, and Hurtado Miller traveled to Washington to begin negotiations.

Despite the heavy toll of these measures on Peruvians' living standards (inflation for August alone neared 400 percent), they did not represent a comprehensive reform package, and the response both in Peru and abroad was tepid. In February 1991, Fujimori appointed a new economics minister with a much stronger commitment to free-market reform and much greater technical expertise, Carlos Boloña. Boloña, an economist from Oxford University, quickly decreed a comprehensive reform package: Tariffs and tarifflike barriers were slashed; the exchange rate system was unified and liberalized; interest rates were allowed to float freely; labor-market provisions that enhanced job security were ended; and public monopolies were eliminated. Boloña also announced that public enterprises would be privatized and that tax collection would be strengthened.

As Chapter III mentioned, at the same time a highly professional economist, Manuel Estela, was appointed to head the Superintendencia Nacional de Administración Tributaria (SUNAT), Peru's tax agency. The strengthening of the SUNAT was the first economic reform that won widespread acclaim for the Fujimori government in international circles. In 1990, the SUNAT—whose poorly paid and poorly trained bureaucrats worked with outdated taxpayer lists in a context of hyperinflation—collected less than 5 percent of GDP in tax revenue (down from 15 percent a decade before). Within a year, the tax agency was transformed into a model of professionalism, and tax revenue almost doubled to more than 8 percent of GDP (and was to increase further subsequently).[8] The transformation was proclaimed "an example to many countries round the world" by IMF director-general Michel Camdessus.[9]

In September 1991, Boloña's efforts yielded international fruits.[10] Peru's reinsertion was beginning: The International Monetary Fund approved Peru's economic-stabilization program. Although arrears with the IMF and the World Bank were not cleared and Peru was not yet eligible for fresh loans from these institutions, Peru's smaller arrears with the Inter-American Development Bank were cleared (with the help of a "Support Group") and the IDB announced a three-year $1.7 billion loan package for Peru, including an immediate $425 million for trade-sector reform. Soon thereafter, Peru's entire $6.6 billion external debt with the Paris Club of creditor nations was rescheduled, some of it over a six-year period and some of it over a twenty-year period. The Fujimori government was delighted.

Another major set of economic reforms was introduced in November 1991 and approved by the congress in the first four months of 1992. Among the most important were measures promoting foreign investment. Controls on foreign investment, including restrictions on profit remittances, were ended, and equal treatment for foreign investors was guaranteed. Also, financial-sector reform was introduced. The operations of state-owned development banks were reduced or abolished, and the development of a commercial banking sector encouraged. A legal framework for Peru's stock exchange was promulgated.

Peru appeared well on its way to the achievement of its goal of reinsertion in the international financial community. The Support Group of industrialized nations that included the United States, Japan, Germany, and Spain was negotiating a bridge loan for Peru of approximately $1 billion. In this set of transactions that would last only a few hours, the U.S. Treasury Department and Japan's Export-Import Bank would transfer funds to a Peruvian government account; these funds would be used to pay Peru's arrears to the World Bank; the World Bank would then disburse credits for virtually the same amount to Peru; in turn, these funds would be used by Peru to repay the U.S. and Japan. The critical benefit for Peru was that it would clear its arrears with the World Bank and be eligible for new loans and credits.

The negotiations were, however, delayed by Fujimori's April 1992 autogolpe, which appeared to portend dictatorial rule (see Chapter VII). The U.S. government and the Inter-American Development Bank suspended loans and other assistance. Only after elections were held for a constituent assembly in October 1992 did the reinsertion process begin again. Another event that facilitated negotiations was the September 1992 capture of Abimael Guzmán and other Shining Path leaders and the subsequent decline in political violence (see Chapter IV).

The key leaders of the negotiations were Boloña and the U.S. Treasury Department's Lawrence H. Summers, who at the time was the treasury's undersecretary for international affairs. Said the Peruvian ambassador to the United States: Larry Summers "worked hand in glove with Peru."[11] At the same time, Peruvian officials were working to settle a lingering conflict with the American International Group (AIG), which had made an insurance claim against Peru for the 1985 expropriation of Belco's offshore oil fields.

Finally, in March 1993 and with human-rights conditions described in Chapter VII, the bridge loan was made.[12] The U.S. Treasury Department transferred approximately $500 million to Peru, and Japan's Export-Import Bank approximately $450 million; Peru's arrears were cleared. Negotiations also continued with the Paris Club, and further rescheduling for the years 1993–1995 was achieved; whereas Peru had been set to repay about $1 billion a year, the sum was reduced by about 60 percent.[13] Further, Peru, AIG, and Belco's representatives agreed that Peru would pay $185 million compensation and that, in return, AIG would withdraw its complaints against Peru. The Fujimori government and the international financial community were pleased.

THE CONSOLIDATION OF PERU'S FREE-MARKET REFORMS, 1993–1997

The free-market economic reforms initiated in 1990–1992 were consolidated in subsequent years. Indeed, Peru was one of the two South American nations widely considered to have made the most dramatic shift toward a free market between 1990 and the mid-1990s.[14] As late as 1995, Peru's score on an index of economic freedom elaborated by the Heritage Foundation tied with Brazil for second to last (above only Nicaragua) among sixteen Latin American nations; in contrast, in 1997 Peru ranked eighth among the sixteen Latin American nations (below Chile, El Salvador, Panama, Argentina, Paraguay, Uruguay, and Bolivia).[15] Peru's economy was judged considerably freer than those of the two largest countries in the hemisphere, Brazil and Mexico.

The consolidation of the economic reforms was led not by Boloña but by his successor, Jorge Camet. For reasons that included conflict between Fujimori and Boloña over Peru's continuing low economic growth and Boloña's star status, Fujimori fired Boloña in an end-of-1992 cabinet shuffle. Industry minister at the time of his appointment, Camet was a successful engineer and entrepreneur who had served twice as the president of Peru's primary business confederation, Confederación de Instituciones Empresariales Privadas (CONFIEP, Confederation of Private Business Institutions), and his appointment strengthened the Fujimori government's ties to Peru's business community. Camet was to become Fujimori's longest-serving minister, and the two enjoyed a friendly relationship. However, Camet (who, as of 2002, was struggling to avoid indictment on charges of illicit enrichment) was lackluster and unsophisticated about economics; in part as a result, Peru's economic policies during his more than five years in office were in large part directed by the international financial institutions, which in turn were greatly influenced by the U.S. Treasury Department.[16]

Under Camet, Peru's reinsertion into the international financial community was completed: A Brady Plan agreement was finalized with Peru's commercial bank creditors.[17] Camet worked closely with Summers on the Brady Plan deal.[18] The negotiations—involving an estimated $10.6 billion commercial bank and supplier debt—led to an agreement-in-principle in October 1995 and concluded in March 1997 with a deal that the Peruvian government touted as one of the most favorable in the region. Creditors were provided several alternatives for the exchange of their debt for bonds; the overall discount that Peru would obtain on the debt was expected to be 40 to 45 percent. The Peruvian government repurchased $2.6 billion of eligible debt under a buyback, officially by Swiss Bank Corporation. Although the agreement increased Peru's interest payments on the debt considerably (see below), the government emphasized that it would enable cheaper international loans to Peru. However, various key components of the deal were not revealed by Peruvian officials; even at the time, concerns that officials had profited personally were raised by opposition leaders.

The Fujimori government's trade liberalization was dramatic. Average tariffs were reduced from about 40 percent under the Belaúnde government and more than 60 percent during the García government to about 16 percent in 1996.[19] For its part, in 1991 the United States passed the Andean Trade Preferences Act (ATPA, an initiative to encourage alternative crops in drug-producing areas) that enabled some goods from Andean nations to be exported to the U.S. tariff-free; the U.S. president designated as a beneficiary country first Colombia, then Bolivia, next Ecuador, and finally, in mid-1993, Peru. However, U.S. trade restrictions, including tariffs up to 30 percent, were maintained on many of the most important goods—textiles, apparel, footwear, canned tuna, petroleum, and watches.[20]

Peru's trade expanded greatly. Although for most of the twentieth century Peru's trade had been increasing, it had declined slightly during the latter half of the second Belaúnde government and much more sharply during the García administration.[21] Then, from 1989 to 1999, Peru's exports more than doubled, from $2.7 billion to $6.1 billion, while imports increased even more, from $2.9 billion to $6.7 billion.[22] In accord with this trend, the value of Peru's exports to and imports from the United States also doubled during this period.[23]

Although the absolute amount of U.S. trade with Peru increased, the relative U.S. share of Peru's trade declined. In contrast to patterns of international investment, however (see below), the United States remained Peru's most important trading partner—by far. The U.S. share of Peru's exports and imports was more than 40 percent until the 1960s but declined thereafter; during most of the 1990s, the U.S. share was around 20 to 25 percent.[24] The U.S. share was increasing at the end of the decade, however; in 1998, the U.S. share was 32 percent of Peru's exports and 26 percent of its imports.[25] Asian nations, in particular China and Japan, were increasing their share of Peru's exports while other Latin American nations, in particular Chile, Colombia, and Brazil, were increasing their share of Peru's imports; but none of these country's shares of exports or imports surpassed 10 percent.[26]

During the 1990s, the composition of Peru's exports and imports changed somewhat from previous decades. As had been the case prior to 1930 and after the mid-1970s, the bulk of Peru's exports were minerals and petroleum.[27] However, the relative importance of specific minerals changed. Gold became much more important, replacing copper as Peru's number one export, and silver and zinc exports increased considerably. Although the amount of petroleum exports was roughly stable during the decade, petroleum declined as a percentage of export revenue.

The importance of agricultural exports decreased during the 1990s. From approximately 1890 through the 1950s, the value of sugar and cotton exports was in the range of 35 to 50 percent of Peru's total; in contrast, the value of Peru's sugar and cotton exports in the late 1990s was barely 1 percent of the total.[28] In the mid- to late 1990s, the only agricultural export that was regularly earning more than $200 million annually was coffee.[29] (Fishmeal, which had begun to be a major export during the 1960s, continued to earn about 15 percent of total export revenue during the 1990s.[30])

As mentioned above, in early 1992 the Fujimori government liberalized Peru's investment laws to welcome foreign investors. Soon thereafter, the government formed the privatization commission, Comisión de Privatización (COPRI), and it prepared an initial for-sale list of some seventy state holdings, including most of the largest. In February 1994, the state telecommunications network became the first large state enterprise to be privatized, and at the time the sale was considered a spectacular success. While the base price for the network had been set at $525 million and the possibility of $800 million had been speculated by government optimists, the winning bid from Spain's Telefónica was more than $2 billion.

Ultimately, between 1990 and 1998, more than 180 state holdings—spanning from telecommunications to banking, tourism, mining, transport, and cement— were privatized, for a total sale value of about $6.6 billion.[31] In 1997, the Heritage Foundation listed Peru's rank on the "government intervention" indicator (composed in good part on the basis of government ownership of state enterprises) as 1—Peru's top score on the scale of ten indicators, and a score achieved by only two other countries in Latin America (Chile and Ecuador).[32]

In general, at the time the performance of COPRI was praised by foreign investors as efficient and honest. Not only did the commission manage the sales, but it also devised strategies for the purchase of small amounts of shares by Peruvians—strategies that helped defuse nationalist resentment against the sale of assets to foreigners. Subsequently, however, it was revealed that as much as one-quarter of the $6.6 billion was used for arms transactions from which both Montesinos and Camet were likely to have received kickbacks.[33]

Privatization was the principal engine behind the overall surge in foreign direct investment (FDI). Whereas FDI flows to Peru had been negative in the later 1980s, they became strongly positive after 1993 (see Table V.1). Total registered direct foreign investment rose from $1.3 billion in 1990 to more than $8 billion in 1999 (from about 16 percent of GDP in 1990 to 24 percent in 1995).

U.S. FDI also skyrocketed (see Table V.1). Between 1990 and 1999, the stock of U.S. direct investment registered in Peru tripled, from about $600 million to about $1.8 billion.[34] During the four-year period 1994–1997, the increase in U.S. direct investment in Peru was greater than in any other South American nation.[35] The largest investments were by mining and oil concerns: Newmont Mining, Southern Peru Copper Corporation, Dominion Energy, BHP Copper, Aguaytia Energy, Duke Energy, Cyprus Climax Metals, Occidental Petroleum, and Mobil Oil.[36] However, important investments were also made by large U.S. companies interested in the Peruvian consumer market—in particular, Coca-Cola, Delta Air Lines, Proctor and Gamble, and McDonald's; further, Chase Manhattan, Bank of Boston, J. P. Morgan, and Citibank became important U.S. investors in Peru's financial sector.[37]

Arguably the most successful investment in Peru during the 1990s was a joint venture among a U.S.-based company, Newmont Mining, the Peruvian company

TABLE V.1

CHANGES IN REGISTERED FOREIGN INVESTMENT STOCK IN PERU, 1991–1999
Millions of Current U.S. Dollars

Year	Change in Total Foreign Investment	Change in U.S. Foreign Investment
1991	33	−5
1992	168	7
1993	139	30
1994	2,809	101
1995	1,091	118
1996	691	375
1997	1,035	236
1998	732	150
1999	575	167

Source: "Inversión Americana en El Perú 1999," Fact Sheet by the AmCham Peru InfoCenter, courtesy of the American Chamber of Commerce in Peru. These figures jibe better with known investment trends than those for total FDI from ECLAC, "Preliminary Overview of the Economies of Latin America and the Caribbean" (Santiago, Chile, 2000), 99, or for U.S. FDI 1990–1999, from "U.S. Direct Investment in LAC: Capital Flows," International Investment Data, Bureau of Economic Analysis, at www.bea.doc.gov/bea/di/longctyx.htm).

Buenaventura, and (until 1998) the French firm BRGM. Headquartered in Denver, Newmont Mining is currently the world's largest producer of gold with major assets spanning five continents. In mid-1992, the joint venture was formed to begin to exploit the gold at Yanacocha, in the highlands of Cajamarca. By the end of the decade, Yanacocha had become the largest gold producer in Latin America.[38] In 1999, Yanacocha's gold exports were valued at $460 million; Yanacocha was responsible for about 8 percent of Peru's total exports, more than any other company save Southern Peru Copper Corporation.[39]

Despite these investments, however, the relative U.S share of Peru's stock of FDI declined. Whereas in 1980 the U.S. was the source of 55 percent of Peru's stock of FDI, by 1998 it was the source of approximately 20 percent.[40] Still, these percentages were skewed by Spain's Telefónica's huge investment; if one of the U.S.-led consortia that had bid on Peru's telecommunications network had won the auction, the U.S. would have continued to hold the largest share of Peru's stock of FDI. Following Spain and the U.S as sources of FDI in 1998 were the United Kingdom, the Netherlands, Chile, and China.[41] Despite collaboration between Japan and Peru during this period, significant investments were not made by Japanese companies.

The increase in foreign investment in Peru was fundamental to the country's high growth rates during 1993 through 1997 (see Table V.2). Another important factor was the decline in political violence, which enabled the resumption of nor-

TABLE V.2

ANNUAL GROWTH RATES IN TOTAL GROSS DOMESTIC PRODUCT
Percentages based on values in constant 1995 dollars

		Average Annual Rate
Year	Peru	Latin America and the Caribbean
1981–1990	−1.2	1.2
1991	2.8	3.8
1992	−0.4	3.2
1993	4.8	4.0
1994	12.8	5.2
1995	8.6	1.1
1996	2.5	3.7
1997	6.7	5.2
1998	−0.4	2.3
1999	0.9	0.3
2000	3.0	4.1

Source: CEPAL, *Preliminary Overview of the Economies of Latin America and the Caribbean* (Santiago: United Nations, 2000), 85, and *CEPAL News* XXII, no. 2 (January 2002), 1.

mal economic activities that had been impossible for many years in much of the country. Real GDP growth averaged above 7 percent over the five-year period from 1993 through 1997, higher than any other Latin American nation save Chile.[42] At the same time, inflation was low: From the triple-digit figures of the previous decade, inflation was only 15 percent in 1994 and continued to fall thereafter.[43] However, the economic heyday was not to last.

Economic Recession, 1998–2000: Origins and Outcomes

In 1998–2000, the Peruvian economy contracted and Peruvians' living standards declined. The economic trends that became apparent during this period were worrisome, and led increasing numbers of Peruvians to question the viability of the free-market model in Peru. However, although privatization slowed, the Fujimori government maintained most key dimensions of the model. Accordingly, despite increasing indications of corruption and politicization of economic policy making, for the most part the international financial community continued to extend its hand enthusiastically to Fujimori.

Table V.2 shows that, during the three years from 1998 to 2000, GDP growth was either negative or minimal. The data in the table are for total GDP growth; the figures for per-capita GDP growth are almost 2 percentage points lower, and accordingly per-capita growth was negative during this period. Preliminary estimates for total GDP growth in 2001 were about 0.1 percent.[44]

What were the reasons for Peru's recession? One important factor outside the control of both the international financial community and the Fujimori government was a devastating 1998 El Niño weather pattern, which hit agriculture and fishing hard. However, most other factors raised questions for Peruvian analysts about the viability of the free-market model in Peru.[45]

First, although in the context of the debt-service and trade trends to be discussed immediately below, foreign investment was essential to economic growth in Peru, it was not increasing during 1998–2000 at the rates that it had during the middle years of the decade (see Table V.1). Although foreign direct investment flows to most Latin American nations were considerably greater in 1997–1999 than they had been in 1994–1996, this was not the case in Peru. Foreign direct investment inflows to Latin America and the Caribbean as a whole increased from an average of $43 billion annually from 1994 through 1996 to an average of $73 billion annually between 1997 and 1999—an increase of almost 70 percent.[46] The inflows to Peru, however, declined from an average of $2.7 billion to $1.2 billion in 1997–1999—a decrease of almost 20 percent.[47] The reasons for this decline are discussed below in the paragraphs about the Fujimori government's economic policy making 1998–2000.

Second, Peru's external debt obligations were rising considerably.[48] Although the Fujimori government had hailed the success of its debt renegotiations, Peru's total external debt increased from $18.5 billion in 1992 to $31 billion in 1998—about 50 percent—and annual debt payments increased from $1 billion in 1992 to $4 billion in 1998.[49] In 1998, Peru's total external debt was 53 percent of its GDP—slightly higher than the figure for Argentina and much higher than the figures for Chile, Mexico, Uruguay, or Brazil.[50] Of Peru's total external debt, about $25 billion was public-sector debt, on which the government owed roughly $2.1 billion annually (about one-third of Peru's export revenue).[51]

A third factor in Peru's economic recession was the country's trade trends. Although not only foreign investment but also export revenue was pivotal to Peru's capacity to service its debt, the rate of increase in Peru's exports continued below the rate of increase in the nation's imports. Between 1990 and 1999, the value of Peru's exports almost doubled, from $3.3 billion in 1990 to over $6 billion in 1999; however, the value of the country's imports more than doubled, from $2.9 billion in 1990 to $6.7 billion in 1999.[52] Peru did not export more than it imported during any year of the decade except 1990, and the average difference between exports and imports was about $2 billion during 1995–1998.[53]

Of particular concern to Peruvians was, of course, the capacity of the free-market model to improve their living standards. Unfortunately, the predominant trends were negative. In 1999, average real wages were below the levels of the first years of the decade and well below the levels of the 1970s.[54] Household consumption was estimated to decline by 18 percent between 1997 and 2001 by Peru's National Statistics and Information Institute (INEI).[55]

Peruvians overwhelmingly identified unemployment as the country's principal problem.[56] The official unemployment rate in Lima—9.2 percent in 1999—and the official underemployment rate in Peru's cities—44 percent in 1998—were slightly higher than in earlier years of the decade.[57] In late 1999, the proportion of Peruvians in poverty and extreme poverty was greater than in 1995: 54 percent versus 48 percent in poverty, and 17 percent versus 14 percent in extreme poverty.[58] The proportion of Peruvians in poverty was increasing despite the government's increases in social expenditure (see below).

Increasingly, Peruvians blamed their plight on the free-market model. Whereas in 1991 72 percent of Peruvians said that free-market economics was appropriate for the country, in 1998 the figure was 58 percent.[59] In 1999, only about 20 percent of Peruvians approved the government's overall economic policy.[60] Peruvians were worried about privatization, tariff liberalization, and Peru's high interest rates and high taxes—which were construed to be part and parcel of the free-market model.

Peruvians were particularly critical of privatization. The approval rate for privatization of state enterprises dropped from 59 percent in October 1992 to 32 percent in October 1998.[61] Majorities of Peruvians blamed privatization for the dismissal of thousands of professionals. Also, many newly privatized companies, in particular the utility companies, charged higher fees (exorbitant fees, many said).

Peruvians worried that patterns of investment and trade were also detrimental to job creation. As mentioned previously, increasingly Peru's exports were from the mining and energy sectors, but these enterprises were capital intensive and provided few jobs.[62] (There was also considerable concern that the development of the new mines was contaminating local land and water supplies and displacing peasants in the area.[63]) Peruvians would have preferred that there be an increase in the country's export of manufactures, which were much more labor intensive. But there was not: Between 1990 and 1999, the real rate of growth of Peru's manufactures was a scant 0.7 percent, versus 10.3 percent regionwide.[64] Whereas in 1965 the value of manufactured exports in Peru was the fifth largest in the region, in 1999 it had fallen to eighth largest.[65] Amid the reduction of tariffs, imports of capital goods approximately doubled between 1990 and 1999; however, imports of consumer goods almost quadrupled.[66] Considerable numbers of Peruvians believed that the increase in consumer-goods imports had provoked the bankruptcies of numerous domestic consumer-goods enterprises.

The Fujimori government also pursued policies that were not core free-market principles but became negatively associated with these principles by many Peruvians. Amid the scarcity of foreign capital and a high bad-debt portfolio, domestic credit was scant and interest rates—often available only in dollars—were very high, in the range of 20 to 30 percent per year.[67] To prevent a resurgence of inflation and facilitate debt service, the government did not take steps to increase credit availability. The lack of credit at reasonable interest rates was, however, a major impediment to the initiation of the small and medium-sized businesses that, within the premises of the free-market model, should have been a key engine for growth in Peru. From 1990 through 2000, it was estimated that twenty-two thousand small businesses went bankrupt in Peru.[68]

The government also increased taxes. As mentioned above, tax revenue increased from less than 5 percent of GDP in 1990 to about 12 percent in 1998.[69] Although taxes were not high in Peru by regional standards, the SUNAT—a model of professionalism in the early 1990s—was increasingly resented. First, tax policy became more regressive; the top marginal rate of corporate and personal income tax was only 20 percent.[70] While a hefty "Solidarity tax"—a payroll tax on employment—was levied on all companies, large companies lobbied the government for tax exemptions.[71] Whereas in 1997 Peru's largest sixty enterprises paid about 65 percent of Peru's corporate taxes, by 2000 these largest enterprises paid less than 50 percent.[72] Second, tax policy became more politicized (see below).

Amid this bleak economic context, President Fujimori was in aggressive pursuit of his third consecutive term. Despite Peruvians' increasing doubts about the free-market model, it was maintained. Indeed, on the Heritage Foundation's index of economic freedom, Peru rose from eighth place in 1997–1998 to fifth place in 1999–2000 (behind only Argentina, Chile, El Salvador, and Panama).[73] Between 1998 and 1999, the Fujimori government was considered on this index to have reduced the fiscal burden of government; lowered inflation, thereby indicating an improvement of monetary policy; and (astoundingly in hindsight) increased the judiciary's professionalism and the security of property rights.[74]

Within the context of overall maintenance of the free-market model, however, the Fujimori government was increasingly unable to focus on the development of a strategy for economic growth in Peru. The government's overarching goal was reelection, and its pursuit of reelection impeded the development of a coherent strategy for growth. Indicative of the government's increasingly erratic economic policy making was a succession of four economic ministers during two years: In June 1998, Camet was replaced by Jorge Baca; before the end of 1998, Baca was replaced by Víctor Joy Way; and in 1999, Joy Way was succeeded by Efraín Goldenberg.

As indicated above, within the context of the free-market model, foreign investment—either through privatization of state companies or through the development of new enterprises—was essential for economic growth. As indicated above also, however, foreign direct investment inflows were declining. For the most part, the Fujimori government sought to explain the decline to Peruvians as a function of the financial crises in Asia, Russia, and Brazil—implying that it was temporary and out of Peru's control. As the data above showed, however, this explanation was false; foreign investment in other Latin American nations was increasing.

In fact, foreign investors were turning away from Peru for various reasons. The most obvious was that the inflows during the mid-1990s were primarily for the purchase of Peru's large state companies, and by the late 1990s most of these had been sold. Commented the Economist Intelligence Unit, for example: "By mid-1998 almost all sales had been completed in telecoms, banking, tourism, and light industry, and about four-fifths in mining and metals, basic industry, transport and cement."[75] Another reason was that forecasts for world prices of minerals and oil—the commodities of greatest interest for investors—were declining considerably.[76] A final reason, however, was the Fujimori government's aforementioned focus on reelection to the exclusion of developing a coherent strategy for the attraction of foreign investors.

The government's privatization initiatives faltered. In 1999, the government said to the IMF that it would realize $800 million from privatization and concessions, but ultimately it secured only $300 million.[77] Major privatizations in 1999 were limited primarily to Paragsha, a zinc and lead mine formerly known as Cerro de Pasco, a railroad concession, and the state's remaining share of the telecommunications network. The government decided not to privatize either Lima's water and sewage utility, Sedapal, or the country's important Mantaro hydroelectric plant; privatization of both these companies was strongly opposed in various quarters and subsequently was not pursued by the Toledo government either. However, other privatizations seemed viable, including regional electricity companies, an oil refinery at Talara, the state's share of a sugar company, and transportation infrastructure (airports, roads, and regional ports).

Among these privatization possibilities, the most viable may have been the concession for the country's busy Lima airport. Ultimately, however, the government was unable or unwilling to develop the legal framework for the sale of the concession.[78] Although numerous foreign investors researched the concession and prepared bids, they ultimately tired of the government's delays and went home.[79]

The Fujimori government was also widely considered ineffective in its negotiation of the most important foreign investment of the 1998–2000 period, the investment for the development of the giant Camisea gas fields in the jungle in eastern Peru. Dubbed "the contract of the century" by Fujimori, estimates of likely foreign investment for Camisea were in the range of $3 billion, with the potential for as much as much as $8 billion in corollary energy businesses. The fields contain natural gas and gas by-products equivalent to about 2.3 billion barrels of oil—nearly seven times the size of existing proven reserves in Peru.[80] Shell Oil Company discovered the immense fields in 1981, but until the early 1990s the prevailing Peruvian view was that the state should develop Camisea. Only in 1996 did the Fujimori government begin negotiations for Camisea with Shell and its minority partner Mobil.

After two years, however, the negotiations between the Fujimori government and Shell-Mobil broke down. Although of course both parties were responsible for the breakdown, most analysts assigned a larger share of the blame to the government's team, which was described as arrogant and insensitive to the changing context of the investment.[81] The key substantive issues in the negotiations were the marketing and pricing of the gas. The Peruvian market was too small to purchase a sufficient quantity of the gas, and the consortium wanted the possibility of exports to Brazil or elsewhere, probably via the construction of a pipeline to Brazil. Apparently, however, there was miscommunication between the two negotiating teams, and serious discussion about the export of gas was not initiated. For Shell-Mobil, if its primary market was to be only Lima, it had to set a price for the gas that would be high by Peruvian standards. However, a Fujimori government guarantee of a high price to Shell-Mobil for its gas was not an attractive option; why would Peruvians want to pay high prices for gas when other kinds of energy were available more cheaply? Peru's negotiating team was unwilling to assure Shell-Mobil the minimum price that it sought for the gas in Peru's market.

During the course of the negotiations, Shell-Mobil was encountering new obstacles to its investment, obstacles that the Fujimori government was apparently disinclined to acknowledge. World gas prices were declining, vast new gas deposits were found in Bolivia (of course, closer to Brazil), and new geological and environmental problems involved in the development of Camisea were identified. In mid-1998, Shell-Mobil decided not to proceed. "The contract of the century is fast turning into the missed opportunity of the century," commented a journalist.[82]

In the wake of Shell-Mobil's withdrawal, the government began to put much more effort into the negotiation of an arrangement that would hopefully be mutually beneficial. The government opted to offer two separate tenders—one for production, the second for transportation and distribution. The state sought to guarantee a domestic market and price through "take-or-pay" contracts. The government also approved the export of gas to other countries (possibly the United States). Finally, in February 2000 a consortium of the Argentina-based Pluspetrol with 40 percent, the U.S.-based Hunt Oil with 40 percent, and the Korea-based SK Corporation with 20 percent, won the first-phase tender. However, this consortium was not as experienced and possibly not as capable as Shell-Mobil, and its investment would be several years later than had been hoped.

Still, not all the negotiations between the Peruvian government and foreign investors were fraught by miscommunication and delay. The negotiations between Peru and a Canadian consortium for the exploitation of vast copper and zinc deposits at Antamina proceeded smoothly; the contract was signed in September 1998. Valued at some $2.2 billion, the Antamina project is located about 380 kilometers north of Lima in the Andean mountains. The mine opened ahead of schedule in July 2001 and was expected to increase Peru's mineral production by as much as one-quarter.[83]

Amid the government's failure to reactivate the economy, it resorted to desperate measures in its effort to secure reelection. A key tactic was outright distortion of data. In the most flagrant example, the government claimed that Peru's 1999 economic growth rate was 3.8 percent, which would have been the best in Latin America.[84] The government achieved this statistical feat by using an out-of-date base year (1979) for its calculation, when in fact an appropriate base year was approximately 1994. The government's claim was refuted by distinguished Peruvian economists in the independent media.[85]

Also in the pursuit of reelection, the government was politicizing expenditure. The politicization of antipoverty initiatives was especially evident. In general, the Fujimori government was praised for its increase of social expenditure in Peru— from approximately 2 percent of GDP in 1992 to 7.6 percent in 1999—which extended access to water, sewage, electricity, and roads and enabled approximately 38 percent of Peruvians to receive daily food rations.[86] (Perhaps one-quarter of the food was provided by the U.S. government.[87]) However, most of these funds were allocated through the ministry of the presidency, which provided the aid to local officials who promised in return to deliver their community's electoral support to the government.[88]

The Fujimori government also spent inordinate amounts on advertising. Even according to official statistics, the government spent at least $35 million on advertising in 1999 and $40 million in the first four months of 2000; during this period, the government was Peru's biggest spender on advertising.[89]

Arguably the government's most worrisome strategy was its politicization of taxation. Many Peruvians believed that tax policy was regressive so that the government would maintain the support of big businesses. Most seriously, the government increasingly used SUNAT to persecute its political opponents.[90] With an apparent vengeance from SIN agents who had developed a presence within SUNAT, the tax agency audited political opponents and demanded huge tax payments. Worse yet, although nonpayment of taxes, if not compounded by deliberate deceit, was an administrative fault incurring fines and penalties rather than a crime, the Fujimori government increasingly moved to immediate criminal prosecution—in special courts whose judges were vulnerable to the government's pressures—of its opponents' alleged tax and customs offenses. Criminal prosecution ruined numerous political opponents' businesses and reputations. In one notorious case in October 1998, SUNAT agents entered without notification the offices of an opposition leader, Guido Pennano, confiscated all accounting books and documents, and then issued a warrant for his arrest.

What did the international financial community think about the Peruvian economic policymaking during 1998–2000? Opinions were mixed. On the one hand, some international economic analysts were not only concerned about Peru's weak democratic institutions but believed that the problem was of such importance that they did not support Fujimori's reelection in 2000.[91] They worried about unstable rules of the game that placed sudden, unexpected obstacles in companies' paths. They were aware that the Fujimori government was increasingly corrupt and that it was subordinating the judiciary to its will. This view, however, was in the minority.

For the most part, officials at international development agencies, U.S. officials responsible for international economic issues, U.S.-based executives of international companies, and Peru-based executives continued to support President Fujimori.[92] In the eyes of these officials and executives, the Fujimori government was the first Peruvian government in decades to "get the basics right."[93] They believed that Fujimori remained a pragmatic, capable president. Consider, for example, comments by Fred Levy, the 1994–98 World Bank representative in Lima, in a February 1998 interview.[94] Asked about President Fujimori's performance with respect to El Niño, Levy replied, "I see President Fujimori as a problem-solver.

He enjoys being confronted by concrete problems that require an engineering solution and strong management." Probed about Fujimori's "authoritarian emphasis," Levy says, "I would rather not comment on that." This positive view of Fujimori at the international development banks continued through June 2000.[95]

In a poll of Wall Street analysts in late 1999, almost all were aware that the Fujimori government was not promoting democracy in Peru; however, a large majority believed that Fujimori was still the best candidate for Peru in 2000.[96] Either they considered the problem of weak democratic institutions relatively minor; or they believed that, having won his third term, Fujimori would change; or they doubted that any other candidate would do better than Fujimori.[97] "Stability" and "continuity" were the watchwords of analysts who considered Peru an "island of calm in the Andes."[98]

The low priority given to democratic institutions by Wall Street analysts was expressed by Carlos Janada, a Peruvian senior economist with New York investment bank Morgan Stanley, in an interview with *The Peru Report* in September 1998.[99] Janada praised Peru as the Latin American nation that, along with Argentina, had advanced fastest with free-market reform, and indicated scant concern about Peru's politics. When asked "Are foreign investors concerned about the judicial system?," Janada replied, "More about the red-tape problems, I'd say." Asked "Are investors more worried about political factors now than they have traditionally been?," Janada answered, "The main concern is political stability, someone who guarantees the rules of the game. Broadly, this administration has done that so far." We noted above that, just as Janada was inclined to dismiss the Peruvian opposition's charges of increasing corruption and politicization of Peru's judiciary, the Heritage Foundation in its index of economic freedom for 1999 ranked the judiciary as more professional and autonomous from government influence than in the past.

Some analysts charge that the international financial community was not greatly concerned by the Fujimori government's bending of democratic rules in large part because its manipulations often benefited major U.S. companies. The most salient example was Newmont Mining's bid for majority control of the Yanacocha gold mine, which pitted the U.S.-based company and its Peruvian partner against the French firm BRGM. An audiotape of a February 26, 1998 meeting in Lima reveals that Newmont Senior Vice President and Chief Administrative Officer Lawrence R. Kurlander discussed the case with Montesinos; apparently, Montesinos promised to "help" with the decision to be made by Peru's Supreme Court, and Kurlander responded "I hope so."[100] A 1998 "vladivideo" shows Montesinos offering a promotion to the court's chief justice to vote in favor of Newmont (which he did—casting a tie-breaker).[101] From prison, Montesinos has charged that U.S. Department of State officials, in particular Peter Romero, asked him to intervene on Newmont's behalf; Romero has acknowledged that he argued for a "level playing field" for Newmont.[102] As of the writing of this book, French businessman Patrick Maugein is alleging that Newmont paid $4 million to Montesinos to manipulate the Supreme Court vote.[103]

The international financial community indicated its support for Fujimori by a lenient stance toward the government's failure to meet agreed-upon economic targets for 1999. Despite Peru's worsening fiscal deficit, the International Monetary Fund maintained its approval for loans to Peru. The IMF seemed to believe, in the words of one journalist, that "Candidate-presidents . . . are allowed some whims."[104]

CONCLUSION

For the U.S. government, Peru's shift from the attempt to lead a regional initiative against debt service under García to one of the region's most dramatic free-market reform programs under Fujimori was extremely welcome. Although the government's privatization initiatives slowed during 1998–2000, its other free-market policies were maintained (or were perceived to have been maintained), and overall the government retained the support of the international financial community.

How should the continuing support from the international financial community for the Fujimori government be understood? On the one hand, the international financial community's fear that Fujimori might be succeeded by a populist president proved valid: In 2001, former president García, who remained anathema to the international financial community at the time, came within six points of victory (see this book's postscript).

Overall, however, the international financial community's continued support for Fujimori was troubling. First, a question should be raised regarding its concern about the election of a populist president in Peru—a concern that was salient even in the 2000 elections, when neither Toledo nor any of the other major candidates was running on a populist platform. Why was the international financial community so dubious that a pro-free-market candidate could win? Put another way, was the international financial community dubious that free-market reform was in Peru's immediate interest? Given the prevalence of these doubts, should not the international financial community have been debating what was going wrong with free-market reform in Peru (and indeed in much of Latin America) rather than looking to a Fujimori to maintain an unpopular model?

Ultimately, the international financial community was prioritizing free-market policy performance—or the appearance of free-market policy performance—over democracy. Although the international financial community is not charged with the advancement of democracy in Latin America, long-standing authoritarian governments in the region have often been particularly corrupt, and the international financial community is indeed charged with analysis of corruption. As this book indicates, by 1998–2000, charges of corruption against the Fujimori government were rampant in Peru. The international financial community was not doing its homework.

In 1998–2000, the international financial community's judgment of the Fujimori government was blinded by fear and ideology. Fearful of the election of a populist successor and persuaded that, despite Fujimori's flawed 1998–2000 economic policy making, he would prove a reliable partner in 2000–2005, the international financial community expressed its desire for "order" and "stability."[105] This desire was similar to that expressed by numerous international political leaders (see Chapter VII)—and similarly oblivious to the implications of illegitimacy for order and stability.

CHAPTER VI

THE BILATERAL AGENDA FROM THE 1980s TO 2000: NARCOTICS CONTROL

IN THE EARLY 1980S, NARCOTICS CONTROL BECAME AN important political issue within the United States. The term "war on drugs" was first coined in 1968 by Richard Nixon; in Latin America, the war began in earnest during the Reagan administration and subsequently intensified under the Bush and Clinton administrations. For the U.S. government, Peru was a priority theater in this war. From the 1970s through 1995, Peru was the world's top producer of coca; the Upper Huallaga Valley, some 50,000 hectares in remote northeastern Peru on the slopes between the Andes and the Amazon, was one of the most fertile coca-producing areas in the world. Most of the coca or coca paste was transported in traffickers' small planes to Colombia, where it was refined into cocaine; from Colombia, the drug was smuggled into the United States and Europe.

The goal of narcotics control was officially endorsed by every Peruvian government between 1980 and 2000. However, narcotics control was not the priority for Peru that it was for the United States. Especially during the 1980s and early 1990s, most Peruvian citizens and their leaders believed that drug production was primarily a problem of U.S. demand, not Latin American supply, and that therefore the U.S. government should bear most of the financial burden of the war. Also, some Peruvians considered coca a licit crop with medicinal properties and important ritual uses; still others wanted to make money from the plant and its derivatives.

During this period, U.S. and Peruvian officials were in considerable disagreement about the appropriate means to the end of narcotics control. Not surprisingly, Peruvian officials worried about the impact of narcotics-control policies on Peru's approximately two hundred thousand coca growers; for the most part, they favored not the use of military force but funds facilitating the cultivation of licit crops in areas where coca was grown (called crop substitution or alternative development). In short, they favored carrots over sticks. In contrast, U.S. officials tended to be less concerned about the lot of the coca producers—considered criminals by many U.S. officials—and more inclined to the use of military force. In short, they favored sticks over carrots.

Amid the distinct U.S. and Peruvian perspectives on the narcotics problem, it is not surprising that tensions emerged on the issue. By the late 1980s, it was evident that, at the relatively low levels of U.S. funding, coca eradication and alternative development were failing to reduce overall production, and the Bush administration pressured for a greater use of military force. This strategy was resisted by President García during his final eighteen months in office and for several years by Fujimori. During 1993 and 1994—the first two years of the Clinton administration and just after the autogolpe in Peru—antinarcotics policy in both countries was uncertain, and agencies and personnel in both countries were at odds.

By 1995, however, the U.S. and Fujimori governments had agreed that military interdiction of traffickers' planes (called "air bridge denial") was an appropriate means to the goal of narcotics control, and the two governments collaborated closely in this effort. The hypothesis behind air bridge denial was that, in the relatively small, unpopulated area between the Upper Huallaga Valley and Colombia, it would be possible to identify traffickers' planes and force them down; if there were no traffickers to purchase the coca, then the price would drop and growers would switch to other crops. It seems possible too, that—unexpectedly for many analysts in Peru—air bridge denial was advantageous against guerrilla movements in the area. While air bridge denial was proposed as early as the mid-1980s in U.S. circles, and apparently advanced for Peru by both the Central Intelligence Agency (CIA) and the Southern Command (SOUTHCOM), by all accounts Montesinos was its Peruvian manager.

From 1995 through 2000, the air bridge denial policy was in place. At the same time, the number of hectares in coca cultivation in Peru declined dramatically. For Clinton administration officials, this decline was their most salient victory in the war against drugs; these officials emphasized that the battle in Peru showed that the war could be won. While air bridge denial was cited as the major reason for the victory in Peru's battle, there was considerable disagreement among scholarly analysts about both the extent of the decline in coca cultivation and the reasons for the decline.

Also, although all analysts agreed that there had been at least some decline in coca cultivation in Peru, success in this battle highlighted serious questions about the war against drugs. First, U.S. success in Peru did not affect the overall strength of an enemy whose networks were international; in 2000, the U.S. government was no closer to its real goal—reducing the supply of cocaine on U.S. streets—than it had been in 1995. Second, U.S. success in Peru was based on an alliance with Montesinos, who was widely believed to be duplicitous in the war in Peru by the mid-1990s and almost universally believed to have been duplicitous by late 2000. Finally, air bridge denial was not initially approved by the U.S. government because of fears that innocent civilians might be killed by mistake; tragically, these fears proved well founded. On April 20, 2001, amid miscommunication between CIA employees on U.S. surveillance aircraft and Peruvian air force pilots, a U.S. missionaries' plane was shot down and a U.S. missionary and her daughter were killed. Air bridge denial was immediately suspended.

PERU AND THE REAGAN ADMINISTRATION: COOPERATIVE EFFORTS, SCANT RESULTS

During the 1970s and early 1980s, the demand for drugs in the United States and the supply from Latin America, as well as drug-related crime, were increasing. Cocaine and crack abuse was skyrocketing and extending into much wider sectors of U.S. society, especially among U.S. youth. In this context, President Ronald Reagan declared a "war on drugs" in 1982. Also, in 1984, after a visit to a class of U.S. fourth-graders, Nancy Reagan initiated the "Just say no [to drugs]" campaign. Although the war on drugs was a Republican initiative, it enjoyed support among many Democrats, especially Democrats who represented drug-racked inner cities. However, U.S. aid for narcotics control was meager by the standards of the 1990s—about $2 to $3 million annually in Peru between 1981 and 1985 (see Table I.2).

The principle of narcotics control was endorsed by the Belaúnde government, which established several programs toward this end in approximately 1983. The most important was Control y Reducción de los Cultivos de Coca en el Alto Huallaga (CORAH, Special Project for the Control and Eradication of Coca in the Upper Huallaga).[1] With an annual budget of about $1.3 million from the Bureau for International Narcotics Matters, the objective of CORAH was the eradication of coca plants by hand. CORAH employed some 450 workers to dig up coca plants, and paid the coca growers a nominal fee in exchange. During the project's peak year in 1985, almost five thousand hectares of coca were eradicated. This figure, however, paled beside the twenty-thousand-odd new hectares that came under cultivation that year.

The eradication effort was complemented by Programa Especial del Alto Huallaga (PEAH, Upper Huallaga Area Development Project).[2] With an annual budget of about $3 million from the Agency for International Development (U.S. AID), this project was intended to promote crop substitution and in general to encourage development in the area. It encountered major obstacles, most fundamental among them that the production of coca was extremely attractive. Not only was coca much more profitable than other crops, but it was also a sturdy, reliable plant, and coca products were lightweight and easy to transport. Infrastructure between the Upper Huallaga Valley and Peru's coast was poor, and there was considerable risk that fruits and vegetables would perish on the hazardous roads.

Another problem was restriction on eligibility for participation in the program to peasants certified by CORAH as noncultivators of coca, which proved to be a complex bureaucratic process. Gradually the fifty-odd employees of PEAH focused primarily on research into viable alternative crops at PEAH's own headquarters.

A third program was Unidad Móvil de Patrullaje Rural (UMOPAR, Rural Mobile Patrol Unit).[3] The goal of this new police unit of the civil guard was to protect CORAH and PEAH personnel, to provide the vehicles and other equipment for their work, and in general to enforce antidrug policies. Its 350-odd men were trained by the U.S. Drug Enforcement Administration (DEA), and most of their salaries were paid directly or indirectly by the U.S. government.

None of the three programs was successful. It was estimated that the area under coca cultivation in Peru tripled between 1980 and 1985.[4] Moreover, the programs severely alienated the coca growers. Both the Shining Path and the Movimiento Revolucionario Túpac Amaru (MRTA) were able to build support among the coca growers by providing them protection against narcotics-control personnel. In November 1984, nineteen CORAH workers were assassinated, and subsequently violent attacks against the headquarters of narcotics-control agencies became common.[5]

In 1986, a young basketball star, Len Bias, died from a cocaine overdose, and his death stirred intense concern in the United States. In part as a result, President Reagan issued National Security Decision Directive No. 221, proclaiming that drug production and trafficking threatened U.S. national security and apparently authorizing CIA participation in narcotics control.[6] U.S. aid for narcotics control approximately tripled, reaching $8 million for Peru in 1988, Reagan's final year in office (see Tables I.2 and VI.1).

At the same time, the U.S. Congress enacted stricter antidrug laws. Among these was the requirement that foreign countries be "certified" by the U.S. president as cooperating in the war against drugs if they were to receive U.S. aid. In the certification process, the United States either (1) certifies a country as fully cooperating with the United States in the war against drugs—"full certification"; (2) does not certify the country as fully cooperating with the United States but grants the country a waiver from the concomitant sanctions on the grounds of U.S. national interests; or (3) denies certification. Against nations that are denied certification, the concomitant sanctions include the withdrawal of most U.S. foreign assistance and U.S. opposition to loans for these countries from the multilateral development banks.

In 1985, President García declared that he would continue his predecessor's cooperation with the United States in the "war on drugs."[7] To the efforts of CORAH and PEAH, another initiative was added: air interdiction of cocaine laboratories and traffickers' airstrips. Named "Operation Condor," this interdiction initiative was carried out predominantly by a police unit formed on the base of

TABLE VI.1

CONTROL OF COCA AND COCAINE IN PERU, 1985–2000

Year	U.S. Antinarcotics Aid (millions $)*	Hectares in Cultivation (excludes seedbeds)**	Hectares Eradicated	Labs Destroyed	Aircraft Seized***
1985	2	95,200	0	44	0
1986	4	107,500	0	19	0
1987	8	109,500	355	24	0
1988	8	115,630	5,130	75	0
1989	11	115,630	1,285****	38	0
1990	10	121,300	0	151	0
1991	19	120,800	0	89	10
1992	13	129,100	0	88	7
1993	18	108,800	0	38	13
1994	8	108,600	0	21	4
1995	15	115,300	0	21	22
1996	19	94,400	1,259	14	7
1997	26	68,800	3,462	18	11
1998	32	51,000	7,825	N.A.	0
1999	75	38,700	13,800	N.A.	0
2000	80	34,100	6,200	N.A.	2

Sources: (except for U.S. anti-narcotics aid): www.state.gov/g/inl/rls/nrcrpt/2000, and Bureau of International Narcotics Matters (BINM) and its successor International Narcotics and Law Enforcement Affairs, *International Narcotics Control Strategy Report* (Washington, D.C.: U.S. Department of State), annual editions. Figures for the number of labs destroyed are not reported in recent editions.

*See Table I.2 for sources and the text in this chapter for discussion. Figures for 1996–2000 are from www.ciponline.org/facts/pe/htm and include U.S. Department of Defense aid.

**After early 1989, the Peruvian government rejected the eradication of mature coca plants. From 1990 through 1995, the Fujimori government was eradicating only seedbeds. The principle was to mitigate the resentment of coca farmers.

***For the years 1991–1994, BINM reports do not clarify the precise actions taken against aircraft. The unit of measurement is "items."

****This figure is from the 1991 and 1992 BINM reports. A higher figure is reported in some subsequent reports.

UMOPAR under DEA auspices; Peru's police unit was supported by U.S. helicopters and U.S. pilots. Peruvian antidrug units destroyed cocaine laboratories and seized the coca and coca paste at the laboratories. Also, the García government agreed to establish the biggest antidrug base in the Americas at Santa Lucía in the Upper Huallaga Valley. Approximately twenty-five DEA agents plus about eight U.S.-supplied helicopters and 450 Peruvians were located at the base, which opened in 1988.[8] Moreover, the García government agreed to study the aerial application of coca herbicides.

The García government's interdiction policy achieved some successes. As Table VI.1 shows, a large number of cocaine laboratories were destroyed, especially in 1985 and 1988. A considerable number of airstrips—as many as forty in 1985—were disabled. The number of arrests for drug-trafficking offenses also increased dramatically, from about 4,275 in 1985 to an estimated 9,000 in 1989.[9]

However, as under Belaúnde, these successes paled within the overall context of failure. As antinarcotics operations centered in Santa Lucía and the city of Tingo María, the coca growers and traffickers moved to other parts of the Upper Huallaga Valley and beyond it. The number of hectares under coca cultivation in Peru continued to increase (see Table VI.1). At the same time, the alliance between coca growers and Peru's guerrilla groups was strengthened, and security conditions for antinarcotics units deteriorated.

PERU AND THE BUSH ADMINISTRATION: BILATERAL CONFLICT

In January 1989, President Bush was inaugurated, and narcotics control became an even higher U.S. priority. Indeed, during the Bush administration narcotics control was arguably at the very top of the U.S. agenda for Peru.[10] In 1988, the Office of National Drug Control Policy had been established; President Bush appointed former secretary of education William Bennett, a prominent hard-liner on the issue, as the office's first head—the first U.S. "drug czar." Two presidential summit meetings on counternarcotics were held, one in Colombia in 1990 and one in Texas in 1992.

In September 1989, Bush announced the Andean Initiative, proclaiming that the United States could most effectively reduce the supply of cocaine by destroying it at its source in the Andean nations. Whereas the Reagan strategy had been eradication and interdiction predominantly by Andean police forces under DEA auspices, Bush promoted a much greater role for the Andean and U.S. militaries, including the U.S. Army Special Forces (Green Berets). The narcotics-control budget included a much larger component of direct military-to-military aid.

For Peru, the Bush administration proposed a $35.9 million military aid package. Under the proposal, the U.S. would station twenty to fifty U.S. Army Special Forces instructors in Peru to train roughly fifty-five hundred Peruvian military personnel; equip the personnel; and refurbish twenty ground-attack planes and supply river patrol boats.[11] It was also expected that the U.S. would support alternative development programs in coca-producing areas, but precise amounts were not specified.

The Bush administration's emphasis on direct military-to-military aid disturbed the García government. The alliance between coca producers and the Shining Path guerrillas in the Upper Huallaga Valley was becoming ever stronger, and guerrillas' attacks against counternarcotics units were intensifying.

While the Bush administration argued that *counternarcotics* and *counterinsurgency* were synonymous, the García administration was coming to the belief that they were at odds, and that the correct role for Peru's military was counterinsurgency. The García government feared that a repressive counternarcotics program, especially if not combined with support for alternative development, would only lose more Peruvian peasants' hearts and minds to the Shining Path.[12] Peruvian officials cited the example of General Alberto Arciniega, who in 1989 had regained control of an area in the Upper Huallaga Valley by relentlessly pursuing guerrillas but ignoring coca farmers and traffickers—much to the dismay of U.S. antinarcotics officials. In general, to many Peruvian officials, the U.S. request that Peru wage a war against drugs was "[to ask] a country that's fighting the Civil War and going through the Great Depression to take on Prohibition as well."[13]

In this context, bilateral cooperation was limited. For much of 1989, counternarcotics operations were suspended. As Table VI.1 indicates, both the number of cocaine laboratories destroyed and the number of coca hectares eradicated declined relative to 1988. President García attempted to highlight the need for economic rather than military assistance by showcasing a coca farmer at the presidential summit in Colombia in 1990. Most important of all, the García government rejected the $35.9 million military aid proposal in April 1990.

A new opportunity for cooperation opened after President Fujimori's inauguration in July 1990. The tone of the dialogue was more cordial. Record numbers of cocaine laboratories were destroyed in 1990 (see Table VI.1). Although the Fujimori government did not resume the manual eradication of coca plants, it did target coca seedbeds for eradication. (These figures are not included in Table VI.1.) However, the Bush administration's proposal that the Peruvian military succeed the Peruvian police as the lead agency for narcotics control continued to meet resistance in Peru. In September 1990, Bush's military aid package was rejected by Fujimori, who cited the same concerns as García.

Finally, however, in May 1991, President Fujimori accepted the $35.9 million military aid package. The shift in Fujimori's position reflected intense U.S. pressure; although U.S. officials denied that U.S. support for Peru in the international financial community was contingent upon Peru's signing the military aid agreement, the Peruvian government repeatedly indicated that it was, and Peruvian journalists routinely interpreted the negotiations in this fashion.[14] A second factor was that, in the course of U.S.-Peruvian negotiations between September 1990 and May 1991, the Bush administration compromised.[15] In particular, the Bush administration promised greater economic aid, especially for crop substitution. Also, the administration modified some of its conceptualization; for example, peasant producers were not labeled criminals.

But tensions continued. The U.S. military aid proposal was under consideration in the U.S. Congress for several months. Human-rights concerns were paramount for many U.S. legislators; they feared that U.S. military aid would undermine Peru's weak civilian institutions and exacerbate the serious pattern of human-rights abuse.[16] Finally, in September 1991, the U.S. Congress reduced the amount of military aid from $35 million to $25 million; the $10 million that had been earmarked for the Peruvian army—the service most often cited for abuses by human-rights groups—was withheld, and the remaining funds were conditioned upon various improvements in the Peruvian security forces' human-rights performance (see Chapter VII).[17]

These conditions and delays appeared to irritate the Fujimori government. Although the destruction of cocaine laboratories and the eradication of seedbeds continued, the high expectations that had emerged after the May 1991 agreement were gradually dashed.[18] Although the agreement had not specified precise figures for U.S. economic support for counternarcotics, Fujimori had assumed a massive allocation. In the event, although U.S. AID reported $19 million for counternarcotics economic programs in 1991 (see Table VI.1), a smaller sum was calculated by Peruvian experts.[19] For their part, U.S. officials expected improved antidrug performance on the part of Peruvian officials, but the pattern of events suggested that official complicity with drug traffickers—a serious problem for many years—was becoming worse.[20] (As Chapter III described, presidential adviser Hernando de Soto resigned in January 1992, citing corruption among counternarcotics officials.) Accordingly, the U.S. government delayed its disbursements of aid, and the delays angered the Peruvians. In February 1992, at a Texas drug summit that President Bush had hoped would showcase counternarcotics successes, U.S. policies were sharply criticized by President Fujimori. Indeed, Fujimori publicly accused the DEA of corruption and complicity in the drug traffic.

Then, on April 5, 1992, the Fujimori government executed its autogolpe. The next day, all U.S. counternarcotics aid (and most other kinds of aid as well) was suspended by the Bush administration. The prospects for anti-drug cooperation appeared dim.

The prospects appeared dimmer yet after April 24, 1992. On that day, two Peruvian fighter jets shot a U.S. Air Force Hercules C-130 flying off the northern Peruvian coast from its base in Panama, causing rapid decompression in the C-130 that sucked an American crewman out of the aircraft to his death. The Hercules C-130 had been on a secret drug surveillance mission in the Upper Huallaga Valley and had not responded to the Peruvians' warnings, probably because of interception rules established for spy planes during the Cold War and misunderstandings.[21]

Although the full story of the shoot-down was still not available at the time of this writing, the event exacerbated tensions between the U.S. and the Fujimori government. The Bush administration maintained that the Hercules C-130 was clearly identifiable as a U.S. aircraft and that the shoot-down was the Peruvians' fault. U.S. legislators, especially Senator Jesse Helms from North Carolina (the home state of the killed crewman), were irate. For its part, the Fujimori government argued that the Hercules C-130 was not identifiable as a U.S. aircraft and that the U.S. pilots were responsible for the accident because of their failure to respond to the Peruvians' warnings. The Fujimori government proceeded to bill the U.S. government $30,000 for its expenses incurred by the attack. U.S. legislators continued to protest; Helms led an effort to condition disbursement of U.S. aid to Peru on compensation to the crewman's family by the Peruvian government. Finally—in December 1993, more than a year later—Peru did provide compensation.[22]

What might the full story behind the Peruvians' shoot-down of the Hercules C-130 have been? At the time, some U.S. authorities charged that Peruvian military officers not only weren't cooperating in the war on drugs but were actually on the enemy's side, trying to discourage drug surveillance by the United States. This interpretation was one reason for the hostility toward the Fujimori government and its military in many U.S. official circles during this period. However, this interpretation was almost certainly incorrect. In 1993, a U.S. investigative journalist hypothesized that the Peruvian military officers who had shot at the plane were angry at the U.S. aid cutoff.[23] This interpretation was probably incorrect also. Most likely, the shoot-down was indeed a simple accident resulting from miscommunication.[24] Apparently, U.S. analysts underestimated the possibility that the shoot-down had been an accident because they did not know that, in fact, U.S.-Peruvian military collaboration was increasing at this time; plans were under way for the program that would become air bridge denial, but these plans were covert.[25]

The Clinton and Fujimori Administrations, 1993–1994: Cooperation and Conflict Amid Bureaucratic Disarray

In 1993–1994, narcotics-control policy was in disarray in both the United States and Peru. Different sectors of both governments upheld different means for narcotics control in the Andean nations. The question of military interdiction of traffickers' planes, or air bridge denial, was especially controversial. It appears that during this period the CIA and Montesinos consolidated a position favoring air bridge denial, and that in December 1994 this position prevailed.

The bureaucratic disarray in the United States was attributable in part to the new president's uncertainty about his counternarcotics policy preferences.[26] During his first two years in office, President Clinton emphasized that international counternarcotics policy was under review. However, numerous steps by the new government suggested that its ultimate policy preference would be a dramatic shift toward antidemand programs, focusing on treatment and rehabilitation, and away from the antisupply priority of the Bush administration.

These steps included changes in both rhetoric and resources.[27] In contrast to presidents Reagan and Bush, during his first two years in office Clinton rarely talked about narcotics control in the Andes. He slashed the staff and budget of the Office of National Drug Control Policy, and appointed as its director Lee Brown, a New York City police commissioner with no international narcotics-control experience. Between 1992 and 1996, appropriations for antidrug international and interdiction programs declined.[28]

While President Clinton was reviewing his administration's narcotics-control policy, however, officials at different ranks and at different bureaucracies were making their own policies. The CIA, Department of Defense (DOD), DEA, and State Department were at odds over policy in the Andean nations. Complained one SOUTHCOM analyst: "With the Department of Defense barely on speaking terms with its number one customer—DEA—[in many areas of Latin America it] is the equivalent of two battalions going into combat, with one having the bullets and the other having the guns."[29]

In Peru, the CIA had begun to collaborate on counternarcotics with Montesinos as early as 1991.[30] In May 1991, the agency hosted Montesinos at its Langley headquarters, and in September an "antidrug" arm was established within Montesinos's Servicio de Inteligencia Nacional (SIN).[31] However, the CIA's collaboration with Montesinos was unwelcome to the DEA and the State Department.[32] Officials at both these agencies were aware of Montesinos's extensive previous work for drug traffickers, and feared that the "fox would be guarding the henhouse."[33] They raised the possibility of a replay of the story of Panama's General Noriega. Apparently, however (as would be the case for many years), they did not have sufficient "proof"—by the CIA's standards of proof—to prevail.[34]

The plan that brought U.S. officials and Montesinos together was the military interdiction of traffickers' flights.[35] This idea had been considered since the mid-1980s.[36] In 1987, for example, during the Reagan administration, U.S. customs commissioner William Von Raab argued at a narcotics-control meeting that the U.S. Air Force should be allowed to shoot down suspected drug-smuggling planes that did not respond to warnings.[37] The argument was rejected amid U.S. judicial rulings that the use of lethal force against fleeing suspects was unconstitutional and fears that tragic mistakes and innocent deaths would culminate in lawsuits against U.S. officials.[38]

However, as of 1991 in Peru, initiatives that would ultimately become the air bridge denial program were being taken. In 1991, the CIA and SOUTHCOM installed radar stations to help Peru's air force to track drug planes.[39] As Table VI.1 indicates, ten traffickers' aircraft were seized in 1991 in some way or another.

(The precise character of these seizures is not indicated in the U.S. Department of State reports; it appears that some were "forced down" but not "shot down."[40]) Immediately after the autogolpe—perhaps in an effort to build CIA and SOUTH-COM support for the autogolpe—military interdiction initiatives increased. President Fujimori and Montesinos placed all airports in Peru's northern drug-producing areas under military control, and apparently at this time persuaded Peru's air force to assume interdiction responsibilities.[41] (As discussed above, it appears likely that it was in the context of this post-autogolpe collaboration that a U.S. Hercules C-130 drug-surveillance plane was downed by the Peruvian air force in April 1992.) Seven traffickers' aircraft were reported seized in 1992 and thirteen in 1993 (see Table VI.1).

This collaboration was not, however, the official policy of either the U.S. or the Peruvian government.[42] In the U.S. government, concerns continued about possible U.S. responsibility if a civilian aircraft were downed on the basis of U.S. intelligence. In Peru, the military was not comfortable with the policy. As indicated in the previous section, at this time—when the Shining Path was at its strongest—the Peruvian army tended to believe that counternarcotics and counterinsurgency were at odds, and that the army's priority should be counterinsurgency. Moreover, when tensions on the Peru-Ecuador border escalated, however (see Chapter IV), this collaboration became increasingly controversial; many officers argued that more attention to Peru's border disputes was necessary.[43]

In 1994, U.S. concern about liability for civilian deaths mounted in the U.S. Justice and Defense Departments.[44] Apparently as a result of civilian deaths amid a U.S military confrontation in Iraq, in May the U.S. Defense Department ordered a review of U.S. air operations worldwide and, pending the outcome of this review, suspended U.S. intelligence-sharing programs in the Andean nations. The suspension was opposed by many antinarcotics officials and numerous members of the U.S. Congress, who were convinced that U.S. intelligence on traffickers' flights was essential to the success of international narcotics control. The suspension also worried narcotics-control personnel in Peru and other Andean nations, who needless to say perceived the disarray of U.S. policy.[45] The upshot in Peru was the seizure of only four traffickers' planes in 1994 (see Table VI.1).

During the latter months of 1994, these tensions were resolved.[46] Led by Democrats, the U.S. Congress passed new legislation authorizing the U.S. president to identify countries under extraordinary threat from drug trafficking; in these countries, U.S. officials were exempted from liability for civilian deaths during the shoot-down of suspected drug-trafficking planes. In any case, U.S. pilots would not be directly responsible; the actual shooting would be done by the host-country air force. The key condition for the exemption was that detailed rules of engagement be stipulated and respected. In December, this legislation was signed by President Clinton.

While the costs and benefits of military interdiction of traffickers' planes were debated, other counternarcotics strategies were advanced in various sectors of the U.S. government. In particular, the U.S. assistant secretary of state for international anti-narcotics strategy, Ambassador Robert Gelbard, was an outspoken advocate of the strategy of the manual and/or aerial eradication of the coca plants. Believing that eradication provoked the alliance between peasants and guerrillas and that security conditions for eradication were inadequate, the Fujimori government rejected this strategy. As is evident in Table VI.1, no mature coca plants were eradicated in Peru between 1990 and 1995.

For this reason—despite Peru's cooperation in the seizure of aircraft—in the annual U.S. certification process, the U.S. Department of State became more critical of Peru's antinarcotics performance. For the first time, on the basis of its performance during 1993, Peru was certified in 1994 only as a result of a national-interest waiver. In the report by the Bureau of International Narcotics Matters (BINM), Peru was sharply criticized for its failure to adopt an eradication program, as well as its failures to develop a national counternarcotics strategy and to reduce drug-related corruption.[47] The report recognized the Fujimori government's disruption of drug-trafficking operations and other achievements, but these were insufficient to secure full certification for the country.

In 1994, the U.S. Department of State and the Fujimori government continued to disagree on the strategy of coca eradication.[48] Although the eradication of coca seedbeds was resumed in Peru, the eradication of mature plants was not. In the context of the suspension of U.S. intelligence for the seizure of traffickers' aircraft, Peru's overall 1994 antinarcotics record was not as positive as in 1993 (see Table VI.1). Assistant Secretary Gelbard sought decertification and a denial of the national security waiver for Peru. Only an emergency effort by the assistant secretary of state for Latin America at the time, Ambassador Alexander Watson, enabled Peru to retain the national security waiver for its 1994 counternarcotics performance.[49]

Although at no time during the 1990s did Peru adopt as aggressive an eradication policy as did Bolivia or Colombia, the conflict on the issue gradually dissipated. As the next section describes, after 1995 virtually all U.S. and Peruvian actors were celebrating the successes of the air bridge denial policy.

THE CLINTON AND FUJIMORI ADMINISTRATIONS, 1995–2000: BILATERAL COOPERATION

A variety of factors led to shifts in both U.S. and Peruvian antinarcotics policy in late 1994 and early 1995. With these shifts, air bridge denial became official U.S. and Peruvian policy. The policy was soon touted by General McCaffrey and other U.S. antidrug officials as the major reason for the decline in coca cultivation in Peru.[50] However, the U.S. claim was disputed by many analysts.[51] Critics charged that the decline was not as dramatic as U.S. and Peruvian officials were reporting. Also, skeptics argued that air bridge denial was not as important to the decline as the emergence of a coca-killing fungus and structural changes in the cocaine industry. Although for various reasons a definitive analysis of this controversy is not possible, it seems likely that air bridge denial was important to the decline— but not as important as the U.S. and Peruvian governments claimed. Also, whatever the impact of air bridge denial, the antidrug battle in Peru raised many questions about the overall war.

In the wake of the Republican victory in the November 1994 midterm elections and the new Republican majority in the U.S. Congress, President Clinton's anti-narcotics policy changed. To a significant degree, the Clinton administration reasserted the traditional U.S. emphasis on international antisupply programs. The White House no longer sent mixed signals about international narcotics control, but endorsed the direct military-to-military programs that the Bush administration had tried to establish. The first indication was Clinton's December 1994 approval of the U.S. congressional legislation to exempt U.S. officials from liability for civilian deaths during the shoot-down of suspected drug-trafficking planes.

A second major indication was President Clinton's appointment of four-star general Barry McCaffrey as director of the White House's Office of National Drug Control Policy in January 1996. As Chapter III indicated, at the time McCaffrey, considered a hero of the Gulf War, was the commander in chief of the U.S. Southern Command in Panama. Whereas it had been clear that former New York City police commissioner Lee Brown was unlikely to focus on international antisupply policies, it was just as clear that General McCaffrey was likely to emphasize them. McCaffrey's prodding was apparently important to the large jump in the Pentagon's expenditures for international narcotics control at this time.[52]

As the commander in chief of SOUTHCOM, McCaffrey had already developed a cordial relationship with President Fujimori, General Hermoza, and other military officers.[53] After January 1996, as drug czar, McCaffrey met with Fujimori on numerous occasions, and McCaffrey spoke highly of the man. Said McCaffrey in May 1997: "I have tremendous admiration for Alberto Fujimori."[54] It appears, however, that the relationship between McCaffrey and Montesinos was cool. Prior to a 1998 visit to Peru, McCaffrey had said to U.S. human-rights groups that he would not meet with Montesinos; accordingly, McCaffrey was angry when a video was released that showed him with Montesinos at an official meeting. Apparently, the video was an attempt by Montesinos to raise his own public image, but it indicated Montesinos's disrespect for the drug czar and frayed their relationship. Such strains probably reflected at least in part lingering tension between non-CIA and CIA actors in Peru's drug war.

A third indication of the Clinton administration's policy shift was a major increase in U.S. support for antidrug international and interdiction programs.[55] Most of the increase in support for interdiction was from the U.S. Department of

Defense.[56] Under Section 1004 of the 1991 National Defense Authorization Act, the Pentagon was authorized to assist and train foreign security forces in counternarcotics. Among the types of support authorized were the operation of bases, the establishment of communication and intelligence services, the maintenance and repair of equipment, and the transport of U.S. and foreign personnel. Also, in 1998, Section 1033 authorized the Pentagon to support riverine counternarcotics initiatives in Colombia and Peru. In contrast to the U.S. Department of State's expenditures, the Department of Defense's expenditures on these and other smaller counternarcotics programs in Latin America were not systematically reported to the U.S. Congress. Figures first became available only in 1996 as a result of the efforts of the Latin America Working Group and the Center for International Policy. In Peru, the amount was estimated to triple—from less than $25 million annually in 1996–1997 to more than $75 million annually in 1999–2000 (see Table VI.1).

At the same time that the Clinton administration was unifying behind international antisupply policies, major Peruvian actors were also becoming much more positive toward them. Whereas Peruvian military and civilian leaders had feared that a repressive counternarcotics program would lose peasants' hearts and minds to the guerrillas, it gradually became clear that there were significant counterinsurgency benefits from the interdiction effort.[57] First, it seems possible that, although the stated goal of the collaboration was counternarcotics, the information provided to Montesinos and other Peruvian authorities by the CIA was also helpful in the tracking of the guerrillas. Second, as a result of the interdiction effort, a greater CIA and Peruvian military presence was established in areas that were at the time largely controlled by the Shining Path or the MRTA. Third, because the target of air bridge denial was not the Peruvian coca growers but Colombian traffickers, the policy did not propel growers toward the guerrillas for protection. Fourth, as the revenues available to the guerrillas from taxation and other levies upon coca growers and drug traffickers declined, the guerrillas' power declined as well. Even for officers who continued to believe that counterinsurgency and counternarcotics were at odds, by 1995 this concern was irrelevant; security conditions in Peru had improved dramatically.

A second factor, not mentioned by U.S. or Peruvian officials at the time, was probably important also: Montesinos's growing power over the Peruvian military. Gradually during the 1990s, Montesinos was able to place his allies throughout the top ranks of Peru's military (see Chapter III). He apparently persuaded U.S. officials that he personally had the capacity to order Peru's officers to fight drugs—or not. According to various U.S. journalists, Montesinos occasionally threatened U.S. officials that he would end Peruvian support for narcotics control if his requests—probably tolerance for authoritarian actions by the Fujimori government—were not met.[58]

In these new U.S. and Peruvian contexts, intensive U.S.-Peruvian collaboration to deny the drug traffickers' air bridge began in early 1995. In an agreement signed by the U.S. ambassador and Peru's foreign minister, intelligence on suspicious planes was to be provided to the Peruvian air force by CIA contractors on surveillance aircraft owned by the Pentagon; the suspicious planes would then be intercepted by the Peruvian air force.[59] The program was dubbed, "You fly, you die."

Gradually, the program expanded.[60] The hundred-odd U.S. officials working for the program in Peru by the mid-1990s hailed not only from the CIA and the Pentagon but also from the DEA and the U.S. Customs Service. Intelligence was collected not only by the CIA but also by the DEA and the National Security Agency, which specializes in eavesdropping and code breaking. The U.S. Customs Service introduced aircraft with more effective radar capability. As many as 175 U.S. military and intelligence personnel were deployed in Peru for short intervals in order to train Peruvians for their drug-war missions.[61]

The program expanded on the Peruvian side as well. The new antinarcotics police unit, called DINANDRO (the Peruvian National Police Drug Directorate), was strengthened. Its primary goal was to work with the Peruvian air force and the U.S. government toward the denial of the air bridge. It also sought to arrest drug traffickers and seize their assets.

Montesinos, however, remained the chief of antinarcotics in Peru.[62] In 1992, Montesinos had underlined the SIN's leadership role when SIN agents had raided the offices of the police counternarcotics intelligence unit and seized its files.[63] As indicated previously, despite apparent tensions between Montesinos and McCaffrey, the U.S. drug czar met with him repeatedly, as did General Charles Wilhelm, the 1997–2000 head of SOUTHCOM.[64] Montesinos's pivotal role was cited by U.S. authorities when they were questioned about U.S. support for the drug intelligence unit of the SIN. During 1996–1998, this SIN unit was the recipient from the U.S. Department of State of approximately $200,000, reportedly for computer equipment and training.[65] Also, the unit received at least $1 million in cash annually for a period of ten years from the CIA.[66]

U.S. officials argued that the effects of air bridge denial were dramatic. They cited air bridge denial as virtually the only reason for the decline of about two-thirds in the number of hectares in coca cultivation in Peru between 1995 and 1999 (see Table VI.1). General McCaffrey's praise was copious; he pronounced the changes in narcotics control in Peru "revolutionary"; "without historical precedent"; and "absolutely astounding."[67] Although the U.S. Department of State continued to urge forced eradication of mature coca in Peru (and the Fujimori government began to comply), it fully certified Peru as a partner in the war against drugs.[68] For U.S. officials, the apparent success of the air bridge denial battle in Peru offered hope of success in other countries and therefore hope of victory in the war; accordingly, it was helpful in the overall promotion of the Clinton administration's narcotics-control policies.[69]

In support of their argument about air bridge denial, U.S. officials cited a range of facts. First, there were clear effects in the skies over the Upper Huallaga Valley. In 1995, some twenty-two drug-transport aircraft were seized (see Table VI.1). The fee demanded by pilots for one drug-transport flight across the border increased from about $30,000 in 1994 to approximately $180,000 in 1997.[70] As the flights became more dangerous and expensive, their number detected plummeted—from roughly 752 in 1992 to 96 in 1996.[71] Second, the prices for coca products declined sharply. By the end of 1995, the price of a kilogram of coca leaf was less than one-quarter of the price at the beginning of 1995—approximately $0.60 versus $2.50 per kilogram of coca leaf.[72] By most accounts, the price remained below $0.80 through 1997.[73] The price of coca was no longer sufficient to cover the cost of production.

However, U.S. officials' claims about the success of air bridge denial program were disputed. First, critics charged that the extent of the success in Peru was exaggerated; they believed that the statistics, which were collected by the CIA's satellite imagery, were inaccurate.[74] Aware of the relationship between the CIA and Montesinos, these analysts worried that the methodology for the data collection was opaque and might have been affected by the interests of the collecting parties. Why, for example, was the emphasis invariably on figures for the number of hectares in coca cultivation, when improved technologies had dramatically increased the amount of coca that could be produced per hectare? In particular, the U.S. statistic for the number of hectares in coca cultivation in 2000 was criticized by the UN Drug Control Program and by Peruvian scholar Hugo Cabieses.[75] Citing the recuperation of the price for coca and many analysts' observation of cultivation trends, Cabieses said that the low U.S. figure was false and politically motivated.[76] In 2002, criticism of U.S. estimates was expressed by the Toledo government, which pointed out that U.S. satellite imagery often failed to detect young coca plants.[77]

Second, critics charged that, whatever the extent of the decline in coca cultivation, air bridge denial was not the key factor to this change. In 1991–1993, a fungus (*Fusarium oxysporum*) devastated coca cultivation in the Upper Huallaga Valley; at least 30 percent of coca plants in the area wilted and died.[78] It appeared most likely that the fungus was not natural, but had been introduced by U.S. researchers contracted by the CIA in the early 1980s and had spread.[79] Although several analysts suggested that the fungus was the only factor in the decline in coca cultivation during the 1990s, this argument is invalid. If the fungus were the only factor, the price of coca in Peru should have increased, not decreased, as supply became more limited. What seems more likely is that the fungus was one among various factors in Colombian traffickers' decisions about the locations from which they would purchase coca.

Critics argued that air bridge denial had not been important to the decline because, as of 1995, Colombian traffickers had already decided to restructure their industry, purchasing most of their raw material in Colombia.[80] In the early 1990s in Colombia, the Medellín cartel was struggling for its survival; in 1993 its kingpin, Pablo Escobar, was killed. Upon the demise of the Medellín cartel, U.S. and Colombian pressure against the remaining Cali cartel increased, and new trafficking groups emerged. Many traffickers decided that it would be less dangerous and more cost effective to vertically integrate their businesses—in other words, to grow and process their raw material in the same place (in this case, Colombia).

Although it is logical that both the fungus and cost issues would have persuaded Colombian traffickers to grow their raw material in Colombia, the relevant available data suggest that air bridge denial was also likely to have been a factor in their decisions. Although coca cultivation began to increase in Colombia prior to 1995, the increases are greater after 1995. Whereas the number of hectares in coca cultivation in Colombia rose by 15 percent from 1993 to 1994 and by 13 percent from 1994 to 1995, the number jumped by 31 percent from 1995 to 1996 and 18 percent from 1996 to 1997.[81] We conclude, as Carlos Basombrío did, that air bridge denial was not the only cause of the decline in coca prices and coca cultivation, but it exacerbated and prolonged the coca growers' crisis.[82]

In any case, while a battle in Peru had probably in part been won, the war certainly had not been. By the late 1990s, it was extremely clear that the drug industry was flexible and could rapidly shift illicit activity from one place to another in reaction to international narcotics-control policies. Of course, the area where coca can be cultivated is vast, spanning not only many Latin American nations but also Indonesia, Sri Lanka, India, and Taiwan, and the potential transportation routes are numerous. It was agreed by critics of air bridge denial and U.S. government officials that a key result of air bridge denial was to move coca cultivation from Peru to Colombia.[83] As indicated above, as the number of hectares in coca cultivation decreased in Peru and Bolivia, the number in Colombia increased; as a result, the total for the three nations was almost exactly the same in 1999 as in 1993.[84]

Not only did traffickers shift cultivation to Colombia, but alternate routes for the export of drugs from Peru were also developed. These routes were through the Amazon and its tributaries to Brazil and also overland to Lima and other Peruvian coastal cities, where drugs were sent to the United States via the Pacific Ocean and often put ashore in Mexico.[85]

For most analysts, it was also extremely disturbing that, to win the battle in Peru, the U.S. government had allied with a man who was ultimately revealed to be a traitor. In early 2002, based on abundant evidence of his charges to traffickers for his assistance and protection, of his receipt of goods yielded by drug trafficking, and of his involvement in money laundering, Montesinos was indicted in Peru on charges of drug trafficking.[86] Indications of Montesinos's involvement in drug trafficking were mentioned in Chapter III: In 1996–1997, he was publicly accused of selling information about antidrug raids and was revealed to have an annual income many times his likely official salary. Prior to 2000, there were numerous other red flags. In 1996, two seizures of huge quantities of cocaine (each seizure would have fetched at least $10 million on the streets of the United States) were made on Peruvian military transports.[87] In the mid-1990s, the DEA detected multimillion-dollar transfers from Peruvian government coffers to overseas accounts that they feared were linked to Montesinos.[88] Montesinos's involvement with the drug trade was alleged to U.S. officials not only by captured drug traffickers but also by a Peruvian DEA informant.[89] Apparently, however, these events and allegations were insufficient to trigger a serious U.S. investigation of its ally.

So far, this section has addressed questions raised by air bridge denial for the U.S. war on drugs. Another set of questions was about the results of the policy for Peruvians. These results were significant not only for peasants in coca-producing areas but also for large numbers of Peruvians in coastal cities.

For peasants in coca-producing areas, the results were mixed. After the collapse in the price of coca in Peru, conditions were favorable for the introduction of licit crops, and the Fujimori government pursued alternative development. A new agency, CONTRADROGAS (literally, "Against Drugs"), was established in approximately 1996, ostensibly to coordinate counternarcotics policy, but (given that this was Montesinos's job) actually to enhance alternative development, prevention, and rehabilitation programs. It is estimated that between 1995 and 2000 the U.S. government spent approximately $85 million—roughly $15 million annually—on alternative development and new infrastructure in coca-producing areas in Peru.[90] At a meeting convened by CONTRADROGAS for international donors in Brussels in 1998, the United States pledged about $125 million and Canada, European nations, the United Nations, and other international organizations a similar amount.[91] It does not appear, however, that all these funds materialized.

The alternative-development funds were advantageous. From the mid-1990s through 1999, about six hundred kilometers of roads were rehabilitated and roughly seventeen bridges constructed.[92] Credit for the cultivation of licit crops was extended to more than thirty-five hundred families in 1999 alone.[93] Gradually, the production of coffee and cacao (crops that had been traditional to coca-growing areas) increased considerably. Also, in part as a result of the research programs of previous years, the cultivation of new crops, including pineapple, citrus, soy, anise, and palm heart, began. Some alternative-development funds were allocated to the provision of basic health and educational services in coca-growing areas, and the percentage of families with access to these services increased significantly.

Still, alternative-development funds did not reach a majority of the peasants in coca-growing areas. One of the regions that received the most alternative-development funding—at least $10 million between August 1995 and the end of 1997—was the Apurímac River Valley; economic trends in the valley were examined by a *Le Monde* journalist in early 1998.[94] The journalist found that about one-quarter of the farmers in the valley had benefited from the program. Most of the problems were endemic to alternative-development efforts. Although credit and technical assistance were more available than previously, they were still scarce and limited by patronage and red tape. Most roads remained inadequate. Ultimately, most peasants in the valley were poorer in 1998 than in 1994, and most—but not all—were hoping for a revival in the price of coca.[95] Lamented one analyst: "They were promised alternative development and instead, they got alternative poverty."[96]

Peruvians in coastal cities were also affected by air bridge denial. For these Peruvians, the result was negative.[97] Traditionally, drug trafficking and addiction were problems that affected only remote, sparsely populated areas of Peru. However, it was noted above that, as a result of air bridge denial, traffickers established alternative export routes through Peru's coastal cities; also, in the context of the coca glut, they were willing to sell cocaine base at very low prices. Suddenly, cocaine base was cheaply available in Lima and elsewhere. In 1999, *bazuco*, a derivative of coca paste smoked like crack cocaine, could be purchased on the streets of Lima for as little as 10 cents a hit.[98] Ironically, just as the U.S. government was hailing Peru's successes against drug trafficking, almost 70 percent of Peruvians reported that drug trafficking had increased considerably or somewhat in the previous year.[99]

CONCLUSION

From the 1980s through the early 1990s, the U.S. and Peruvian governments agreed on the goal of narcotics control, but for the most part disagreed on the appropriate means to this goal. After fits and starts, however, in early 1995 the U.S. and Fujimori governments forged agreement not only on the goal but also the means: air bridge denial. Supported by U.S. surveillance aircraft staffed by CIA contract employees, Peruvian pilots interdicted scores of drug traffickers' planes and effectively closed the air bridge between Peru and Colombia. The U.S.-Peruvian collaboration for air bridge denial was applauded by U.S. officials and routinely cited as the key reason for U.S. support of the Fujimori government.

Despite U.S. applause for air bridge denial, in many respects the fruits of U.S.-Peruvian collaboration on counternarcotics were less evident than U.S.-Peruvian collaboration on security threats and on free-market reform. First, air bridge denial did not result in an actual decrease of the supply of cocaine in the United

States; rather, production simply shifted to Colombia (a shift that, as critics emphasized, was under way prior to air bridge denial and would probably have continued to at least some degree without the program). Second, as was tragically clear when a U.S. missionary and her daughter were killed in April 2001 as a result of a miscommunication between CIA employees and Peruvian air force pilots, air bridge denial risked the loss of innocent lives. From the Peruvian perspective, the results of air bridge denial appeared particularly negative: For the first time, significant quantities of drugs were exported out of coastal cities, and addiction became a more serious problem in Peru.

Accordingly, the benefits of air bridge denial did not appear to warrant the obvious cost of the program: partnership with Vladimiro Montesinos. U.S. authorities were concerned by the mounting allegations of Montesinos's involvement in drug trafficking and by the possibility that, eventually, another U.S. ally in the drug war would be proven a traitor—but these concerns did not prevail.

In hindsight, it seems likely that air bridge denial was evaluated positively in some U.S. and Peruvian circles in part because of its implications for security. Although in the late 1980s and early 1990s the Peruvian military feared that antidrug programs would fuel the flames of insurgencies in Peru's remote coca-growing areas, in the event air bridge denial (which of course targeted not coca growers but traffickers) appeared advantageous for counterinsurgency purposes. With a larger military presence in the coca-growing areas and with only meager revenues from the drug trade, it was more difficult for guerrilla groups to operate. This assessment was a factor in the Toledo government's call for the resumption of air bridge denial (see this book's Postscript). It also seems possible, especially given Montesinos's emphasis on the importance to the United States of his support for Plan Colombia, that air bridge denial was helpful to U.S. goals in Colombia in ways that are not precisely clear at this time.[100]

In the context of the strong emphasis of the George W. Bush administration on counterterrorism and counternarcotics, and the evident complex relationship between the two in the Andean nations, it seems likely that counternarcotics collaboration between the United States and Peru will be sustained. At the same time, however, it appears probable that the Toledo government will reassert Peru's long-standing concerns about Peruvian coca growers' plight and accordingly seek more carrots—well-financed and carefully designed alternative-development programs—from the U.S. government.

CHAPTER VII

THE BILATERAL AGENDA FROM THE 1980s TO 2000: DEMOCRACY AND HUMAN RIGHTS

Whereas issues of democracy and human rights had not led to confrontation between the United States and the García government, they were the issues that most strained the relationship between the U.S. and the Fujimori government during the 1990s. Twice during the 1990s—first after the Fujimori government's April 1992 autogolpe, and second amid the rigged 2000 elections—the question of democracy was at the top of the bilateral agenda. However, on both occasions the U.S. government ultimately decided to continue to extend its hand to Fujimori.

In our conclusion to this book, examining why the Clinton administration chose not to prioritize democratic standards, we integrate material from our various chapters and consider broad questions about U.S. officials' priorities during the 1990s. It is germane to this chapter, however, that we indicate several important problems of international democracy promotion.

First, whereas clear guidelines about free-market reform have been established by the international financial community and clear guidelines about antinarcotics programs have been set by the United States, standards for democracy and human rights remain vague. Even by 2000, after more than twenty years of formal international promotion of democracy and human rights, definitions are not precise. In the United States, democracy tends to be defined first and foremost as free and fair elections—with much more emphasis on a fair election-day count than on a level electoral playing field.[1] Although the U.S. State Department issues annual reports on human-rights practices, these reports often list violations without rigorous attempts to assess whether the violations reach a threshold where the nation should not be considered democratic and its electoral playing field should not be considered level.

The U.S. failure to establish precise democratic standards reflects in part the low priority that the U.S. government has traditionally placed on democracy promotion. Although democracy promotion has been salient in the rhetoric of recent U.S. administrations, it has not enjoyed strong bureaucratic or financial support within the U.S. government. As discussed in Chapter III, in recent years the U.S. Department of State—the department primarily responsible for democracy promotion—became less influential relative to other agencies. U.S. resources for democracy promotion are meager; in Table I.1, it is evident that democracy is not even one of the rubrics under which U.S. aid is classified. The budget for the Democratic Initiatives and Training office within the U.S. Agency for International Development (U.S. AID), the primary relevant office during this period, budgeted $2 to $3 million annually for Peru in the second half of the 1990s.[2]

To a much greater degree than with respect to any other item on the U.S.-Latin America agenda, the United States chose a multilateral strategy on democracy promotion. This choice was appropriate; there was long-standing fear among many Latin American nations that "democracy promotion" could be a pretext for U.S. intervention against a government that, for whatever assortment of reasons, the U.S. did not like. During the 1990s, the Organization of American States (OAS) was building its capacity to monitor elections rigorously and to promote democracy in general. In particular, in 1991 in Santiago, the OAS passed Resolution 1080; this resolution committed the OAS secretary-general to convene a meeting of the OAS Permanent Council when there is "a sudden or irregular interruption of the democratic political institutional process or of the legitimate exercise of power by a democratically elected government...."

At the same time, of course, if a multilateral strategy is to succeed, the United States and other key nations must be active in the relevant organizations. For the most part, the Clinton administration's level of engagement with the OAS was insufficient for the task of democracy promotion in the hemisphere. In part as a result, thresholds for free and fair elections and for respect for human rights were not clarified by the OAS; also, the language of Resolution 1080 was not modified to respond to the Latin American context at the beginning of the new millennium. Also, a multilateral strategy does not absolve the U.S. government from responsibility for its own statements and decisions about democratic erosion or breakdown, especially if the country in question (such as Peru) is a major recipient of U.S. aid.

The various problems of democracy promotion were deftly exploited by the Fujimori government. To a remarkable degree, both during the 1992 autogolpe and the 2000 rigged elections, the Fujimori government was able to play on U.S. fears that Peru's opposition leaders were incompetent and/or hostile to U.S. interests. In retrospect, whatever these leaders' deficiencies may have been, they paled against the Fujimori government's corruption and authoritarianism.

1980–April 1992: Agreement on Electoral Standards, Tensions on Human Rights

The Reagan and Bush Sr. administrations said that democratization was a primary U.S. goal in Latin America. Given that these U.S. administrations defined democracy almost exclusively as free and fair elections and that by this definition Peru was democratic between 1980 and April 1992, democracy was a point of consensus between the two countries during this period. At the same time, however, the Belaúnde and García governments were facing increasingly serious challenges from the Shining Path and the Movimiento Revolucionario Túpac Amaru (MRTA; see Chapter IV). Amid the guerrilla challenge, the Peruvian military committed serious human-rights violations. These violations prompted concern and criticism in both Peru and the United States. However, neither the Reagan nor the Bush Sr. administration seriously joined the question of how the Peruvian government might develop a counterinsurgency strategy both effective and respectful of democratic norms.

In Peru between 1980 and April 1992, elections were free and fair. Presidential and legislative elections were held concurrently in Peru in 1980, 1985, and 1990, and the results were not seriously questioned by the losing political candidates. Most citizens believed that the electoral process was fair, and that no sector was discouraged from participation by the government.[3] Especially by the end of the 1980s, violence against electoral candidates, poll-watchers, and voters was chilling, but these attacks against the electoral process were perpetrated almost exclusively by the Shining Path guerrillas, not the government.[4]

Peru's achievement of electoral democracy was hailed by the United States. Each U.S. State Department report on human rights during this period began with the statement that Peru enjoyed a "freely elected democratic government."[5] Indeed, despite the conflicts between the U.S and García governments on many points of the bilateral agenda, the U.S. government rejected any attempt at a military coup. During the one short period in late 1989 when it appeared that some sectors of the Peruvian military might be plotting a coup against the García government—which by that time was extremely beleaugered—U.S. ambassador Watson merely confirmed the Bush administration's commitment to democracy, and apparently this confirmation was sufficient to stop the plotting.[6]

Unfortunately, however, the bilateral consensus about democracy meant not that the two countries worked together to enhance democratization, but that they took it for granted. Democratization was not in the "to do" box; rather, it had been "done." Successive U.S. ambassadors spoke very little about democratization; especially by the late 1980s, international narcotics control was their primary articulated emphasis, and was their primary perceived emphasis by Peruvians.[7] Neither the U.S. government nor any multilateral institution allocated significant resources for democratization in Peru or elsewhere. A "democracy program" did not even exist within the U.S. Agency for International Development until the early to mid-1980s.[8]

This lackadaisical attitude was especially unfortunate because, although Peru enjoyed an electoral democracy between 1980 and 1992, its democratic institutions were not working well and political violence was increasing. As the Shining Path and MRTA guerrilla movements expanded, human-rights violations multiplied. Although information about the total number of forced disappearances between 1980 and 1992 is still being collected at the time of this writing, the toll is now estimated at nearly six thousand during these twelve years.[9] This toll was among the highest in the world.[10]

The toll provoked concern in both Peru and the United States. In Peru in the early 1980s, numerous nongovernmental organizations (NGOs) began to focus on the defense of human rights against the violence of both the military and the guerrilla movements; in 1985, they decided to collaborate in an umbrella organization called the National Coordinator of Human Rights or, more simply, the Coordinadora.[11] Funded to a significant degree by international organizations and foundations, these Peru-based human-rights NGOs worked closely with U.S.-based groups such as Amnesty International, Américas Watch, and the Washington Office on Latin America. A key human-rights group recommendation during this period was the prohibition of U.S. military aid to Peru; their pressure was one of the reasons for the small amounts of U.S. military aid to Peru in the 1980s (see Table I.2).

Not surprisingly, these groups' criticisms of human-rights violations in Peru displeased both the Belaúnde and García governments. President Belaúnde even declared that Amnesty International was "a tool for the destruction of Peruvian democracy" and immediately relegated one of its letters of complaint to the garbage can.[12] At the start of his administration, García was committed to the respect for human rights, but this commitment dissipated as the resolution of the guerrilla challenge proved extremely difficult.

For its part, during the 1980s the U.S. Department of State acknowledged the reports of human-rights organizations and the tragic number of political killings, disappearances, and abuses in Peru.[13] In its annual reports, the Department of State invariably described the year's most salient violations—for example, the massacre of eight journalists in the Andean community Uchuraccay in 1983, the summary execution of more than two hundred terrorist suspects after prison riots in 1986, and the killing of about thirty peasants in the Andean community Cayara in 1988. At the same time, however, the U.S. Department of State emphasized that these human-rights violations occurred in response to violence instigated by the guerrilla movements and were not condoned by the Peruvian government. Also, the U.S. government rarely commented on human-rights violations in Peru outside the annual State Department report.[14]

Neither the Reagan nor the Bush Sr. administration appeared to join seriously the question of how Peru's human-rights performance could be enhanced. For example, Peru's judiciary was pivotal to human-rights performance; for a variety of reasons, however, the rate of convictions of persons charged with terrorism was very low, and this problem was a factor in the military's resort to forced disappearances. Still, despite recommendations by the U.S. Congress and U.S. human-rights groups—beginning by at least 1985—that the U.S. government support Administration of Justice programs in Peru, Peru's judiciary began to receive U.S. support only in 1989, and the total budget for the three-year program was a mere $3.4 million.[15] Perhaps even more important than U.S. resources would have been U.S. encouragement of dialogue about the counterinsurgency strategies for a democratic Latin American nation. Such a dialogue might have been particularly valuable in the late 1980s when President García tried but failed to launch judicial reforms.[16]

The tone of the U.S. Department of State became more critical in 1988 and subsequent years. Information provided by the Coordinadora and other human-rights groups was increasingly fundamental to its annual reports. In the late 1980s, the García government was still claiming an effort to maintain respect for human rights, but this claim was losing credibility. In particular, the García government did not provide the support that was necessary for an investigation of the 1988 deaths in Cayara; ultimately all the witnesses of the massacre were killed and, amid death threats, the government prosecutor fled Peru. For the first time, in its 1989 report the U.S. Department of State placed actual blame on Peru's military for human-rights violations.[17]

Upon the inauguration of President Fujimori, the Peruvian government's human-rights performance did not improve. The government's rhetorical commitment to human rights ended; by 1991, President Fujimori was calling human-rights groups "the legal arms of subversion," "accomplices of terror," and the "front organizations" of terrorists.[18] Fujimori and Montesinos sought to increase—without conditions—the power and prerogatives of Peru's armed forces.

At the same time, however, Peru's human-rights performance was becoming more intensely scrutinized by the U.S. government. As discussed in Chapter VI, in 1990–1991 the Bush administration was trying to secure a $35.9 military aid package for Peru, officially for the purpose of narcotics control; in May 1991 this package was accepted by President Fujimori. It was then submitted to the U.S. Congress; in September 1991, after considerable debate about human rights in Peru, the U.S. Congress released $25 million of the $35 million that the administration had requested but conditioned the delivery of these funds on Peru's compliance with specific human-rights provisions.[19] Among these conditions were the establishment of a central public registry of detained persons and access for the International Committee of the Red Cross (ICRC) and public prosecutors to all detention centers. Eager for the military aid, the Fujimori government quickly met these U.S. conditions, but its overall disdain for human rights continued; indeed, as will be discussed below, a government-authorized death squad was becoming responsible for numerous executions.[20]

BILATERAL CONFLICT AMID THE AUTOGOLPE

On April 5, 1992, President Fujimori, with the strong support of the military, executed the autogolpe. Proclaiming a "Government of National Emergency and Reconstruction," Fujimori suspended parts of Peru's constitution and dissolved its congress. Fujimori said that his goals were to end the corruption in the judiciary and the legislature and thereby achieve successes against Peru's guerrilla challenge and on other fronts as well.

However, the autogolpe appeared to portend indefinite dictatorial rule. On April 5, the government not only took the actions mentioned above but also repressed opposition media and political leaders. Troops occupied the offices of most of Peru's main newspapers, newsmagazines, and television and radio stations. At least twenty-three journalists and twelve political leaders (eleven of whom were members of Alan García's APRA party) were detained.[21] A determined but ultimately unsuccessful attempt was made to capture Alan García; in the security forces' effort to locate him, his secretary was detained and her husband badly beaten when he tried to intervene.[22] The presidents of both houses of congress and several other legislators were placed under house arrest. A deed that was of special concern to the United States was the detention of Gustavo Gorriti, an internationally respected journalist with numerous American friends and colleagues.

The autogolpe surprised and outraged most U.S. officials. The U.S. assistant secretary of state for Latin America, Bernard Aronson, had just arrived in Lima, expecting to offer Fujimori an ambitious new alternative development and counternarcotics program the next day; Aronson canceled the meeting. In the first few days after the autogolpe, Aronson, an articulate former trade unionist affiliated with the Democratic party who had been appointed assistant secretary in part to facilitate collaboration between the Republican executive and the Democratic Congress, lobbied swiftly and effectively for a strong U.S. response.[23] Secretary of State James A. Baker III was actively engaged in the decision-making process as well. It is possible, however, that the autogolpe was neither a surprise nor an outrage to some U.S. officials in the security sectors of the U.S. government.[24]

On April 6, the United States decided to "suspend immediately all new assistance to Peru and to review all of its assistance to that country."[25] The U.S. government froze 1991 aid that had not yet been disbursed—approximately $30 million of economic aid and $15 million of military aid for 1991—and reviewed the $275-million-plus allocated for 1992.[26] A few days later, as a result of the review, some $100 million of economic aid allocated for 1992 was frozen as well as the $39 million of military aid allocated after the intense controversy described above.[27] However, the $120 million allocation for humanitarian aid (almost entirely food aid) and most narcotics-control aid remained.[28] Also, on April 14, the Bush administration withdrew twenty to thirty U.S. Army Special Forces (Green Berets) who had been counternarcotics trainers; Drug Enforcement Agency (DEA) officers remained, however.[29]

Even more important than U.S. aid to Peru was the international financial community's support for its return to the global lending system—what was commonly called Peru's "reinsertion." At the time of the autogolpe, Peru was negotiating with a "Support Group" of industrialized nations for a bridge loan of roughly $1 billion that was necessary for the country's reinsertion (see Chapter V). After April 5, not only the United States but also Spain and Germany suspended their participation in the Support Group; without these countries, negotiations halted.[30] Another indicator of the international financial community's opposition was the April 6 decision of Inter-American Development Bank (IDB) officials not to sign a $221 million financial-sector loan for Peru.[31]

Other international bodies were also critical. The OAS reacted swiftly. On April 6, the OAS secretary-general invoked Resolution 1080, convening an emergency meeting of the OAS Permanent Council; the council condemned the autogolpe and called an ad hoc meeting of Latin America's ministers of foreign affairs for April 13.[32] Venezuela and Panama suspended diplomatic relations with Peru; Argentina recalled its ambassador; and European nations expressed their opposition.

These rapid negative reactions to the autogolpe appeared to dissuade Fujimori from a blatantly repressive course. Within a week, Gorriti and most other political detainees were released and media outlets reopened. Fujimori stated that he would not govern past 1995.[33] Commented Eduardo Ferrero, who was later to serve as Fujimori's foreign minister:

> Faced with the disapproval of key foreign governments and other international lenders, Fujimori had to acknowledge that maintaining his break with democracy would mean the dashing of his country's hopes for economic recovery and national reconstruction. This realization—which set in fairly quickly—was to play a significant motivating role in his dealings with the OAS in the weeks following the autogolpe.[34]

At the same time that the Fujimori government was realizing that the international reaction to the autogolpe had been more adverse than it had expected, the international community was realizing that the autogolpe was more complex than it had anticipated. First, of course, Fujimori was a democratically elected president. Also, it quickly became evident that Peruvians' reaction to the autogolpe was favorable. In public-opinion polls, more than 75 percent of Peruvians approved Fujimori's administration and his actions against the legislature and the judiciary.[35] It was clear, too, that the autogolpe was acceptable to Japan, whose leaders had established considerable rapport with the Latin American president of Japanese descent.

Accordingly, within about a week the intensity of the crisis abated. Neither the United States nor most other Latin American nations favored a trade embargo or other economic sanctions against Peru similar to what had been enacted against the 1991 military coup in Haiti. At the April 13 ad hoc meeting, Latin America's foreign ministers did not impose OAS sanctions. Rather, they issued a resolution deploring the events and authorizing an OAS mission to Peru for the promotion of dialogue between the authorities and the opposition.[36] At the meeting, U.S. secretary of state Baker repeated the U.S. suspension of all new assistance to Peru and said:

> The actions taken by President Fujimori, whatever the justification given, are unjustified. They represent an assault on democracy that cannot and will not be supported by the United States of America. . . . This Organization of American States is founded on one unswerving principle: Representative democracy is the key to peace, it is the key to economic opportunity, and it is the key to legitimacy in this hemisphere.[37]

From mid-April to mid-May, negotiations between key international actors and the Fujimori government were intense.[38] On April 20, President Bush called Fujimori, speaking with him for about thirty-five minutes; Bush was reported to have told Fujimori that the United States was "disappointed with the measures taken by Peru" and urged him to move back to a constitutional government "as soon as possible."[39] However, Bush issued no threats or ultimatums, and said also that he "understood the pressures fragile democracies are under."[40] Assistant Secretary Aronson returned to Peru to speak with Fujimori, and three OAS missions led by Uruguayan foreign minister Héctor Gross Espiel also met with him. In these meetings, Fujimori proposed a July 5 plebiscite on his rule, after which his cabinet would draft constitutional reforms; in this proposal, the schedule for a new national congress was indefinite at best. By contrast, international actors favored scheduling elections that would reestablish a congress, charging the congress rather than Fujimori's cabinet with the drafting of a new constitution.

Meanwhile, the Peruvian opposition tried to make its case. It argued that the 1979 constitution remained in effect; since Fujimori's actions had violated the constitution, first vice president Maximo San Román was Peru's legal president. A declaration of San Román as Peru's president was made by the dissolved congress on April 21. To advance their arguments, Peru's traditional parties and unions successfully organized a large rally in downtown Lima on May 15. However, San Román, who had become Fujimori's vice presidential candidate as a representative of Peru's small and medium-sized businesses, was an international nonentity; probably, unflattering portraits of San Román were painted for U.S. officials by the Fujimori government's allies. There is no indication that the U.S.

or any other government seriously considered San Román as an alternative to Fujimori. The U.S. disinclination to consider the replacement of Fujimori by his vice president contrasts with subsequent U.S. support for this action in somewhat similar crises in Guatemala in 1993 and Ecuador in 2000.[41]

Nor was the United States inclined to look favorably upon what was called a "countercoup." The autogolpe worried a considerable number of Peruvian officers; they feared that Peru might be internationally isolated and that Montesinos would further politicize promotions within the military. It is apparent from declassified U.S. documents that the U.S. government was keenly aware of the problem of Montesinos's politicization of appointments and of the possibility of a countercoup, but that the U.S. was not favoring such an event.[42] When retired General Jaime Salinas Sedó was arrested on November 13 on charges of conspiring to lead a countercoup, the U.S. government was mute.

Surprisingly, the negotiations between the U.S. and Fujimori governments did not appear to be dramatically affected by Peru's April 24 shoot-down of a U.S. drug-surveillance jet (see Chapter VI). The main effect of the shoot-down was to suspend indefinitely U.S. military aid, primarily because the U.S. congressional opposition now included not only Democrats concerned about human-rights violations but also Republicans angry about the shoot-down.

On May 18, at a second ad hoc OAS meeting of Latin America's foreign ministers in the Bahamas, Fujimori yielded to the international community's demand for the election of a congress that would both draft a new constitution and assume conventional legislative functions. In a surprise appearance, Fujimori promised the election within five months. Moreover, on the advice of adviser Hernando de Soto (see Chapter III), Fujimori shrewdly proclaimed himself not a destroyer of democracy but a builder of it; he claimed that prior to April 5 Peru's political system was not true democracy but a "*partidocracia* (party-ocracy)," in which political participation was controlled by elite-dominated political parties.[43] Fujimori's concessions were apparently negotiated primarily among de Soto, Gross Espiel, Aronson, and U.S. deputy secretary of state Lawrence Eagleburger.[44]

The foreign ministers at the Bahamas meeting were relieved. Prior to Fujimori's speech, the possibility of more severe international economic reprisals had continued to loom.[45] After it, however, in their resolution at the end of the meeting, they not only eschewed sanctions against Fujimori but did not criticize his actions.[46] Still, it was decided that—for the first time—the OAS would monitor Peru's election for a constituent assembly (the Congreso Constituyente Democrático, CCD). Eagleburger was the U.S. representative at the meeting, and his official statement was cautious, referring respectfully to Fujimori as Peru's president and praising his economic policies, but emphasizing that the U.S. government would not resume its leadership of the Support Group until Peru had made its return to democracy.[47] He indicated that international monitoring of this return would be close: The "devil is in the details," he said.[48]

Despite the official "wait-and-see" U.S. attitude, most Peruvian analysts believed that, unless the CCD elections were blatantly fraudulent, Peru's reinsertion into the international financial community would proceed. After all, the post of U.S. ambassador was soon to be vacant; soon too, U.S. attention would be upon its own November presidential elections. At the same time, the relationship between Fujimori's economic team and the international financial community was becoming increasingly cordial.[49]

At first, the Peruvian view appeared correct. For the CCD elections, the Fujimori government shifted electoral authorities, procedures, and schedules to its benefit; in part as a result, the election was boycotted by most of Peru's major traditional parties (American Popular Revolutionary Alliance, APRA; Acción Popular; and the larger left parties).[50] None of these developments received significant comment from OAS or U.S. officials; OAS foreign ministers described the elections as an important step in the restoration of democracy in Peru, and the tone of the U.S. State Department human-rights report for 1992 was optimistic about Peru's return to democracy.[51] By the end of 1992, the IDB had disbursed the full U.S. $390 million that it had planned to provide to Peru that year.[52]

In fact, however, "normalization" (the common term) of the bilateral relationship had not been achieved. Amid the various events of 1991–1992, human-rights violations continued; although the number of disappearances declined, the number of extrajudicial executions increased. Opposition activists and human-rights groups charged that a government-sponsored death squad coordinated by Montesinos, which would eventually be called the Grupo Colina (Colina Group), was responsible for these executions.[53] Two cases were notorious: the November 1991 massacre of seventeen people at a chicken barbecue in the Barrios Altos neighborhood in downtown Lima and the July 1992 disappearance of nine students and a professor from La Cantuta University in Lima. As the U.S. Department of State emphasized, the Fujimori government's investigations into these two cases were insufficient.[54] Concerns gradually mounted, too, about the disappearance of at least thirty-five students from the Universidad del Centro in Huancayo during the latter months of 1992. Also, after the autogolpe, Peru's laws for cases of terrorism were transformed; suspects were tried before "faceless" judges or even in military courts, and most legal defense rights were denied.

In January 1993, Clinton was inaugurated, and greater priority was placed on human-rights concerns.[55] Led by Richard Feinberg, the senior director for Western Hemisphere affairs at the National Security Council (who, due to appointment delays, was for several months the only Latin Americanist on Clinton's foreign policy team), the Clinton administration immediately criticized Peru's human-rights performance and conditioned the U.S. role in the Support Group on improvements.[56] In particular, the Clinton administration demanded that ICRC access to military and police detention centers be resumed.[57] The new

U.S. government also supported an investigation of the administration of justice in Peru by the Commission of International Jurists (led by Robert Goldman and accordingly called the Goldman Commission), which issued a highly critical report in March 1993.

Gradually, however, many officials in the Clinton administration came to the view that, if the U.S. government were to achieve its free-market and other substantive objectives in Peru, it was necessary that relations be normalized.[58] Accordingly, after ICRC access to detention centers was resumed and several other human-rights conditions were met by the Fujimori government, in March the Clinton administration approved the Support Group's bridge loan for Peru (see Chapter V). Peru's arrears were cleared with the International Monetary Fund (IMF) and the World Bank, and Peru took its most important step toward its key goal of "reinsertion." Although U.S. military aid to Peru was not resumed, U.S. economic aid for 1993 almost reached its 1991 level (see Table I.1); in 1993, Peru was second after Bolivia as the largest recipient of U.S. aid in Latin America.[59]

During 1993 and 1994, the Clinton administration and the Fujimori government warmed to each other.[60] The Clinton administration was pleased that the Shining Path was decimated without as much loss of civilian life as had often been the case in Latin America (see Chapter IV). In the context of the decimation of the guerrillas as well as the administration's clear pressure, human-rights violations began to decline. The Clinton administration was also delighted that Peru's free-market reform was among the region's most dramatic (see Chapter V). Despite tensions on the issue of narcotics control during this period, collaboration was to improve soon (see Chapter VI). In 1994, Peru was the top recipient of U.S. aid in Latin America and fourth in the world.[61]

In this context of increasing partnership, the Clinton administration looked the other way at the Fujimori government's manipulation of democratic processes. In October 1993, a referendum was held on the new constitution that had been drafted by the CCD; the new constitution was approved only narrowly (52 percent yes to 48 percent no, in the official result). Numerous flaws in the referendum process were identified by critics.[62] As in the 1992 CCD election, the Fujimori government tightly controlled decisions about the scheduling and format of the referendum. Also, in highland areas where the military continued to wield maximum authority under state-of-emergency provisions, it was argued that ballots and tallies were manipulated. Six weeks elapsed between the referendum and the announcement of official result—an unprecedented delay in the post-1980 era—and one member of the Peru's electoral commission denounced the result as fraudulent. However, the referendum was pronounced fair by the OAS's observer group, and the OAS's assessment was followed by the U.S. State Department.[63]

THE 1995 ELECTIONS AND THE FUJIMORI GOVERNMENT'S SECOND TERM

In the context of his government's counterinsurgency and economic successes, Fujimori won the 1995 presidential election handily. The U.S. government was delighted; by the conventional U.S. definition of democracy—free and fair presidential elections—Peru was again squarely back in the democratic camp. Even in the aftermath of the 1995 elections, however, the government's commitment to free and fair elections was questioned. Moreover, serious human-rights violations continued; also, the government's pursuit of a third consecutive term mocked Peru's constitution and led to flagrant violations of the democratic process. While some of these issues prompted public U.S. comment, others did not.

The 1995 presidential election was indeed a landslide for Fujimori. His tally was an impressive 64 percent of the valid votes in a field of fourteen candidates. The runner-up, with 22 percent of the valid votes, was Javier Pérez de Cuéllar, a distinguished former secretary-general of the United Nations but ineffective campaigner. However, Pérez de Cuéllar charged that his campaign had been sabotaged in various ways, including wiretapping of his phones. Despite Pérez de Cuéllar's international stature, his charges had little resonance with the OAS or the Clinton administration. Presumably, it was believed that the sabotage could not have affected the presidential outcome; still, it is surprising that such charges by a former UN secretary-general were not investigated.

Moreover, the 1995 legislative election was seriously flawed.[64] Fujimori's political vehicle, called Cambio 90/Nueva Mayoría at this time, was officially reported to have won 51 percent of the votes and a majority of the seats.[65] This result was at odds with the predictions of public-opinion polls, which had indicated that opposition parties would win a legislative majority and that Cambio 90/Nueva Mayoría would win only 25 to 35 percent of the vote.[66] However, on election night the legislative electoral result was endorsed by international and national observer groups—namely, the OAS Misión de Observación Electoral (Election Observation Mission) and the Peru-based Associación Civil Transparencia (which was barely a year old at the time).[67]

A few days after the announcement of the results for the legislative race, it was apparent that vote counting had gone terribly awry: a whopping 40 percent of the ballots had been declared invalid. This percentage was more than four times the percentage for the presidential election and more than three times the percentage for legislative elections in 1985 and 1990.[68] Indeed, more ballots were declared invalid than were cast for Cambio 90/Nueva Mayoría.

The massive invalid vote was attributed by Peru's electoral officials primarily to problems in voters' casting and voting-table officials' tabulating of the "preferential vote" (the voter's indication of up to two preferred candidates from a political party's list of candidates). Electoral officials said that voters had cast their preferential vote incorrectly; that voting-table officials had calculated these votes incorrectly; and that incorrect voting tally sheets had been rejected by electoral officials' computers. It was indeed the first time that Peru had used computers for electoral tabulation.

These claims were countered by a considerable number of Peru's opposition leaders and electoral analysts.[69] Opposition leaders pointed out that the preferential vote had been in use in Peru since 1985, and that it was unlikely that, suddenly, such an unprecedented percentage of voters and voting table officials would have erred. They hypothesized that the computers were programmed to invalidate certain tallies that favored candidates who were particularly distasteful to the Fujimori government.

Given the importance of this controversy (with a legislative majority, the executive was able to secure almost any law it wanted for the next five years), an appropriate OAS and U.S. action would have been a request for an investigation of the problems in the legislative vote. However, no request was made. Rather, Peruvian officials' explanations were accepted by both the OAS and the U.S. government.[70]

One of the most salient political abuses by the Fujimori government during its second term was its denial of due process to persons charged with terrorism. Despite the decline in the strength of Peru's guerrilla movements, many cases of terrorism continued to be tried in military courts without due process. In January 1996, U.S. citizen and MRTA sympathizer Lori Berenson was convicted of treason in a faceless military tribunal and sentenced to life imprisonment. Dismayed, human-rights groups, U.S. legislators, and the U.S. Department of State urged the Fujimori government to resume open trials in civilian courts, not only for Berenson but for all persons charged with terrorism. These requests were to no avail.

Ultimately, in mid-1999, Peru's failure to meet international standards of due process was repudiated by the Inter-American Court of Human Rights, an arm of the OAS based in Costa Rica that was established to provide plaintiffs in human-rights cases an alternative to their own countries' judicial systems. The Court declared invalid Peru's military trial of four Chileans who had been charged with involvement in the MRTA and convicted of treason. The Court called for a new civilian trial for the four Chileans. In response, the Fujimori government declared that it would withdraw Peru from the jurisdiction of the Court. Fujimori's decision was influenced by the fact that numerous other cases were pending against Peru at the Court.[71] The Court countered that Peru's withdrawal from its jurisdiction was "inadmissible" but had no means by which to enforce this decision.

Arguably, the Fujimori government's pursuit of a law allowing a third consecutive term for Fujimori was the most obvious indicator of its fundamentally authoritarian nature. As Catherine M. Conaghan wrote, the reelection project "became the political equivalent of a cluster bomb, as it spewed out its destructive effects across institutions and Peru's legal system."[72] At no time, however, was

Fujimori's pursuit of a third consecutive term criticized by U.S. officials. When questions about the reelection project were raised off the record, a customary U.S. response was a sigh, accompanied by a comment about the weakness of Peru's opposition. In public, U.S. officials said the question was a matter of internal Peruvian politics (even though at almost the same time U.S. officials were saying to Haiti's Aristide that they would not countenance his running for a *second* consecutive term).[73]

The reelection project began in August 1996 when Fujimori's congressional majority passed a law permitting Fujimori to run for a third consecutive term, a law that was called the "Law of Authentic Interpretation of the Constitution." According to this law, the provision in the 1993 constitution that limited a president to two consecutive terms could not be applied retroactively; in other words, because Fujimori had been elected in 1990 under the auspices of the 1979 constitution, his first term did not count.

The "Law of Authentic Interpretation" was considered absurd by most constitutional experts. They pointed out that Fujimori had been Peru's president between 1993 and 1995 under the new constitution, and derided the government's mathematics: 1 plus 1 plus 1 equals 2. As previously mentioned, in 1992 Fujimori had promised not to run even in 1995, and the vast majority of Peruvians had assumed that his 1995–2000 term would be his last.

To enable the "Law of Authentic Interpretation" to prevail, the Fujimori government ran roughshod over a spectrum of political institutions. Amid a controversy over the law, in 1997 the government effectively neutralized the Constitutional Tribunal, a judicial entity of seven judges that reviewed the constitutionality of laws. First, at a press conference in January 1997, three of the seven judges ruled that the law was "inapplicable" to President Fujimori. The precise legal implication of this ruling by a minority of the judges was not clear; six of the seven judges' votes were necessary for a ruling that a law was unconstitutional.[74] However, the government was angry at the judges' attempt to obstruct the reelection project; in May 1997, a congressional committee accused the three judges of inappropriate conduct and voted to remove the three judges from office. Of course, with only four judges remaining on the Constitutional Tribunal, it was impossible to secure the six votes necessary for a ruling of unconstitutionality, and the tribunal could not exercise its primary function.

The Fujimori government also obstructed Peruvians' right to a referendum. Aware that public-opinion polls consistently showed that at least two-thirds of Peruvians opposed a third consecutive term, opposition leaders vigorously sought a referendum on the issue. Spearheaded by the Foro Democrático (Democratic Forum), opposition leaders began to collect the 1.2 million signatures that were necessary for the referendum to be held. However, the Peruvian congress responded with a law conditioning the referendum not only on the 1.2 million signatures but also on the votes of 48 of the 120 members of congress. For a period, this new congressional condition for a referendum was rejected by the Jurado Nacional de Elecciones (JNE, National Elections Board), but a series of new congressional laws changed the composition and procedures of the JNE; the JNE reversed its previous ruling. As a result, when the Foro Democrático presented 1.4 million signatures for the referendum to government officials in July 1998, its referendum initiative was submitted to the congress. In August, the referendum initiative fell three votes short of the necessary forty-eight votes. Various legislators who had been expected to support the referendum were absent on the day of the vote; it was suspected (and subsequently confirmed) that the absences were due to co-optation, intimidation, or both.[75] No official declaration about the death of the referendum was issued by the U.S. Department of State; its demise was mentioned critically, but very briefly, in its report on human-rights practices for 1998.

The government was also responsible for major human-rights violations during 1996–1997.[76] To most analysts, it was obvious by this time that the mastermind of the abuses was Montesinos, operating through the Servicio de Inteligencia Nacional (SIN) and the Servicio de Inteligencia de Ejército (SIE, Army Intelligence Service). It was obvious also that Montesinos had spearheaded the Grupo Colina, the death squad that included both SIN and SIE members and was responsible for the massacres at Barrios Altos and La Cantuta.

First, in November 1996, government officials briefly arrested General Rodolfo Robles (who in 1993, when he had been the third-highest-ranking officer in the army, had sought refuge in the U.S. embassy while his wife distributed a document identifying members of the Grupo Colina death squad). Recently returned to Peru upon Peru's 1995 amnesty law, Robles charged that members of the Grupo Colina were responsible for the recent bombing of a radio station in Puno.

Next, in early 1997, the dismembered body of SIE agent Mariela Barreto was found on the outskirts of Lima. Soon, it became apparent that Barreto was a former member of the Grupo Colina who had probably leaked information about the activities of the death squad and been killed by SIE agents. Then, in April, another SIE agent, Leonor La Rosa Bustamante, was brutally beaten; however, she was able to announce on television that she had been tortured by her former colleagues, also due to their suspicion that she had leaked information.

The revelation of the human-rights violations led the Fujimori government to a much more concerted effort to control Peru's media. The media magnate at the forefront of the critical broadcasting was Baruch Ivcher, an Israeli-born majority stockholder of the Channel 2 television station. Ivcher's station reported not only the attacks against the SIE agents but also systematic wiretapping by the SIN and Montesinos's income (see Chapter III). The Fujimori government retaliated quickly. In July 1997, immigration authorities revoked Ivcher's Peruvian citizenship. Because a Peruvian law was interpreted to deny the right to own a television station to a foreigner, Ivcher's minority partners gained control over the station. Ivcher went into exile; Channel 2's critical investigative reporting ceased.

In part because of intensive lobbying on Ivcher's behalf by the former assistant secretary of state for Latin America, Elliott Abrams, Ivcher's plight provoked sharp criticism in many sectors of Washington. The Fujimori government's abuse of Ivcher was deplored by Ambassador Jett.[77] Also, in a speech to the Institute for International Education in October 1999, Secretary of State Albright reproached the Fujimori government for its mistreatment of Ivcher. There was criticism as well from the U.S. Congress and the U.S. media. In February 1999, when presidents Mahuad and Fujimori visited Washington to celebrate the Ecuador-Peru peace agreement, the *Washington Post* praised the agreement in an editorial, but rebuked the Fujimori government for its abuse of Ivcher.[78]

Criticism of the Fujimori government's political abuses was not restricted to the Ivcher case. This was especially so as threats and attacks against journalists increased in 1998 and 1999.[79] Ambassador Jett spoke out frequently against the government's abuse of freedom of expression in general. The tone of the U.S. Department of State's annual human-rights report became more critical. Also, in 1999 the sharp decline in media freedom in Peru was faulted by the OAS's Inter-American Commission on Human Rights, the Committee for the Protection of Journalists, and Freedom House.[80]

Yet the Fujimori government's increasing authoritarianism was not seriously and consistently challenged by the U.S. government.[81] Even Ambassador Jett, considered a harsh critic of Fujimori, did not state that Peru was not democratic or that a third term for Fujimori was not legitimate—or was even problematic in any way.[82] Most importantly, Jett's criticisms were not echoed by his superiors. Rather, Jett's criticisms were considered counterproductive—failing to produce concessions from the Fujimori government but prompting it to sever some communications and jeopardizing cooperation on other parts of the bilateral agenda.[83]

U.S. officials were restricted by the belief that, if the U.S. were to "get things done" in Peru, it had no choice but to work not only with the Fujimori government in general but with Montesinos in particular. As mentioned in Chapter V, for example, U.S. Department of State official Peter Romero asked for Montesinos's help on behalf of Newmont Mining in a multi-million dollar legal dispute being heard in Peru's Supreme Court in 1998.[84] Elaborated journalist Karen DeYoung:

> Montesinos, it seemed, had his hand in everything. When a commercial deal involving a U.S. company ran into problems, a call to the doctor— sometimes directly from Washington—could resolve it. When the Peruvian air force and army got into a jurisdictional dispute and held up a counter-narcotics operation, or if the budget for air interdiction of drug flights was in danger of being cut, Montesinos could fix it.[85]

Also, as the U.S. government considered its options at this time, its perceptions were shaped by the Fujimori government's concerted attempts to isolate U.S. officials from the Peruvian opposition and to malign opposition leaders. As early as 1992, after U.S. ambassador Anthony Quainton met with Alan García, Quainton was called by an angry Peruvian government official and asked, "How could you meet with a disgraced crook?"[86] In April 2000, Ambassador Hamilton was reproached by Peru's foreign minister merely for meeting with opposition candidate Alejandro Toledo.[87]

The Rigged 2000 Elections and the Demise of the Fujimori Government[88]

As Peru's 2000 elections neared, the Clinton administration was poorly positioned to cope with the difficult challenges it would soon confront. The Clinton administration was in its last eighteen months in office, and was mired in the Monica Lewinsky scandal. As Chapter III indicated, not only was the president's interest in Latin America limited, but so was that of his secretary of state, Madeleine Albright.[89] As Chapter III indicated as well, Acting Assistant Secretary Peter Romero said little publicly about Peru's upcoming elections. Although Romero reported that he argued at inter-agency meetings for the rupture of the U.S. relationship with Montesinos throughout 2000, to date there is no available evidence of this.[90]

Without clear leadership and without a clear definition of U.S. priorities, State Department officials were very cautious about their position on Peru's elections. Requests to the U.S. Department of State for presentations at conferences were accepted, but by different officials and rarely by Romero; no one person seemed to want to be in charge.[91] Statements were terse; they were not only without criticism of the Fujimori government's past political abuses but without reference to them; it was as if this nine-year-old government had a clean democratic record. Also, after Fujimori officially proclaimed his presidential candidacy, the U.S. Department of State issued a brief statement that it was "neutral on whatever government is elected in Peru, but not neutral about the process."[92] At a conference in January 2000, Deputy Assistant Secretary of State for Inter-American Affairs William Brownfield said: "Reasonable minds will differ on the definition of 'free and fair.' Reasonable minds have differed in Peru. We're looking at the process as it's unfolding. We are where we are."[93] Commented the U.S. Department of State report on human-rights practices in Peru in 1999: "Questions remain about the openness and fairness of the electoral process."[94]

In this context, considerable influence devolved to the new U.S. ambassador to Peru, John Hamilton. As indicated above, the U.S. Department of State had been disappointed by the outcome of Jett's ambassadorship, and Hamilton was asked to renew dialogue with Fujimori. He did so—being very careful, for example, in his first interviews with the Peruvian media to blame democratic deficiencies not on the government but on the weakness of Peru's political parties.[95] A strong rapport developed quickly between Hamilton and Fujimori. Trying to forecast the 2000 elections, Hamilton was quickly persuaded that Fujimori was a strong candidate who was likely to win without resort to significant repression or fraud.[96]

Hamilton's role was widely considered very important by Peruvians. In the 2001 survey of elite Peruvians about power in the country, he was judged the foreigner with the greatest power in Peru.[97] Also, in November 1999, discussing U.S. policy toward Peru's 2000 elections with Peru's armed forces commanders, Montesinos said, "Hamilton is good. We're lucky that we have an ambassador with his outlook at this time, because with Jett we would have had many problems. . . ."[98]

However, Hamilton's perspective was not the only U.S. view. Although at this time there is insufficient information to describe definitively the positions held by the variety of U.S. actors, it was reported by one Peruvian insider that, while Hamilton's "pragmatism" was shared by most key players (see Chapter III), pro-democracy positions were advanced by Morton H. Halperin (Director, Policy Planning), Harold Koh (Assistant Secretary of State for Democracy, Human Rights, and Labor), and Luis Lauredo (U.S. Ambassador to the OAS).[99]

Also during 1999–2000 U.S. AID's Democratic Initiatives and Training Office allocated unprecedented sums to election-monitoring initiatives in Peru. Although in mid-1999 some U.S. AID officials were disappointed that funding for these initiatives was only at conventional levels, ultimately money was transferred from the suspended Haiti program and elsewhere to make some $7 million available for Peru.[100] The most important U.S.-based effort was by the Carter Center/National Democratic Institute (NDI), which sent four pre-election delegations and one post-election delegation to Peru, as well as maintaining an office in Lima from January through May. U.S. AID also provided about $1 million for Peru's most prominent domestic observer group, Asociación Civil Transparencia.[101]

Probably in the hope that the low electoral standards of previous OAS electoral missions would continue, the Fujimori government vigorously sought the establishment of an OAS mission for the 2000 elections. Finally, in mid-February 2000, U.S. State Department provided about $560,000 for the OAS Misión de Observación Electoral.[102] The head of the delegation, former Guatemalan foreign minister Eduardo Stein, was a Fujimori acquaintance invited for his role by OAS secretary-general César Gaviria; for these reasons, the mission was at first viewed suspiciously by the Peruvian opposition.[103]

As the various election observation missions began their work, it still appeared possible that Fujimori could win without resort to significant repression or fraud. Despite his government's authoritarianism and Peru's so-so economic performance, Fujimori appeared focused and capable to most citizens. In contrast, the two leading opposition candidates during this period, Alberto Andrade and Luis Castañeda Lossio, could not persuade either Peruvians or international actors of the viability of their candidacies.[104]

Of course, these perceptions of the character and abilities of the candidates were shaped by a broadcast media that was managed by Montesinos. In 2001, "Vladivideos" revealed that the owners of Peru's three largest television networks and numerous prominent journalists had been bribed to assassinate the characters of opposition candidates and applaud President Fujimori. The amount of the bribes was staggering; as of November 1999, Ernesto Schultz, the owner of Peru's most-watched television station, was receiving $1.5 million a month, for a total of some $9 million, from Montesinos.[105] Not surprisingly, the bias of Peru's television coverage was blatant, and it was duly noted by Carter Center/NDI and the U.S. Senate.[106]

The prospects that Fujimori would win without rigging the election diminished on February 29, when a major scandal erupted. Peru's most serious newspaper, *El Comercio,* published a five-page report on the falsification of 1.2 million signatures for the inscription of Perú 2000 (Fujimori's electoral vehicle) as a competing party in the 2000 elections. Although the Fujimori government regularly mocked the spirit of the law, it tried to appear to stay within its letter; now, however, there was proof that it had violated that letter. For U.S. government officials and for election monitors who were not familiar with recent Peruvian politics, the scandal eroded Fujimori's credibility. For Peru's political opposition, the scandal represented a new opportunity for its message to be heard both within Peru and abroad.

This opportunity was seized by Alejandro Toledo of Perú Posible. Born in poverty in highlands Peru, the dark-skinned Toledo boasted an impressive record of achievement; as a teenager, he had secured a fellowship for study in the United States and had eventually earned a Ph.D. from Stanford University. In contrast to the previous front-runners, Toledo was a committed campaigner and effective speaker; his emphasis on job creation resonated among Peruvian voters. Although the government hoped to malign Toledo as it had the previous front-runners, better-educated Peruvians had become aware of the government's tactics, and its attempts at character assassination were less successful. For the first time, there was an opposition candidate who appeared viable—against whom Fujimori might have to resort to serious fraud.

Amid Peru's changed domestic context, the U.S. government became critical of the Fujimori regime. On March 9, U.S. Department of State spokesperson James P. Rubin called for a complete investigation of the signatures scandal and of reports of harassment against opposition candidates and election observers. Resolution 43—calling for "modifications" in U.S.-Peruvian relations if the elections were not free and fair—was passed on March 29 in a joint resolution by the two houses of the U.S. Congress and signed on April 5 by President Clinton.

On April 9, the balloting for the first round of the presidential race went smoothly, but the counting did not. Traditionally, exit polls were within 1 or 2 percentage points of the official tally in presidential elections, and results were clear a few hours after the polls closed. However, on this date, exit polls predicted that the vote for Toledo had surpassed the vote for Fujimori. Then, an hour or two later, Fujimori was placed at 48 percent and Toledo at 42 percent by Transparencia's quick count—a result that mandated a second round but put Fujimori close to the 50 percent plus one vote that he needed for a first-round victory.

That night, Toledo rallied his supporters in Lima, charging fraud. For several days, Peru's electoral authorities issued incomplete results in which Fujimori hovered at about 49 percent of the vote. International actors mobilized vigorously around the demand for a second round; appeals to this effect were made by both Albright and McCaffrey. It appeared that the Fujimori government was divided between "hard-liners" who wanted to end the electoral process at any cost and "soft-liners" who hoped to mollify international actors. Finally, on April 12 the election authorities announced that Fujimori's tally was below 50 percent and that a second round would be held.

After the decision that a second round would be held, political dynamics changed once again. Despite abundant evidence that Peru's electoral playing field was blatantly tilted and that its chief electoral officials were controlled by the Fujimori government, U.S. Department of State officials became less critical. The reasons are not entirely clear. Probably, one important factor was that the controversy after the first round was about a simple, easily verifiable issue (the accuracy of the vote count) rather than a complex one (the skewed playing field).

Also, U.S. officials became more skeptical of Toledo. One comment was: "He's off the reservation"—in other words, he was not behaving as the U.S. deemed appropriate.[107] In both the United States and Peru, there was concern about Toledo's behavior on the night of the first round. As noted above, Toledo had rallied his supporters in Lima and charged fraud. In the course of the demonstration, there was property damage. In the view of the Peruvian opposition, it was necessary that Toledo demonstrate his capacity for protest; Toledo had to show that a third Fujimori government would be unstable. However, in the view of a good number of Peruvians and most U.S. officials, it was Toledo himself who looked unstable. Wearing an Inca-style red headband, Toledo appeared fiery. Unflattering images of Toledo's leadership of the protest—suggesting that he was drunk—were broadcast ad nauseam on Peru's government-controlled noncable television. In part as a result, support for Toledo was not increasing; he and Fujimori remained neck and neck in opinion polls.

There have been no revelations to date about conversations that occurred at this time between U.S. and Peruvian officials about Toledo. Probably, however, Montesinos made comments to U.S. officials that were similar to those he made to Peruvian elites. In these comments, Montesinos emphasized the geopolitical problems facing the U.S. government in the Andean countries, in particular Colombia, and said that opposition leaders did not have the capacity necessary to cope with these problems.[108] For example, in his conversation with a newspaper publisher in April 2000, Montesinos said that the U.S. Secretary of Defense considered Peru a Latin American country with pivotal security implications for the region; Montesinos (in whose words his own identity blends with that of the U.S. Secretary of Defense) claimed,

> We're analyzing the profiles of the people who could succeed Fujimori and we're seeing that . . . first, they don't have experience in the leadership of a state, that they don't have experience in the management of these problems, and, third, we don't know how their relations with the armed forces will be, if they will truly lead the armed forces or if there will be a divorce. If there's a divorce, it won't work. . . . If there's no management or authority or knowledge of the issues of drug trafficking and terrorism, it won't function either. So, it does not suit their purposes under any point of view.[109]

For their part, however, international election observers no longer trusted the Fujimori government's electoral authorities. In April and May, negotiations about the electoral process proceeded among the various actors, but did not go well. Suddenly, in mid-May, Peru's electoral authorities announced that it was introducing a new computer program for the vote count; on May 18, a dismayed Stein announced that his team could not verify the new program in the mere ten days before the May 28 runoff, and asked for a postponement. That afternoon, Toledo announced that he would boycott the runoff unless it were postponed until June 18 and improvements in electoral conditions were achieved. A few hours later, the Fujimori government indicated that the date would not be postponed.

To Stein and most scholars—fully persuaded that the government would not allow a Toledo victory—Toledo was sensibly registering his refusal to legitimate a rigged process.[110] This view was not shared by the U.S. Department of State. On May 20, a U.S. Department of State spokesperson said, "We regret both the unilateral decision of the opposition candidate to withdraw and the hasty ruling by the National Board of Elections. . . ."[111]

The next week, the various parties negotiated intensely. Stein, U.S. officials, and Latin American leaders urged the postponement of the runoff. Finally, however, on May 25 these appeals were rejected by the Fujimori government. The May 28 exercise proceeded as scheduled, but it was not monitored by the OAS or any other group; Toledo called on his supporters to spoil their ballots or abstain. The official result was 51 percent of the vote for Perú 2000, 31 percent null or blank, and 18 percent for Perú Posible (which remained on the ballot).

At the U.S. Department of State, the response to these events was makeshift.[112] The Monday after the May 28 exercise (the Memorial Day holiday in the United States), an unidentified U.S. Department of State spokesperson declared to reporters that "no president emerging from such a flawed process can claim legitimacy" and that "we do not see the election as being valid." These comments apparently enraged Peruvian government officials, who complained directly to their U.S. allies. Tuesday, the comments were called mere "talking points," and the official U.S. characterization of Peru's 2000 electoral process became bland: the process was merely "flawed." Although all election-monitoring groups agreed that Peru's electoral process did not meet international standards for freedom and fairness, none of their members was sufficiently prestigious to gain significant attention in the media. Neither President Carter nor any member of the U.S. Congress was among the election monitors.

In part because the annual OAS General Assembly meeting was imminent, U.S. officials decided that the U.S. response to the failed election would be first and foremost multilateral. However, this response was not carefully prepared.[113] Most obviously, there had not been a prior effort to revise the wording of Resolution 1080 so that a fraudulent election would be one of the catalysts for OAS action. Also, Mexico's PRI and Venezuela's Hugo Chávez were among the governments represented, and it seemed very unlikely that they would support OAS repudiation of Peru's elections. U.S. officials said that they tempered their comments about Peru on May 29 in order not to preempt debate within the OAS; however, if the U.S. government did not reject the legitimacy of a third Fujimori term, Peru's neighbors would be reluctant to do so, given that the government was likely to survive.

In any case, on May 31, Stein delivered his critical report on Peru's elections to an emergency meeting of the Permanent Council of the OAS in Washington. Although U.S. officials sought Resolution 1080 at this meeting, this initiative was apparently only a tactical maneuver to ensure that the question about Peru's elections would be raised at the General Assembly meeting, scheduled for the beginning of June in Windsor, Ontario.[114] At Windsor, after intense negotiations, the General Assembly did not apply Resolution 1080; it resolved only to send a High-Level Mission to Peru, charged with "strengthening democracy" in the country. The OAS mission, however, was only to propose reforms for the future; its mandate did not include a review of the 2000 elections.[115] With limited leverage, the mission yielded few substantive fruits during June through August 2000 (although its role was constructive in numerous respects after the events of September).[116]

From the time of the rigged elections through the Fujimori government's demise, the Clinton administration took no bilateral action against the Peruvian government. No bilateral aid to Peru was suspended.[117] Although in July 2000 about $42 million in counternarcotics aid from Plan Colombia was not added to Peru's allocation, Ambassador Hamilton assured the Fujimori government that it would be.[118] Despite fervent opposition from U.S.- and Peru-based human-rights groups, Ambassador Hamilton attended Fujimori's inauguration on July 28. Although Toledo organized a protest against Fujimori's inauguration, called La Marcha de los Cuatro Suyos, no support for this protest was signaled by U.S. officials. During the protest, violence erupted and six guards at the Banco de la Nación died in a fire; it was ultimately revealed that the Fujimori government was responsible for the fire, but at the time the government largely succeeded in shifting blame to Toledo's militants.[119] Although Toledo called for an investigation, his call was not echoed by U.S. officials.

At this time, the conventional wisdom within the U.S. Department of State was that the Fujimori government would serve out its term.[120] However, U.S. officials were increasingly disturbed about Montesinos's behavior. First, in approximately June and July 2000, as U.S. officials assessed Peru's 2000 elections, they became persuaded that Montesinos had been the mastermind of the electoral "dirty tricks."[121] Second, in August, U.S. Department of State officials were dismayed by the scandal in which Montesinos was alleged to have smuggled arms to the Fuerzas Armadas Revolucionarias de Colombia (FARC; see Chapter IV). On September 8, at a meeting of the United Nations, Berger and Albright met with Fujimori and encouraged him to "restructure" Peru's intelligence service; the High-Level OAS Mission was also urging this "restructuring." U.S. and OAS officials were diplomatic, however; they did not name Montesinos or explicitly call for his removal from power.[122] The U.S. and OAS premise was that Fujimori and Montesinos were separable—not "Siamese twins," as Peru's opposition believed.

On September 14, 2000, the key event triggering the demise of the Fujimori government occurred: the release of a video that showed Montesinos bribing an opposition congressman. Presumably leaked by one or more of Montesinos's colleagues (see Chapter IV), the video showed the security chief handing wads of bills to a congressman and agreeing to a sum of $15,000. Peruvians exploded in disgust and demanded Montesinos's prosecution. In a survey of 110 Peruvians in Lima in July 2001, more than half the respondents identified the video as the key factor in the regime's downfall.[123] (Specifically, 54 percent opted for the video, 16 percent for Peruvian civil society and the political parties in general, 15 percent for Toledo and his La Marcha de los Cuatro Suyos; only 2 respondents for the OAS and one for the U.S. government.[124])

On September 16, two days after the release of the video, Fujimori made a stunning announcement: He would dismantle the SIN and resign in July 2001 after new elections had been held. Apparently, Fujimori hoped that these promises would defuse the crisis and make possible a transition to one of his political allies as the next president. For his part, Montesinos went into hiding; the opposition's calls for his prosecution were intensifying.

On September 24, in a private jet, Montesinos fled to Panama, receiving a tourist visa but hoping to be granted political asylum. After the Panamanian government had rejected Peruvian requests on Montesinos's behalf, high-level U.S.

government officials as well as OAS Secretary General Gaviria had called the Panamanian government, and it had agreed that Montesinos could land.

U.S. support for Montesinos's flight from Peru was one of its most controversial actions during 2000.[125] Ambassador Hamilton's explanation was that Montesinos and his military allies were threatening a military coup and were generally working to destabilize the country. U.S. concern was not groundless; it is clear that Montesinos was making various threats, and that his behavior was becoming increasingly irrational. However, to almost all scholarly analysts and even other U.S. government officials, it seemed very unlikely that Montesinos and his allies would actually stage a military coup. Obviously, a coup attempt would have faced overwhelming opposition, both internationally and domestically, including serious opposition from other sectors of the Peruvian military. In the view of many journalists, the coup threat was merely "a story cooked up by Fujimori and senior officers to solve the problem of what to do with Montesinos and avoid the public trial that the opposition were demanding" (a public trial in which these senior officers were likely to have been incriminated).[126] Further, for some skeptics, U.S. support for Montesinos's flight raised a further question: was there "a deal between Lima and Washington," probably about Montesinos's library of videotapes, which might have included videotapes of U.S. officials (in particular covert CIA agents)?[127]

For several weeks, it appeared that Fujimori would continue to lead Peru's political transition. In late September, Fujimori traveled to Washington for several days; he met with Albright and Berger, and his transition plan was supported.[128] However, contact between Fujimori and Montesinos apparently continued, and Fujimori's commitment to the transition was increasingly doubted by the opposition. Then, on October 23, having failed to secure amnesty in Panama, Montesinos suddenly flew back to Peru, where he immediately went into hiding.

Montesinos's return was a devastating blow to Fujimori. To the opposition, the spy chief's return and Fujimori's subsequent farcical search for him proved that the two were continuing to collaborate—that the Siamese twins had not separated.[129] To the United States and the OAS, which had acted on Montesinos's behalf, it was at a minimum embarrassing. Still, the international community did not appear to question its support for Fujimori's transition plan.[130] Hamilton and Fujimori met frequently at length; Hamilton took long-distance runs with Fujimori's daughter Keiko as she prepared for the New York Marathon.[131]

As the rumors swirled, more and more Peruvians were convinced that Fujimori was complicit in Montesinos's wrongdoing. In an interview to the Mexican weekly *Epoca*, Montesinos said he had evidence of Fujimori's guilt. The pace of defections from Fujimori's electoral coalition Perú 2000 escalated; his vice president, Francisco Tudela—a leader probably more widely respected than any other in Fujimori's circle at this time—resigned. It was clear that the opposition would soon gain control of Peru's congress and that it would then initiate an investigation of Fujimori's finances. Unable to govern as in the past and fearing prosecution, on November 13 Fujimori left Peru for Asia.

CONCLUSION

For most of the Fujimori government's two terms, conflict between the U.S and Peru on the issues of human rights and democracy was considerable; during the 1992 autogolpe and 2000 rigged elections, the U.S. government considered prioritizing democracy over the other components of the bilateral agenda. During both crises, U.S. and OAS pressure achieved certain results. Ultimately, however, President Fujimori prevailed, and democratic standards for the region were lowered—at least in the short run. Most Peruvians were at least somewhat critical of the U.S. role.[132]

At the same time, there were many differences between the two democratic crises. During the 1992 autogolpe, partnership between the U.S. and the Fujimori government was fledgling at best. In their negotiations with the Fujimori government, the Bush and Clinton administrations wielded a very large carrot: U.S. funds for Peru's reinsertion in the international financial community. Wielding this carrot and collaborating with the OAS—where Resolution 1080 was clearly applicable to the autogolpe—the Bush administration was able to push the Fujimori government away from the outright dictatorship that it had apparently planned. Still wielding this carrot, the Clinton administration was also able to achieve some improvements in Peru's human-rights performance in 1993.

Given the security context of the autogolpe—the Shining Path guerrillas were threatening to take power—and also Peruvians' strong support for it, U.S. and OAS achievement on the front of democracy in Peru in 1992 was not insignificant. At the same time, especially as the Fujimori government proved successful on other fronts in the mid-1990s, the United States and the OAS failed to monitor rigorously the government's democracy and human-rights performance. Whereas an autogolpe attempt in Guatemala in 1993 was foiled by the international community and an important democratic precedent set in the region, the autogolpe attempt in Peru not only stood, but was then by and large forgiven and forgotten as the international community hailed the Fujimori government's achievements.

By 2000, the Clinton administration and the Fujimori government had developed a close cooperation on most items of the bilateral agenda. In this context, the Fujimori government was able to press its case with U.S. officials that, if the political opposition achieved power, such cooperation would not be maintained. It appeared that the Fujimori government's effort was particularly successful with the new U.S. ambassador, John Hamilton, who had been explicitly asked by his superiors to reestablish dialogue with Peruvian officials. Hamilton's role in decision making about Peru in 2000 became considerable in part because the U.S. Department of State was largely focused on other issues. In any event, the sticks and carrots available to the U.S. government in 2000 for pressure against the Fujimori government were not as large as they had been in 1992, and Resolution 1080 was not clearly applicable to the problem of Peru's fraudulent election. On the other hand, by 2000 the Shining Path appeared largely defeated and most informed Peruvians considered the Fujimori government corrupt and authoritarian.

Amid considerable controversy, the U.S. government and the OAS decided to extend their handshakes once again to Fujimori. No U.S. aid was suspended, the U.S. ambassador attended Fujimori's inauguration, and the mandate of the OAS mission in Peru did not include the possibility of review of the 2000 elections.

The decision was in considerable contrast to U.S. and OAS policy toward the 2000 Haitian elections. In legislative elections in Haiti in May 2000, the electoral authorities' counting procedure allowed numerous government candidates to win without the runoffs that were constitutionally required. Arguably, this problem in Haiti's legislative elections was of roughly similar dimensions as the issue of 40 percent of the ballots declared null in Peru's 1995 legislative elections, and considerably less pervasive than those in Peru's 2000 presidential election. However, the U.S. government immediately decided to continue suspending most of its aid for Haiti; no U.S. official was present at the inauguration of President Aristide some months later. Also, a call for new elections was within the mandate of the OAS mediation effort for Haiti, and ultimately the Haitian government did indeed offer to rerun the flawed legislative elections.

Still, there were important positive dimensions to the U.S. and OAS roles in Peru in 2000. U.S. AID was a primary supporter of international and domestic election observation efforts in the country. For the first time in the history of OAS electoral observation, a Latin American election was clearly and carefully judged illegitimate. Amid the controversy about the 2000 elections that was raised by the various observation efforts, the U.S. government became considerably warier of Montesinos. Finally, when in September 2000 Peruvian outrage against Montesinos became explosive, it is very likely that the international criticism of the 2000 elections and the certain international repudiation of any military coup attempt shaped Fujimori's decision making.

CONCLUSION

CHAPTER VIII

THE RELATIONSHIP BETWEEN THE UNITED STATES AND FUJIMORI'S Peru was a test of U.S. policy priorities. In particular, during the rigged 2000 elections, analysts in both the United States and Peru asked whether the United States would seek to maintain its partnership with the Fujimori government on security, free-market reform, and narcotics control despite the government's increasingly authoritarian nature.

Within the Clinton administration, there was tension both within and among agencies about the outcome of this test of U.S. policy priorities. At numerous intervals and in numerous ways, various U.S. actors sought to prod the Fujimori government toward democracy. Ultimately, however, the U.S. government chose to prioritize its collaboration with the Fujimori government on the substantive issues of the bilateral agenda over its democracy objective. In June through October 2000, after the rigged election, the United States did not take the step that would have been most appropriate: repudiation of the fraud and a call for new elections. Not only did the U.S. government express little criticism of the 2000 electoral process, but at no time did it suspend any of the large amounts of U.S. aid that were allocated to Peru. The U.S. ambassador to Peru attended Fujimori's inauguration in July 2000 and maintained a close relationship with the president.

The U.S. response to the Fujimori government's rigged 2000 elections was uncommonly bland. At virtually the same time that the Clinton administration was looking the other way in Peru, it suspended most U.S. economic aid to Haiti to protest the Haitian government's counting procedure in its May 2000 legislative elections—a procedure that allowed numerous governing-party candidates to win without the runoffs that were constitutionally required. As of 2001, U.S. aid remained frozen despite President Aristide's offer to hold the runoffs; no U.S. official was present at Aristide's inauguration.[1]

Why did the Clinton administration compromise democratic principles in Peru? The conventional answer is that, just as anti-Communism was more important to the United States during the Cold War, narcotics control was more important during the 1990s. However, this answer begs the question: Why did the U.S. government not place a higher priority on democracy in Peru in 2000?

First, especially in the final months of its term, the Clinton administration was not poised to articulate a vision of the importance of democracy in Latin America. As indicated in Chapter III, President Clinton was for the most part disinterested in Peru; the Latin American issue of primary interest for Clinton and his top advisers was trade and free-market reform. Although Clinton administration officials denied the criticism that their foreign policy was ad hoc and "pragmatic," the critics' argument is sustained by the administration's contrasting policies toward Peru and Haiti.[2] The administration would stand up for democracy if—as in Haiti—it did not thereby seem to jeopardize other objectives and interests, but would bend if—as in Peru—it did seem to jeopardize them. The Clinton administration was improvising.

At the same time, however, it is not clear that any U.S. administration would have vigorously upheld democratic standards in Peru. As indicated in Chapter VII, even among career foreign-service officers at the U.S. Department of State, there was little will to confront the Fujimori government about its authoritarian abuses. In many U.S. officials' views, the things that the Fujimori government was doing right trumped the things that it was doing wrong—and this was especially important because no Peruvian government in decades had been doing them right. For these officials, free-market reform was a sine qua non for development; development in turn was a sine qua non for democracy; and, without Fujimori, there was a real threat that Peru would return to a more statist or "heterodox" economic policy. In other words, these U.S. officials could argue that the Fujimori government was in the interest of the consolidation of democracy in Peru over the long term.

Of course, it would have been very difficult for U.S. officials to make this argument if there had been more blood on Fujimori's hands. Although U.S. officials were knowledgeable about the accusations against the La Colina death squad and about serious human-rights violations in the late 1990s and 2000, the number of victims was considerably smaller than in, say, Pinochet's Chile. Also, a considerable number of officials were inclined to blame the human-rights violations exclusively on Montesinos, absolving Fujimori of guilt. Finally, many of the Fujimori government's authoritarian abuses were shrouded in complex legalities (as in the cases of the Constitutional Tribunal and Baruch Ivcher) or difficult to prove (as in the case of reprisals by the tax agency SUNAT).

Although there is accordingly a logical interpretation of U.S. officials' toleration of the Fujimori government's abuses, ultimately U.S. policy toward the Fujimori government indicated a disturbing disregard for democratic principles.

At a minimum, U.S. officials made policy toward Peru with insufficient thought and analysis. To a surprising degree, as had been the case during the Cold War, *stability* became a mantra—without consideration of the implications of an illegitimate election for stability.[3] Again as had been the case during the Cold War, U.S. officials tended to adopt the interpretation of events advanced by Peru's authoritarian leadership and ignore the interpretation advanced by Peru's opposition.

Yet, for some analysts, U.S. disgregard for democratic principles in Peru was a result of more than U.S. failure to do its homework. For some, U.S. disregard for democratic principles in Peru could be understood as a reflection of a U.S. cultural tradition that persisted despite a contrary U.S. rhetoric. In the book *Beneath the United States,* for example, Lars Schoultz argues that, since the 1800s, most U.S. government officials have perceived Latin American culture as inferior and authoritarian; in his argument, U.S. officials do not believe that most Latin American nations are capable of democratic consolidation.[4] In other words, in these officials' views, a country as traditionally wayward as Peru was fortunate to have a "strong leader" like Fujimori.

For other analysts, a U.S. disregard for democratic principles in Peru would be understood as reflection of U.S. evaluation of the costs and benefits of its preferred policies in Peru, at least over the short run. Simply put, U.S. officials were confident that Peru's authoritarian regime, beholden to the U.S. government in numerous respects, would respond positively to U.S. concerns. More generally, U.S. officials may have doubted that the free-market and antidrug policies undertaken by the Fujimori government were likely to benefit Peru's majorities and develop a solid base of support within the country. Accordingly, just as authoritarian leadership was often considered necessary by the U.S. government during the Cold War given the appeal of Communism, it was now considered necessary given the appeal of the reversal of free-market reform and other policies of cooperation with the United States.

In any case, for whatever variety of reasons, the U.S. government failed the test of policy priorities posed by Fujimori's Peru. Fortunately for both the United States and Peru, however, the demise of the Fujimori government was rapid and relatively peaceful. Also fortunately for the United States, the winner of Peru's 2001 elections was Alejandro Toledo, who emphasized the positive dimensions of the U.S. and OAS roles during 2000 and was decidedly eager for a constructive relationship with the George W. Bush administration.

Still, the story of U.S.-Peruvian relations from 1990 through 2000 was a sad one: a story of a missed opportunity. As indicated in Chapter II, the relationship between the U.S. and Peruvian governments had been tense during the Cold War, and by and large Peruvians were not favorably disposed toward the United States.

At the end of the Cold War and during the early 1990s, Peruvians' attitudes about free-market reform and narcotics control were shifting in directions that facilitated much greater cooperation with the U.S. government. At the same time, major security threats in Peru engaged the U.S. government in the country to a surprising degree, and cooperation between the relevant U.S. and Peruvian actors was considerable. As a result, there was an unusual opportunity for the development of community beyond the two nations' governments.

This was not to happen. The Fujimori government's relentless pursuit of power, and many key Peruvian actors' toleration of its abuses, led to the test of policy priorities facing the U.S. government in 2000. During this test, the Clinton administration was a poor judge of its Peruvian partners and did not adhere to the ideals it had frequently proclaimed. Although most Peruvians placed the blame for the continuation of the Fujimori government primarily on themselves, there was also a certain bitterness and suspicion as they considered the gap between U.S. rhetoric and U.S. policy. This legacy can be overcome, and community built—but not without significant new effort.

CHALLENGES FOR PERU AND THE UNITED STATES IN THE CONSTRUCTION OF A NEW BILATERAL RELATIONSHIP

On November 13, 2000, with an unusually large amount of luggage that was surmised to include lucre as well as "Vladivideos," Fujimori left Peru for a meeting of the Asia-Pacific Economic Cooperation (APEC) in Brunei. Four days later, Fujimori flew to Tokyo, where he faxed his resignation to Peru. However, the opposition-controlled congress rejected Fujimori's resignation, declaring Fujimori "morally unfit" to serve and Peru's presidency vacant. Fujimori's first vice president had already resigned and his second soon did as well; accordingly, the head of Peru's congress, Valentín Paniagua, became Peru's next president.

President Paniagua, an experienced constitutional lawyer and long-standing Acción Popular political leader, formed an effective government and presided over impeccable presidential elections. In the first round of the elections in April 2001, Alejandro Toledo's Perú Posible won 37 percent of the valid vote to 26 percent for Alan García's American Popular Revolutionary Alliance (APRA) and 24 percent for Lourdes Flores's Unidad Nacional; four other parties garnered the remaining percentage. In the May runoff, Toledo defeated García 53 percent to 47 percent. On July 28, 2001, Toledo was inaugurated president, with a five-year term.

The return of democracy to Peru opens new opportunities and new challenges for the relationship between Peru and the United States. On the one hand, contradicting U.S. fears about the possible successor to Fujimori, Toledo's desire for friendship and cooperation with the George W. Bush administration has been remarkable. Having completed his undergraduate and graduate studies in the United States on a fellowship, Toledo knows and likes the United States and appreciates its power. Toledo has indicated his commitment to the full bilateral agenda—not only democracy and human rights, but also security and narcotics cooperation and free-market reform. For his part, President Bush extended not only a handshake but also an embrace to Toledo during his March 23, 2002 visit to Peru, the first to the country by a U.S. president.

On the other hand, these are difficult times for both nations. The Toledo government is trying to reconstruct democracy amid pervasive cynicism and prolonged economic recession. The Bush administration's plans for a "Century of the Americas" were ended amid the terrorist attacks of September 11.

DEMOCRATIC INSTITUTION BUILDING

The Toledo government hopes to place Peru at the forefront of the promotion and defense of democracy in the hemisphere. In part toward this end, it was one of the catalysts of the Inter-American Democratic Charter, which was signed by Latin America's foreign ministers at the OAS General Assembly meeting in Lima on September 11, 2001. Whereas previously OAS action was triggered only by a "sudden or irregular interruption" of democracy (such as a military coup), it was now authorized more broadly, in the case of "an unconstitutional alteration of the constitutional regime." Democratic breakdown in a Latin American nation could lead to the exclusion of the nation from the OAS or, in the future, the Free Trade Area of the Americas. Also, on September 17, 2001, Peru's congress ratified the Rome Statute for the International Criminal Court.

The immediate goal of the Toledo government is to rebuild democracy at home. Toward this end, the government sought in particular to hold accountable those who subverted democracy in the past—most obviously, Fujimori and Montesinos. The Toledo government hoped that the George W. Bush administration would help Peru's efforts to prosecute the two leaders, primarily by the declassification of U.S. documents that would prove the leaders' guilt in various crimes. At the same time, declassification of U.S. documents was likely to reveal the identities of U.S. officials who had tolerated the lowering of democratic standards in Peru; declassification accordingly became an important indicator to Peruvians of U.S. willingness to acknowledge its own errors and reaffirm its own commitment to democracy.

Soon after the downfall of Fujimori and Montesinos, it became clear that their government was much more corrupt than even its harshest critics had charged. The network of corruption was the largest that has ever been documented in Peru's history—implicating as many as fifty-eight people and amounting to more than $1.9 billion.[1] To date, Peru has not been able to advance toward the trial of Fujimori, who remains in safe haven in Japan; however, supported by the Federal Bureau of Investigation (FBI), the Peruvian police seized Montesinos from his hideout in Venezuela in June 2001, and he is awaiting trial in a Peruvian jail.

In Japan, Fujimori claimed Japanese citizenship. As we noted in Chapter III, Fujimori's birthplace was questioned during the 1990s; however, the Japanese government reported that Fujimori had been born in Peru but had also been registered at the Japanese consulate in Lima as a citizen of Japan. Because the Japanese are not permitted dual citizenship, Fujimori should have renounced his

Japanese citizenship for his Peruvian citizenship many years ago, but he had not done so. Still, in a controversial decision, the Japanese government recognized Fujimori as a Japanese citizen, requiring only that he complete a bureaucratic procedure for the reactivation of his nationality. The Toledo government argued that Japan's procedure was incorrect and that Fujimori's Japanese citizenship should be declared null—but to date to no avail. With Japanese citizenship, Fujimori enjoys a safe haven in Japan; there is no extradition treaty between Japan and Peru, and the Japanese government has indicated that it would reject Peruvian requests for his extradition.

The accusations against Fujimori were varied. On October 30, 2001, after a six-month investigation, Peru's attorney general accused Fujimori of illicit enrichment and embezzlement in the amount of $371,781,872.[2] Among the attorney general's charges were Fujimori's appropriation of funds from privatization and arms sales and also the use of public revenues for the purchase of one of his houses at an exorbitant price. An accusation that has been especially intensely investigated is Fujimori's siblings' embezzlement of $12.5 million from Japanese citizens' donations for poor Peruvian children, an allegation levied by the president's former wife, Susana Higuchi. As of early 2002, these charges have not been proven; the most compelling evidence against Fujimori is his signature on a secret decree in September 2000 to divert $15 million in defense funds for an illegal payoff to Montesinos so that he would leave Peru for Panama.[3] None of these charges has been resonant in Japan.

Also, the Toledo government is hoping that charges of homicide and forced disappearance against Fujimori will constitute "crimes against humanity" and will lead to an international arrest warrant against the former president, which Japan would find difficult to ignore. Specifically, on August 27, 2001, Peru's congress approved charges against Fujimori as "coauthor" (with Montesinos) of the death-squad killings at Barrios Altos in 1991 and La Cantuta in 1992 as well as of torture and disappearances. To date, however, no documents or other evidence have been introduced to confirm Fujimori's involvement in death-squad activity. The Toledo government is vigorously lobbying the Bush administration for the declassification of U.S. documents, in particular documents that could confirm the former president's involvement. Still, it is not clear that such evidence would persuade the Japanese government to extradite Fujimori or to try him in Japan; only the charge of torture is clearly covered in an international agreement (signed by Japan in June 1999) and subject to judicial action anywhere in the world.

While the possibility that Fujimori would be tried in Peru is uncertain and to date U.S. support for this effort has been limited, Montesinos will be tried in Peru, and U.S. support for this effort was very helpful. After his attempt to secure political asylum in Panama failed, on October 23, 2000, Montesinos flew back to Peru and immediately went into hiding. At this time, Montesinos's house was raided; the contents of his wardrobe—including twelve hundred Christian Dior shirts, 120 French and Italian suits, and numerous gold and diamond-encrusted watches—were displayed on Peruvian television.[4] After an eight-month hunt by Peru's police and the FBI, Montesinos was captured in Caracas, Venezuela, in June 2001. The FBI's pivotal role was to trap one of Montesinos's associates in Miami and persuade him to report Montesinos's hideout. Imprisoned, Montesinos faces charges of gun running, drug trafficking, money laundering, and masterminding the La Colina death squad. As of January 2002, the sum that was frozen in international banks was $265 million, of which about $65 million had been returned to Peru.[5]

A second priority for the Toledo government was the reconstruction of institutions that had been undermined to serve the personal goals of Fujimori and Montesinos. As this book has described, Peru's diplomatic service, its military, and its intelligence service were subverted during 1990–2000; promotions and demotions were made according to the interests of Fujimori and Montesinos. The Toledo government launched a campaign for reinstitutionalization in the three sectors.

For the reinstitutionalization of Peru's diplomatic service, the Toledo government immediately restored the rights of the diplomats who had been illegally and arbitrarily suspended by the Fujimori government in December 1992. With the approval of Law 0978–2001-RE, some 117 officials were reincorporated to duties in Peru's diplomatic service. Also, a commission chaired by Peru's ambassador to the United States, Allan Wagner, was charged with the preparation of a new law of diplomatic service that would reestablish correct internal procedures and institutional norms.

For the reinstitutionalization of Peru's military, numerous steps were taken first under President Paniagua and then under Toledo. At least a dozen high-ranking military officials—including General Hermoza—were imprisoned on charges of corruption. There have been successive purges at the top ranks; the largest was at the end of 2001, when as many as 486 officers, including 20 brigadier generals, were retired.[6] For the most part, the top ranks of Peru's military were so discredited by their association with the Fujimori regime that they could not resist the new governments' purges. Also, in its effort to subordinate Peru's military to democratic authority, the Toledo government appointed a civilian as minister of defense. Currently, the Toledo government is working with the new heads of the armed forces for reform, in particular to secure civilian authority over the military.

A third major reinstitutionalization effort is directed at Peru's intelligence service. Not surprisingly, the Toledo government terminated the Servicio de Inteligencia Nacional (SIN). Of the SIN's twenty-four-hundred-odd members, only thirty were approved for the country's new intelligence service, named the Consejo Nacional de Inteligencia (CNI, National Intelligence Council).[7] The Toledo government sought to keep the CNI to a reasonable size—about 400 employees—and to subordinate it to civilian authority. At the head of the CNI was a civilian, and a supervisory role was authorized for the congressional committee on intelligence.[8] The CNI would be the governing board of a System of National Intelligence (SINA), where not only the heads of intelligence at the various military services but also officials of the ministries of foreign affairs, education, and the economy would be represented.

As of early 2002, the Toledo government and the Bush administration have been sounding similar chords about the importance of democracy in the hemisphere. On March 23, 2002, for the first time in history, a U.S. president visited Peru; the primary reason given by George W. Bush for his visit was to support Peru's democratic transition. Although the declassification of U.S. documents was not a major theme during the U.S. president's visit, Bush did apparently promise Toledo a speedier and more efficient process.[9] To date, numerous declassification requests have been filed, and the U.S. government has released a considerable number of documents to the Peru commission investigating Montesinos as well as to the U.S.-based National Security Archive.[10] However, believing that the most revealing documents remain secret, critics have asked: "Where's the beef?"[11]

To date, the Bush administration's democracy agenda has been somewhat different from Peru's. Unfortunately in our view, given the aftermath of the September 11 terrorist attacks and the fact that many important documents would be recent, providing insights about current U.S. intelligence procedures and possibly current U.S. covert agents, it appears unlikely that the Bush administration will demand that the CIA declassify all its documents on Peru. At this time, the top priority of the Bush administration's democracy agenda has been Latin American action against the Fidel Castro government in Cuba. During his March 23 visit, Bush pressed Toledo to take the lead on a resolution in the OAS criticizing human-rights violations in Cuba; this issue was the topic of some 30 to 40 percent of the two presidents' conversation.[12]

Also, there remains much more concern within the United States than within Peru about the plight of Lori Berenson. Images of a fiery Berenson denouncing poverty in Peru and appealing for social change were broadcast repeatedly on Peruvian television at various intervals between 1995 and 2001; these images persuaded the vast majority of Peruvians of her guilt. In June 2001, Berenson was retried in Peru in a civilian court; she was convicted of aiding the Movimiento Revolucionario Túpac Amaru (MRTA) in a thwarted plot to seize Peru's congress and sentenced to twenty years. The Toledo government has said that it will not give a presidential pardon to Berenson. However, the case is to be reviewed by the OAS's Inter-American Commission on Human Rights, and the Bush administration hopes that, after this review, Peru will "take another look at what might be possible."[13] During the March 23 meeting, Bush expressed concern for Berenson but did not specifically request either a pardon or clemency.

NATIONAL SECURITY AND NARCOTICS CONTROL

As indicated previously, the problems of insurgency and narcotics have become increasingly linked in Peru. Unfortunately, between the late 1990s and 2002, both insurgency and drug production appeared to be expanding again.

The resurgence of guerrilla activity in Peru was tragically signaled by the explosion of a car bomb less than a block away from the U.S. embassy in Lima three days before President Bush's visit, killing nine people. Upon examination of the available evidence, the Toledo government concluded that the Shining Path was responsible for the attack. Today's Shining Path—based in Peru's primary drug-producing area and possibly in contact with Colombia's guerrillas—is likely to prove quite different from the doctrinaire, disciplined Shining Path under Guzmán's leadership of 1980–1992, but it could yet pose a significant security threat. Its resurgence was widely attributed to the erosion in Peru's intelligence capabilities—as the SIN had been charged with the harassment of Peru's domestic opposition and then restructured under Toledo—and also to reversals in Peru's narcotics-control efforts.

There has been scant indication of the kinds of support that the Bush administration might offer the Toledo government as it seeks to counter the renewed insurgency. For President Bush's part, indicating that he would travel to Lima despite the car bomb, he dismissed the insurgents as "two-bit terrorists." However, it seems likely that at least some bilateral attention is being given to the problem, in part in conjunction with the drug problem.

In 2001–2002, the advances toward narcotics control of the 1990s were in jeopardy for various reasons. First, the drug mafia's interest in Peru as a source for coca leaf rebounded. The drug mafia was reacting primarily to Plan Colombia, which hampered drug production and trafficking in Colombia, and perhaps in part also to the suspension of the air bridge denial program in Peru. As indicated in Chapter VI, this suspension followed the tragic April 21, 2001, shoot-down of a U.S. missionaries' plane, killing U.S. missionary Veronica Bowers, thirty-five years old, and her daughter Charity, seven months. In any case, between 1999 and 2002, the price of coca leaf in Peru quadrupled, reaching $5.00 per kilogram, its highest level of the decade.[14]

Second, global prices for licit crops such as coffee were plummeting.[15] Some peasants believed that they had little choice but to return to coca production.

These trends were vigorously condemned by the Toledo government's "drug czar," Ricardo Vega Llona. Vega Llona has spearheaded requests for various kinds of international support against the resurgence of the drug trade. For example, he has requested $1.4 billion for new highways so that the transport of goods from the Upper Huallaga Valley to Lima is not more expensive than transport from New York to Lima.[16] The Bush administration has been somewhat responsive; it has pledged to triple U.S. counternarcotics aid to Peru—from approximately $50 million to $150 million.[17]

Apparently for the dual purposes of counterinsurgency and counternarcotics, the Toledo government is also asking for the resumption of the air bridge denial program. By the time of President Bush's visit to Lima, a U.S. congressional committee had concluded that the primary cause of the tragedy was miscommunication between the U.S. and Peruvian pilots and haphazard implementation of safeguards. Apparently, the U.S. Congress was open to persuasion that it was possible to resume the program with sufficient safeguards. However, negotiations remained ongoing between the Bowers family and the U.S. government over the shoot-down. U.S. officials have suggested that air bridge denial will be resumed after these negotiations are completed.

Free-Market Reform and Economic Cooperation

As indicated in Chapter V, the international financial community feared that, without Fujimori, Peru's free-market economic policies would not be sustained. Indeed, just as in many Latin American nations, unemployment and poverty have worsened in Peru, and the Toledo government has been buffeted by intense protests against free-market policies. In the event, however, to date President Toledo has stayed the economic course.

While former president Alan García made a dramatic comeback at the polls in 2001, his economic policy proposals were much more tempered than in the past. Although Peruvians questioned various dimensions of free-market reform, a considerable majority was enjoying many benefits from globalization (in particular, greatly enhanced global communication) and did not want to risk renewed international economic isolation.

In July 2001, the Toledo government signaled its commitment to free-market economic policies by its appointment of Roberto Dañino, a respected international lawyer, as prime minister and its appointment of Pedro-Pablo Kuczynski, a well-known international businessman and former minister of energy and mines in the second Belaúnde administration, as economics minister. Despite domestic pressures for expenditure in order to fulfill Toledo's campaign promises, Kucyznksi's top priority is that Peru meet IMF fiscal targets.

After a scant 0.1 percent economic growth in 2001 (attributed in part to September 11 and the U.S. recession), Peru's economic team is forecasting 3 to 4 percent growth for 2002.[18] It is not clear, however, that Peru can achieve this growth rate. Growth depends in part on increased mineral exports (primarily as a result of the completion of the first full year of operations of the huge copper and zinc mine at Antamina), but international mineral prices have been low. Growth also depends in part on the development of the Camisea gas fields; as noted in Chapter V, however, the consortium that is to develop these fields includes the Argentina-based Pluspetrol, and this company's operations have been hurt by Argentina's financial collapse. Growth depends further on privatization initiatives and the attraction of new investments; however, domestic opposition to privatization is intense, and some international investors are cautious toward Latin America in general and Peru in particular. Investors fear that considerable corruption remains within the judiciary and that, as a result, some business disputes may be settled unfairly. It appears that privatization initiatives for 2002 may be limited to the electricity sector, with a total value to the Peruvian government of less than $200 million.[19]

Peru's economic growth also depends in part on the reinstatement of the Andean Trade Preferences Act (ATPA). Enacted in 1991 as a reward for Andean countries that cooperated in the war against drugs, ATPA provided duty-free access to the U.S. market for certain products. ATPA was fundamental to the growth of various Peruvian agricultural exports during the 1990s, in particular asparagus. In December 2001, however, ATPA expired. Currently, the Andean countries are lobbying vigorously not only for the reinstatement of ATPA but also for its expansion to include other labor-intensive products, in particular apparel. President Toledo estimated that, if ATPA were expanded to include apparel, land cultivated in cotton in Peru would increase five times, at least 250,000 jobs would be created, and some $300 million would be earned from additional exports.[20]

The Andean governments fervently hoped that President Bush would visit Lima bearing the "gift" of the extension and enlargement of ATPA. However, as of March 23, the bill remained mired in the U.S. Congress. It was confronting strong protectionist sentiments, in particular from Republican congressmen representing states with important textile industries. President Bush promised the Andean presidents that the bill would be passed by May 16, but its prospects remain uncertain. In the context of other protectionist policies under the Bush administration as well as various negative effects from the Argentine financial collapse, the possibility of a backlash against free-market reform in Peru and elsewhere in Latin America is increasing.

A FINAL WORD

When President Bush visited Peru, he emphasized that his trip was in support of Peru's return to the democratic path. We hope that President Bush's emphasis will be sustained, and supported by the various actions indicated in this postscript. Unfortunately, as this book has shown, historically it has mattered little to Washington whether or not Peru's government was democratic. We believe that it is fundamental that, on the new bilateral agenda, the values of democracy and respect for human rights be reasserted and prioritized. The revelation of the Fujimori government's crimes is a forceful reminder to the hemisphere that "Power corrupts, and absolute power corrupts absolutely"; also, the Fujimori government's sudden demise is a forceful reminder that, in Latin America today, an authoritarian government cannot be a stable, effective government.

CHAPTER I

1. During 1987–1989, Peru's voting coincidence with the United States in the United Nations was 15 percent or below; see the U.S. Department of State, *Voting Practices in the United Nations,* 1986–1989 (Washington, D.C., annual editions). A low rate of coincidence for the entire 1980s is suggested in Miguel Marín-Bosch, *Votes in the UN General Assembly* (Cambridge, MA: Kluwer Law International, 1998), 212. (Unfortunately, only Peru's voting coincidence with Mexico is provided in this volume; Peruvian coincidence with Mexico was very high, as was most South American nations' coincidence.)

2. U.S. Department of State, *Voting Practices in the United Nations,* 1986–1989 and 1995–1998 (Washington, D.C., annual editions). Information for recent years is available at the U.S. Department of State Web site.

3. Figures from International Trade Administration, U.S. Department of Commerce.

4. As of 1997, American earned 90 percent of all operating profits earned by U.S. air companies in the region, according to the *Wall Street Journal* (January 9, 1998), A1 and A12.

5. *Ibid.* It appears, however, that an incident between an American Airlines agent and Fujimori on an American flight in June 1999 soured the president's attitude toward the airline.

6. Real values for the figures in Table I.1 calculated from U.S. Department of Commerce, *Statistical Abstract of the United States* (Washington, D.C.: U.S. Government), Table No. 751.

7. U.S. Agency for International Development, *U.S. Overseas Loans and Grants and Assistance from International Organizations: Obligations and Loan Authorizations* (Washington, D.C., July 1, 1945-September 30, 1998, and annual editions). Following Peru as major recipients were Bolivia and Haiti.

8. Beginning in approximately 1997, the U.S. Department of Defense was responsible for the allocation of military and police assistance to Latin America, via the

"emergency drawdown," provision and "Section 1004" and "Section 1033" of U.S. counterdrug assistance. On these sections and on U.S. assistance to Peru, Colombia, and other Latin American nations through these provisions, see Adam Isacson and Joy Olson, *Just the Facts: A Civilian's Guide to U.S. Defense and Security Assistance to Latin America and the Caribbean* (Washington, D.C.: Latin America Working Group, 1998 and 1999).

9. For example, while the hardcover U.S. AID report cited throughout this chapter specifies a total of $168 million in U.S. aid to Peru for 1998, the figure at the U.S. AID Web site (www.usaid.gov) is $102 million. Asked about this discrepancy, Joseph L. Dorsey, U.S. AID, said in an author's interview on July 20, 2001, that the question is common but that the answer is not clear.

10. U.S. Agency for International Development, *U.S. Overseas Loans and Grants*, and Isacson and Olson, *Just the Facts*.

11. Information on the amount of aid for democracy initiatives from author's interview with Carrie A. Thompson, head of the Office for Democratic Initiatives, U.S. AID, Lima, July 15, 1999.

CHAPTER II

1. Rosemary Thorp and Geoffrey Bertram, *Peru 1890–1977: Growth and Policy in an Open Economy* (New York: Columbia University Press, 1978).

2. Thorp and Bertram, *Peru 1890–1977*, 23.

3. Lawrence A. Clayton, *Peru and the United States: The Condor and the Eagle* (Athens: University of Georgia Press, 1999), 58.

4. Ronald Bruce St John, *The Foreign Policy of Peru* (Boulder, CO: Lynne Rienner, 1992), 9.

5. Clayton, *Peru and the United States*, 75–76.

6. *Ibid.*, 20–32.

7. St John, *The Foreign Policy of Peru*, 112–113; Clayton, *Peru and the United States*, 65–70.

8. St John, *The Foreign Policy of Peru*, 127 and 140; Clayton, *Peru and the United States*, 72.

9. St John, *The Foreign Policy of Peru*, 157.

10. Clayton, *Peru and the United States*, 101.

11. *Ibid.*, 87.

12. James C. Carey, *Peru and the United States, 1900–1962* (Notre Dame, IN: University of Notre Dame Press, 1964), 57.

13. Clayton, *Peru and the United States*, 121.

14. *Ibid.*, 74.

15. *Ibid.*, 95.

16. Carey, *Peru and the United States, 1900–1962*, 72.

17. St John, *The Foreign Policy of Peru*, 159.

18. The Peruvian interpretation was that the U.S. favored Colombia because it was trying to compensate Colombia for previous territorial losses that had enabled the establishment of the Panama Canal.

19. Rosemary Thorp, *Progress, Poverty, and Exclusion: An Economic History of Latin America in the 20th Century* (Washington, D.C.: Inter-American Development Bank, 1998), 349.

20. Rosemary Thorp and Geoffrey Bertram, *Peru 1890–1977: Growth and Policy in an Open Economy* (New York: Columbia University Press, 1978), 338.

21. Clayton, *Peru and the United States,* 178–183.

22. Gonzalo M. Portocarrero, *De Bustamante a Odría: El Fracaso de Frente Democrático Nacional, 1945–1980* (Lima: Mosca Azul, 1983), 91–92 and 138–143.

23. On the points in this paragraph, see Carey, *Peru and the United States, 1900–1962,* 168, and Peter H. Smith, *Talons of the Eagle: Dynamics of U.S.–Latin American Relations,* 2nd edition (New York: Oxford University Press, 2000), 123–127.

24. Clayton, *Peru and the United States,* 179.

25. *Ibid.,* 181.

26. Charles T. Goodsell, *American Corporations and Peruvian Politics* (Cambridge, MA: Harvard University Press, 1974), 40.

27. Stephen G. Rabe, *Eisenhower and Latin America: The Foreign Policy of Anticommunism* (Chapel Hill: University of North Carolina Press, 1988), 39–41.

28. David P. Werlich, *Peru: A Short History* (Carbondale: Southern Illinois University Press, 1978), 248.

29. St John, *The Foreign Policy of Peru,* 189.

30. On U.S. support for Haya de la Torre, see Jane S. Jaquette, *The Politics of Development in Peru,* Latin American Studies Dissertation Program, Cornell University, June 1971, 122.

31. The first statements of the military government even included the date of the new elections; see Jaquette, *The Politics of Development in Peru,* 121.

32. Werlich, *Peru: A Short History,* 274–275.

33. Enrique Chirinos Soto, *Conversaciones con Belaúnde: Testimonio y Confidencias* (Lima: Minerva, 1987), 88, and Adalberto J. Pinelo, *The Multinational Corporation as a Force in Latin American Politics: A Case Study of the International Petroleum Company in Peru* (New York: Praeger, 1973), 112 and 115.

34. Pedro-Pablo Kuczynski, *Peruvian Democracy Under Economic Stress: An Account of the Belaúnde Administration, 1963–1968* (Princeton, NJ: Princeton University Press, 1977), 125. Higher amounts were reported in U.S. Agency for International Development, *U.S. Overseas Loans and Grants: Series of Yearly Data, Vol. II Latin America and the Caribbean* (Washington, D.C., 1986).

35. Kuczynski, *Peruvian Democracy Under Economic Stress,* 125.

36. Data on this point are provided in *ibid.* See also Barbara Stallings, "Peru and the U.S. Banks: The Privatization of Financial Relations," in Richard Fagen, ed., *Capital-*

ism and the State in U.S.-Latin American Relations (Stanford, CA: Stanford University Press, 1979), 217–253.

37. Werlich, *Peru: A Short History,* 294. See also Pinelo, *The Multinational Corporation,* 119.

38. This explanation was favored by Belaúnde himself; see Clayton, *Peru and the United States,* 239.

39. This explanation is offered by Ernest H. Preeg, *The Evolution of a Revolution: Peru and Its Relations with the United States, 1968–1980* (Washington, D.C.: National Policy Association Committee on Changing International Realities, 1981), 7, and by George M. Ingram, *Expropriation of U.S. Property in South America: Nationalization of Oil and Copper Companies in Peru, Bolivia, and Chile* (New York: Praeger, 1974), 93.

40. This point is made in particular by Clayton, *Peru and the United States,* 236–241.

41. Werlich, *Peru: A Short History,* 291–292.

42. Kuczynski, *Peruvian Democracy Under Economic Stress,* 107.

43. For a review of the legal issues in this dispute, see Werlich, *Peru: A Short History,* 289–291.

44. Peter F. Klarén, *Peru: Society and Nationhood in the Andes* (New York: Oxford University Press, 2000), 265.

45. Werlich, *Peru: A Short History,* 295.

46. Pinelo, *The Multinational Corporation,* 115.

47. *Ibid.,* 118.

48. *Ibid.,* 122–123.

49. Kuczynski, *Peruvian Democracy under Economic Stress,* 121–124.

50. George M. Ingram, *Expropriation of U.S. Property in South America: Nationalization of Oil and Copper Companies in Peru, Bolivia, and Chile* (New York: Praeger, 1974), 151.

51. Daniel M. Masterson, *Militarism and Politics in Latin America: Per from Sánchez Cerro to Sendero Luminoso* (New York: Greenwood Press, 1991), 221. Masterson also reported that, prior to the requests from Chile and Peru, the United States had sold attack bombers to Argentina.

52. St. John, *The Foreign Policy of Peru,* 197.

53. Werlich, *Peru: A Short History,* 294.

54. Kuczynski, *Peruvian Democracy Under Economic Stress,* 260–261.

55. An excellent assessment is Jaquette, *The Politics of Development,* 195–197.

56. Jorge I. Domínguez, "US-Latin American Relations During the Cold War and Its Aftermath," in Victor Bulmer-Thomas and James Dunkerley, eds., *The United States and Latin America: The New Agenda* (Cambridge, MA: Harvard University Press, 1999), 42–43.

57. Smith, *Talons of the Eagle,* 157–162.

58. Preeg, *The Evolution of a Revolution*, 13.

59. Richard J. Collings, "Public and Private Dimensions of Dependency: A Peruvian Case Study," paper prepared for delivery at the 1984 Annual Meeting of the American Political Science Association, Washington, D.C., 6–7.

60. Collings, "Public and Private Dimensions," 6–7.

61. Shane Hunt, "Direct Foreign Investment in Peru: New Rules for an Old Game," 302–349 in Abraham F. Lowenthal, ed., *The Peruvian Experiment* (Princeton, NJ: Princeton University Press, 1975).

62. Klarén, *Peru: Society and Nationhood in the Andes*, 346.

63. Preeg, *The Evolution of a Revolution*, 13.

64. The most complete source on the information about the relationship between the Soviet and Peruvian militaries is Rubén Berrios and Cole Blassier, "Peru and the Soviet Union (1969–1989): Distant Partners," *Journal of Latin American Studies* 22 (May 1991).

65. James D. Rudolph, *Peru: The Evolution of a Crisis* (Westport, CT: Praeger, 1992), 58.

66. Masterson, *Militarism and Politics*, 259, and Preeg, *The Evolution of a Revolution*, 15.

67. Masterson, *Militarism and Politics*, 259.

68. In a CIA "Intelligence Information Cable" distributed August 21, 1973, the agency describes the position of key Velasco ministers about the nationalization of Cerro de Pasco Corporation; the cable is MORI DocID 20455 and Cite Tdfir D3–315/37861–73.

69. In 1975, Peru's external debt was \$3.99 billion, representing 29 percent of Peru's GDP, versus an average of 18 percent for Latin America as a whole; in 1978, the debt was 44 percent of GNP, versus an average of 28 percent for the region as a whole. For an excellent discussion, see Stephen M. Gorman and Ronald Bruce St John, "Challenges to Peruvian Foreign Policy," in Stephen M. Gorman, ed., *Post-Revolutionary Peru: The Politics of Transformation* (Boulder, CO: Westview, 1982), 182–183.

70. Collings, "Public and Private Dimensions of Dependency," 12.

71. U.S. Arms Control and Disarmament Agency, *World Military Expenditures and Arms Transfers 1972–1982* (Washington, D.C., 1984). In Peru's defense, overall Chilean military expenditures far surpassed Peru's, and Peruvians believed that they needed more weapons than Chile because, in their view, Chileans were the braver fighters.

72. Gorman and St John, "Challenges to Peruvian Foreign Policy," 188–189.

73. Gorman and St John, "Challenges to Peruvian Foreign Policy," 188.

74. Preeg, *The Evolution of a Revolution*, 19–20.

75. *Ibid.*, 19 and 22.

76. *Ibid.*, 24.

77. Fernando Tuesta Soldevilla, *Perú Politico en cifras 1821–2001* (Lima: Friedrich Ebert Stiftung, 2001). In 1985, the PPC ran in coalition with a small, makeshift party and garnered about 12 percent of the presidential and legislative vote.

78. The importance of this issue was highlighted by U.S. Ambassador to Peru Anthony Quainton in an author's interview, April 21, 1999, in Washington, D.C.

79. Rudolph, *Peru*, 83.

80. John Crabtree, *Peru Under García: An Opportunity Lost* (Pittsburgh: University of Pittsburgh Press, 1992), 29.

81. Crabtree, *Peru Under García*, 28–29.

82. Masterson, *Militarism and Politics*, 270.

83. *Ibid.*, 271.

84. Eduardo Ferrero Costa, "Peruvian Foreign Policy: Current Trends, Constraints, and Opportunities," *Journal of InterAmerican Studies and World Affairs*, 29, no. 2 (summer 1987), 63.

85. U.S. Arms Control and Disarmament Agency, *World Military Expenditures and Arms Transfers 1986* (Washington, D.C.: U.S. Arms Control and Disarmament Agency, 1987), 145.

86. *Ibid.*, 131.

87. *Ibid.*, 106–131.

88. Gustavo Gorriti, *The Shining Path: A History of the Millenarian War in Peru* (Chapel Hill: University of North Carolina Press, 1999), 211–212.

89. In two volumes on Peru's international relations during this period that number about eight hundred pages, less than twenty pages were devoted to the drug issue. See Eduardo Ferrero Costa, ed., *Relaciones del Perú con los Estados Unidos* (Lima: CEPEI, 1987), and Eduardo Ferrero Costa, ed., *Relaciones Internacionales del Perú* (Lima: CEPEI, 1986).

90. Tuesta Soldevilla, *Perú Politico en cifras*, 530–532. APRA enjoyed just over 50 percent of the presidential and legislative tallies, Izquierda Unida about 25 percent, and Acción Popular, the PPC, and the PPC's coalition party just under 20 percent.

91. "President Alan García's Inaugural Address to Congress, July 28, 1985," *The Andean Report* (August 1985), 16.

92. Interview with U.S. ambassador Anthony Quainton, April 21, 1999, in Washington, D.C.

93. Interview with U.S. ambassador Alexander Watson, December 6, 1987, in Lima.

CHAPTER III

1. Among the numerous scholars making this point, see Peter H. Smith, *Talons of the Eagle: Dynamics of U.S.-Latin American Relations*, 2nd edition(New York: Oxford University Press, 2000), 358.

2. Smith, *Talons of the Eagle*, 246; Richard N. Haass, "The Squandered Presidency: Demanding More from the Commander-in-Chief," *Foreign Affairs* 79 (May–June

2000), 140; and Michael Shifter, "United States–Latin American Relations: Shunted to the Slow Track," *Current History* 97, no. 616 (February 1998), 49–54. The point was also made by Arturo Valenzuela, who had served as deputy assistant secretary of state for inter-American affairs during Clinton's first term, speaking at the Woodrow Wilson Center Dinner Club, Washington, D.C., May 9, 1995.

3. Abraham F. Lowenthal, "United States–Latin American Relations at the Century's Turn: Managing the 'Intermestic' Agenda," Pacific Council on International Policy, Los Angeles (September 1998), 5; Joseph S. Tulchin, "The United States and Latin America in the World," in John D. Martz, ed., *United States Policy in Latin America* (Lincoln: University of Nebraska Press, 1995), 345–346; G. Pope Atkins, *Latin America in the International Political System* (Boulder, CO: Westview Press, 1995), 130–131; and Smith, *Talons of the Eagle,* 249.

4. Anne W. Patterson, deputy assistant secretary of state for Central America and the Caribbean, speaking at the Mid-Atlantic Council, Washington, D.C., January 23, 1996, and Mack McLarty, special envoy to Latin America, speaking at the National Press Club, April 9, 1998.

5. Samuel P. Huntington, "The Erosion of American National Interests," *Foreign Affairs* 76, no. 5 (September–October 1997), 37–38.

6. David E. Sanger, "Rounding Out a Clear Clinton Legacy," *New York Times* (May 25, 2000), A1. See also David E. Sanger, "Economic Engine for Foreign Policy," *New York Times* (December 28, 2000), A1 and A12–A13, and Jane Perlez, "With Berger in Catbird Seat, Albright's Star Dims," *New York Times* (December 14, 1999), A12.

7. *Foreign Policy* editors, "Clinton's Foreign Policy," *Foreign Policy* (November–December 2000), 18.

8. See, for example, Luis Peirano and Carlos Reyna, "Estados Unidos y la Triple 'D'" [interview with U.S. ambassador Dennis Jett], *QueHacer* 107 (May–June 1997), 30–38.

9. Sanger, "Economic Engine for Foreign Policy," A1.

10. Anonymous, "Clinton's Foreign Policy," *Foreign Policy* 121 (November–December 2000), 18.

11. William G. Hyland, "A Mediocre Record," *Foreign Policy* 101 (winter 1995–1996), 69.

12. Haass, "The Squandered Presidency," 140.

13. James Risen, "The Clinton Administration's See-No-Evil C.I.A.," *New York Times* (September 10, 2000), 5.

14. Evan Thomas, "A James Bond Wanna-be?" *Newsweek* (May 28, 2001), 34.

15. The information in this paragraph is based on numerous author's interviews, including Arturo Valenzuela, senior director for Western Hemisphere affairs at the National Security Council, 1999–2000, December 20, 2001, in Washington, D.C., and with Theodore J. Piccone, a member of the Office of Policy Planning in the U.S. Department of State, 1998–2000, December 13, 2001, in Washington, D.C.

16. Karen DeYoung and Steve Mufson, "A Leaner and Less Visible NSC," *Washington Post* (February 10, 2001), A1 and A6.

17. Michael Hirsh, "Albright's Old World Ways," *Newsweek* (March 29, 1999), 34, and R. W. Apple Jr., "A Domestic Sort with Global Worries," *New York Times* (August 25, 1999), A10.

18. Apple, "A Domestic Sort with Global Worries," A10.

19. See Apple, "A Domestic Sort with Global Worries," A1 and A10, and John F. Harris, "Berger's Caution Has Shaped Role of U.S. in War," *Washington Post* (May 16, 1999), A1 and A24.

20. David Scott Palmer, "Las Relaciones entre Estados Unidos y Perú Durante los Gobiernos del Presidente Clinton," in Andrés Franco, ed., *Estados Unidos y los países andinos, 1993–1997: poder y desintegración* (Bogotá: CEJA, 1998), 116.

21. Author's telephone conversations with Arturo Valenzuela, 1999–2000, and interview, December 20, 2001, in Washington, D.C.

22. See, for example, Thomas F. McLarty III, "Back to the Future on Trade Among the Americas," *Miami Herald* (February 26, 2001), B7.

23. "Mack McLarty, Friend of Bill," *The Economist* (March 14, 1998), 29–30.

24. See "Remarks of Thomas F. McLarty III," at the Dante B. Fascell North-South Center, Coral Gables, Florida, June 11, 2001, 4.

25. Joshua Cooper Ramo, "The Three Marketeers," *Time* (February 15, 1999), 35–42; David E. Sanger, "The Administration's Fiscal Closer," *New York Times* (May 13, 1999), C1 and C6; Paul Blustein, "Rubin Resigns Treasury Post," *Washington Post* (May 13, 1999), A1 and A18; "Larry Summers's Little Prize," *The Economist* (May 15, 1999), 36.

26. Jacob Weisberg, "Keeping the Boom from Busting," *New York Times Magazine* (July 19, 1998), 25.

27. Karl Taro Greenfeld, "Taking the Handoff," *Time* (May 24, 1999), 56.

28. Weisberg, "Keeping the Boom from Busting," 27; Greenfield, "Taking the Handoff," 56; Michael Hirsh, "Grooming Mr. Summers," *Newsweek* (May 24, 1999), 53.

29. Ambassador Ricardo Luna, "U.S.-Peruvian Relations 1992–1999: Assessment and Prospects for the Future," George Washington University Andean Seminar on Culture and Politics, June 10, 1999.

30. Gustavo Gorriti, "The Betrayal of Peru's Democracy: Montesinos as Fujimori's Svengali," *Covert Action* 49 (summer 1994), 55. Gorriti's observation was confirmed in various off-the-record interviews by the author.

31. Karen DeYoung, "'The Doctor' Divided U.S. Officials," *Washington Post* (September 22, 2000), A22. DeYoung's observation was confirmed in off-the-record interviews by the author.

32. Anthony Faiola, "U.S. Allies in Drug War in Disgrace," *Washington Post* (May 9, 2001), A28. Also, author's interviews with Richard Dawson, Peruvian analyst, and off-the-record interviews.

33. The CIA's emphasis on the Peruvian government's narcotics-control cooperation is clear from numerous accounts, including DeYoung, "'The Doctor.'" On the basis of the facts about Montesinos's record, however (see next section and Chapter

VI), Montesinos's cooperation on this issue would not have appeared sufficient to earn the degree of support from the CIA that he in fact enjoyed.

34. On General McCaffrey's appointment and role, see Coletta Youngers, "'The Only War We've Got': Drug Enforcement in Latin America," *NACLA Report on the Americas* XXXI, no. 2 (September–October 1997), 13–18, and Weston Kosova and Daniel Klaidman, "A Reluctant Campaigner," *Newsweek* (October 21, 1966), 36.

35. Author's off-the-record interviews.

36. Elaine Sciolino, "2 Key Advisers in a Bitter Duel on U.S. Policy," *New York Times* (September 23, 1994), A1 and A19; Steven Erlanger, "Albright Picks 2 Diplomats for Top Posts," *New York Times* (January 23, 1997), A9; Jane Perlez, "With Time Short, Albright Stays Aloft," *New York Times* (July 3, 2000), A7; and Perlez, "With Berger in Catbird Seat," A12.

37. Between 1985 and 1999, the overall international affairs budget at the U.S. Department of State shrank 40 percent in real terms. See Steven Mufson, "State Dept. Faces Further Cutbacks," *Washington Post* (September 30, 1999), A21.

38. As of January 1996, Christopher had visited the Middle East fifteen times, versus a total of about twenty-four working hours in Latin America (one quick trip to Mexico and two quicker trips to Haiti); see George Gedda, "Latin America? Donde Está?" *Foreign Service Journal* (January 1996), 42.

39. Interview with Peruvian ambassador Ricardo Luna, May 19, 1999, in Washington, D.C. For comprehensive information on Albright's speeches and travels, see http://secretary.state.gov. The secretary's most frequent destination was Haiti.

40. Sanger, "Economic Engine for Foreign Policy," A12.

41. In December 2001, Secretary Albright declined a request to be interviewed for this book.

42. Ambassador Alexander Watson, speaking at the Latin Americanist Dinner Club at the Woodrow Wilson Center, October 11, 1996.

43. See for example Al Giordano, "Borderline Behavior," *Boston Phoenix* (December 16–23, 1999), at www.bostonphoenix.com/archive/features/99/12/16.

44. This paragraph is based to a considerable degree on author's telephone interview with Ambassador Peter F. Romero, January 7, 2002.

45. Statement by Ambassador Peter F. Romero, acting assistant secretary for Western Hemisphere affairs, before the Western Hemisphere Subcommittee of the House International Relations Committee, on "Current Issues in the Western Hemisphere Region," September 29, 1999.

46. Heather Draper, "Romero on Newmont Payroll," *Rocky Mountain News*, June 7, 2002.

47. "El Poder en el Perú," *Debate* XXI (July–August 1999), 39.

48. See sources in Chapter VII, footnote 83.

49. Adrian Karatnycky, "Flat-Footed in Peru," *Washington Post* (October 25, 2000), A31.

50. Author's interview with Arturo Valenzuela, December 20, 2001, in Washington, D.C.

51. "El Poder en el Perú," 39.

52. Samuel P. Huntington, "The Lonely Superpower," *Foreign Affairs* 78 (March–April 1999), 40.

53. *Ibid.*

54. Search of *Washington Post* for the dates indicated.

55. John E. Rielly, "Americans and the World: A Survey at Century's End," *Foreign Policy* 114 (spring 1999), 101.

56. Stephen M. Walt, "Two Cheers for Clinton's Foreign Policy," *Foreign Affairs* 79 (March–April 2000), 79. Percentages are not indicated.

57. Rielly, "Americans and the World," 99.

58. See, for example, Luigi Einaudi, "The Peruvian Transition and the Role of the International Community," in Cynthia Arnson, ed., *The Crisis of Democratic Governance in the Andes* (Washington, D.C.: Woodrow Wilson International Center for Scholars, 2001), 128–129.

59. Cecilia Valenzuela, "Dónde Nació? Buscando la Cuna de Fujimori," *Caretas* 1475 (1997), 27.

60. On Fujimori's youth, see Sally Bowen, *The Fujimori File: Peru and Its President 1990–2000* (Lima: Peru Monitor, 2000), 3–10, and Rei Kimura, *The President Who Dared to Dream: President Fujimori of Peru* (Great Britain: Eyelevel Books, 1998), 1–44.

61. Luis Jochamowitz, *Ciudadano Fujimori: la construcción de un político* (Lima: Editorial Peisa, 1993), 185.

62. Kimura, *The President Who Dared to Dream*, 40.

63. Laura Mayoral, "Inversión japonesa en el Perú es una de las más bajas de América Latina," *La República* (May 31, 1999), 13. See also Chapter V.

64. The information in this paragraph is drawn primarily from César Delgado and Wilo Rodríguez, *Los Viajes del Presidente: 1822–1998* (Lima: Servicio de Investigación Parliamentarias, 1998), and Juan Zegarra Salas, "Y dónde está el presidente," *El Comercio* (January 17, 1999), 1.

65. Maria Elena Castillo, "Un país pobre con un presidente turista," *La República* (September 13, 1998), 17–18.

66. Fujimori made arguments similar to those in Keith Hamilton and Richard Langhorne, *The Practice of Diplomacy, Its Evolution, Theory and Administration* (London: Routledge, 1995), cited in Luis Castro Loo, "Globalización y diplomacia: Fin de diplomacia global?" *Política Internacional* 45 (1996), 95–96.

67. Jochamowitz, *Ciudadano Fujimori*, 181–187.

68. Quoted in Bowen, *The Fujimori File*, 219.

69. Anonymous, "Hombres del Presidente," *Caretas* 1145 (1991), 34–37.

70. Bowen, *The Fujimori File*, 37.

71. *Ibid.*, 38.

72. *Resumen Semanal,* XVIII, no. 886 (September 4–10, 1996), 3–5. Various explanations for the resignation are discussed.

73. These annual surveys were published in the July–August issue of *Debate,* a respected magazine published by Apoyo in Lima.

74. The exception is the year 1996, when he was ranked fifth.

75. Bowen, *The Fujimori File,* 44. This was a characterization of Fujimori, but it is applicable to Montesinos as well.

76. On Montesinos's activities during the 1970s, see Gustavo Gorriti, "The Betrayal of Peru's Democracy: Montesinos as Fujimori's Svengali," *Covert Action* 49 (summer 1994), 4–11; Gustavo Gorriti, "Montesinos, la Sombra de Régimen," *Gatopardo* 1 (April 2000), 35–44; Francisco Loayza Galván, *El Rostro Oscuro del Poder* (Lima: Ediciones Referéndum, 1998); Anonymous, "El Doctor Vladimiro Montesinos," *Debate* XX, no. 103 (November–December 1998), 24–32; and Bowen, *The Fujimori File,* 52–55.

77. Francisco Igartúa, "El Secretísimo," *Debate* 103 (1998), 31–32.

78. Gorriti, "The Betrayal," 8.

79. Anonymous, "Armas y firmar," *Caretas* 1599 (1999), 20–23.

80. Gorriti, "The Betrayal," 8–9. See also Anonymous, "El Asesor," *Caretas* 1163 (1991), 19–21.

81. A 1980s relationship is asserted by Clifford Krauss, "Our (and Their) Man in Peru," *New York Times* (October 8, 2000), 3, but not by other scholars or journalists.

82. Bowen, *The Fujimori File,* 58–59. See also anonymous, "La Mala Sombra, Entrevista a Francisco Loayza," *Caretas* 1153 (1991), 25–27.

83. Bowen, *The Fujimori File,* 59.

84. Fernando Rospigliosi, *Montesinos y las fuerzas armadas: Cómo controló durante una década las instituciones militares* (Lima: Institituto de Estudios Peruanos, 2000), 26–30; Enrique Obando, "Fujimori and the Military," in John Crabtree and Jim Thomas, eds., *Fujimori's Peru: The Political Economy* (London: Institute of Latin American Studies, University of London, 1998), 199–200; and Philip Mauceri, "Military Prerogatives with a Civil-Military Alliance: The Case of Peru," paper presented at the Latin American Studies Association Meeting, September 24–26, 1998, 3–5.

85. Gorriti, "The Betrayal," 55. See also Karen DeYoung, "'The Doctor' Divided U.S. Officials," *Washington Post* (September 22, 2000), A1 and A22.

86. Gorriti, "The Betrayal," 55.

87. *Ibid.,* and DeYoung, "'The Doctor,'" A22.

88. Diario Oficial El Peruano, *D.L.* 25635 (Lima: Editora Perú), July 23, 1992, 108274.

89. On the SIN, see Rospigliosi, *Montesinos y las fuerzas armadas,* 190–213, and Coletta Youngers, "Deconstructing Democracy: Peru Under President Alberto Fujimori," Washington Office on Latin America, February 2000, Washington, D.C.

90. The resistance of the military institution to its politicization is elaborated by Obando, "Fujimori and the Military," 200–203.

91. This point is especially well made by Obando, "Fujimori and the Military," 204–208.

92. This point is especially well made by Rospigliosi, *Montesinos y las fuerzas armadas,* 163–164 and 229–239. See also *Resumen Semanal,* XX, no. 982 (August 19–25, 1998), 1–3.

93. Rospigliosi, *Montesinos y las fuerzas armadas,* 163–164, and Mauceri, "Military Prerogatives," 17–18.

94. John T. Fishel, "Fujimori's Peru: The Rise and [Apparent] Fall of a Quasi-Democratic Regime," paper presented at the Latin American Studies Association Meeting, September 6–8, 2001, in Washington, D.C., 24–25.

95. Fishel, "Fujimori's Peru," 27.

96. Anonymous, "Qué tal escándalo," *Caretas* 1459 (1997), 17.

97. Anonymous, "Lo que debe hacer Aljovín," *Caretas* 1599 (1999), 22–24.

98. Bowen, *The Fujimori File,* 31–32. On de Soto's background and his book, see Jeremy Main, "How to Make Poor Countries Rich," *Fortune* (January 16, 1989), 101–106.

99. On Estela and the various phases of tax reform at Peru's SUNAT, see Francisco Durand and Rosemary Thorp, "Reforming the State: A Study of the Peruvian Tax Reform," *Oxford Development Studies* 26, no. 2 (1998), 133–151.

100. Anonymous, "Nos Llamaban Los Wisconsin Boys," *Caretas* 1519 (1998), 36–39.

101. The source for this list is Peruvian newspapers.

102. Compare "Ley Orgánica del Ministerio de Relaciones Exteriores," *El Peruano,* 26112 (Lima: Editora Perú, 1992), 111586, and El Peruano, "Ley Orgánica del Ministerio de Relaciones Exteriores," 113 (Lima: Editora Perú, 1981), 240.

103. "Ley Cesan Personal del Servicio Diplomático," *El Peruano,* 453 (Lima: Editora Perú, 1992), 111588.

104. Anonymous, "Las de Caín," *Caretas* 1244 (1992), 26–28.

105. David Scott Palmer, "Relations Between the United States and Peru: Dynamics, Background, and Projections," *International Politics* 53 (1998), 32.

106. Anonymous, "Entrevista a Ludwig Meier: Los empresarios son los principales promotores de inversión," *Gerencia* 203 (1993), 16.

107. David Scott Palmer, "Las Relaciones entre Estados Unidos y Perú Durante Los Gobiernos del Presidente Clinton," in Andrés Franco, ed., *Estados Unidos y los países andinos, 1993–1997: poder y desintegración* (Bogotá: CEJA, 1998), 123–125.

108. Raúl Vargas, "Torre Tagle, La Tercera Ola, Entrevista al canciller Fernando De Trazegnies," *Caretas* 1557 (1999), 16–18.

109. Eduardo Ferrero Costa, "El proceso para la ejecución plena del Protocolo de Río de Janeiro: Un Testimonio," *Análisis Internacional* 15 (July–December 1998), 7.

110. Anonymous, "El cuento de lobby feroz," *Caretas* 1594 (1999), 14–15.

111. Author's off-the-record interviews.

112. Anonymous, "Error sin fronteras, Entrevista al embajador Felipe Valdivieso," *Caretas* 1296 (1994), 32.

113. Apoyo survey, in Lima, September 1998. Data were courtesy of Alfredo Torres at Apoyo. No precise answer was provided by 23 percent of respondents.

114. Reasons were not asked in the questionnaire. Probably, concerns about the Peru-Ecuador border accords were paramount, although the terms of the settlement were not known at this time. International economic policy, which was rejected by larger majorities, was likely also a factor.

115. Apoyo survey in Lima, March 1999. Data were courtesy of Alfredo Torres at Apoyo.

116. Apoyo survey in Lima, March 1999. Data were courtesy of Alfredo Torres at Apoyo.

117. All data in this paragraph are based on "Imagen de Países," Apoyo survey in Lima, February 1999. Data were courtesy of Alfredo Torres at Apoyo.

CHAPTER IV

1. Among the numerous excellent discussions of the "national security" concept, see Margaret Daly Hayes, *Latin America and the U.S. National Interest: A Basis for U.S. Foreign Policy* (Boulder, CO: Westview, 1984), 7.

2. For the sources for the following paragraphs about the Shining Path, see Cynthia McClintock, *Revolutionary Movements in Latin America* (Washington, D.C.: U.S. Institute of Peace Press, 1998), 63–90.

3. *Ibid.*, 47–48.

4. *Ibid.*, 86–89.

5. *Ibid.*, 117. In 2002 it became apparent that previous estimates had been low.

6. Enrique Obando, quoted in Charles Lane, et al., "Peru into the Cross Fire," *Newsweek* (August 19, 1991), 29, and Gustavo Gorriti, quoted in James Brooke, "Marxist Revolt Grows Strong in the Shantytowns of Peru," *New York Times* (November 11, 1991), A1.

7. This section draws upon interviews between 1981 and 1991 with U.S. officials, including Deputy Chief of Mission John Youle, July 14, 1986; Ambassadors David Jordan, July 30, 1987 (in Washington, D.C.), and Alexander Watson, December 6, 1987, and July 6, 1989; U.S. embassy officials Dan Clare, July 11, 1983; Charles Loveridge, July 7, 1989, and April 7, 1990; Gene Bigler, August 17, 1991; and Steve McFarland, August 20, 1993. See also Lawrence A. Clayton, *Peru and the United States: The Condor and the Eagle* (Athens: University of Georgia Press, 1999), 272.

8. "U.S.-Peru Joint Manuevers," *Lima Times* 636 (August 21, 1987), 1, and author's interview with U.S. ambassador Alexander Watson, December 6, 1987, in Lima. At the conference "Soviet Activities in Latin America," U.S. Department of State, on May 7, 1987, 1984–1986 U.S. ambassador David Jordan said that one of his instruc-

tions had been to break the tie between the Soviet and Peruvian militaries, that he had made some headway, but that ultimately his initiatives did not receive financial support from the U.S. Congress.

9. Gustavo Gorriti, "The Betrayal of Peru's Democracy: Montesinos as Fujimori's Svengali," *Covert Action* 49 (summer 1994), 49.

10. Joel Brinkley, "Administration Seeks to Double Aid for Peru," *New York Times* (January 30, 1985), A4.

11. McClintock, *Revolutionary Movements*, 242.

12. The Aprista congressman Hector Vargas Haya, quoted in *Christian Science Monitor* (May 3, 1990), 3.

13. Gorriti, "The Betrayal," 54; author's interview with Agustín Mantilla, in Lima, June 16, 1997.

14. Author's interviews with knowledgeable U.S. Department of State officials. A later date—early 1991—is given for Aronson's concern in Charles Lane, "'Superman' Meets Shining Path: Story of a CIA Success," *Washington Post* (December 7, 2000), A29.

15. Lane, "'Superman,'" A29. Lane's story is based largely on the account by Colonel Benedicto Jiménez, who headed the GEIN throughout this period. In this account, Benedicto Jiménez asked for support from CIA officials in Lima in March and received it in June. According to Mantilla and knowledgeable U.S. Department of State officials, however, Washington decided to provide the support in March. Both accounts may be accurate.

16. Cynthia McClintock, "The Decimation of Peru's Sendero Luminoso," in Cynthia Arnson, ed., *Comparative Peace Processes in Latin America* (Stanford, CA: Stanford University Press, 1999), 235–241.

17. For an account of the GEIN's two-and-a-half-year pursuit of Guzmán, culminating in his capture, see McClintock, "The Decimation," 230–235.

18. The information about the relationship between the CIA and the GEIN became public in Colonel Benedicto Jiménez, "El contacto era directo con la CIA," *La República* (June 23, 2000), 11, and in Lane, "Superman," A29. However, prior to the publication of these accounts, the author conducted numerous interviews on the issue, most of which were unfortunately stipulated to be off-the-record. The most knowledgeable on-the-record confirmation of the CIA's role was with Agustín Mantilla (interior minister under García), in Lima, June 16, 1997. The author also interviewed Colonel Jiménez on June 30, 2000, in Lima. Among the published accounts that include discussion of the relationship between the CIA, on the one hand, and the SIN and the GEIN on the other, see Christopher Simpson, *National Security Directives of the Reagan and Bush Administrations: The Declassified History of U.S. Political and Military Policy, 1981–1991* (Boulder, CO: Westview Press, 1995), 641; Carlos Reyna, "Cómo fue realmente la captura de Abimael Guzmán," *Debate* 17, no. 82 (1995), 46–50; Clifford P. Krauss, "The U.S. Reaction Is Mixed," *Houston Chronicle* (September 14, 1992), 5;

Sally Bowen, "Political Indicators," *Peru Report* 5, no. 2 (1991), 44; and Jonathan Cavanagh, "Political Interview," *Peru Report* 6, no. 8 (1992), 3.

19. Colonel Jiménez contends that the GEIN's initial contact with the CIA was direct, not indirect via the SIN; see Jiménez, "El contacto," 11, and also author's interview, June 30, 2000. However, this belief was not common among other actors.

20. Author's interview, Fernando Rospigliosi, Lima, July 23, 1996.

21. Lane, "'Superman,'" A29.

22. Jiménez's account was disputed by Vidal, but the available evidence supports Jiménez.

23. Gorriti, "The Betrayal," 56, among the many reports.

24. The CIA's attitude toward information linking Montesinos and the Grupo Colina has become increasingly clear from declassified documents. See the summary statement in "U.S. Knew Early of Montesinos Allegations," *Washington Post* (January 23, 2002), A13. A further discussion is provided in Chapter VII.

25. The number of disappearances in the small highlands city of Huancayo, for example, was estimated at more than one hundred in various interviews by the author in Huancayo during the 1990s. The capacity of human-rights organizations to investigate the reports of disappearances in highlands areas was limited.

26. Of course, this statement cannot be fully documented at this time. Our conclusion is largely based on interviews with several journalists based in Peru who were privy to CIA activities in the country, in particular Sharon Stevenson, July 26, 2001, in Lima.

27. It is not clear who issued these warnings or whether they were made with any sense of urgency. Ultimately, police authorities rather than intelligence services were blamed for the lax security, but there has been no thorough public investigation of the relevant facts. Still, many analysts believe that the SIN had proven ineffective in detecting the movement of the MRTA into Lima, and that, in general, Peru's intelligence capabilities had been weakened amid the conflict between Vidal and Montesinos over credit for the capture of Guzmán. See Yusuke Murakami, *El Espejo del Otro: El Japón ante la crisis de los rehenes en el Perú* (Lima: Instituto de Estudios Peruanos, 1999), 32–77, and the *Latin American Weekly Report* 18 (May 6, 1997), 208.

28. Murakami, *El Espejo*, 113–115; and the video *Endgame*, broadcast on *CNN Perspectives*, August 15, 1999.

29. Larry Johnson, former deputy director of the U.S. State Department's Office of Counter-Terrorism, interviewed on *ABC News Nightline*, April 22, 1997, and Jeremy Bigwood, investigative journalist, in his comments on a draft of this chapter, fall 2001.

30. "El mosquito espía," *Cambio* (Colombian newsweekly; February 14–21, 2000). Available at www.revistacambio.com/20000214/El_Pais_02.asp. The presence of the plane was confirmed by former hostage and vice president Francisco Tudela, September 8, 2000, in Washington, D.C. Both Johnson on *ABC News Nightline*, April 22, 1997, and Admiral Luis Giampetri on *Endgame*, August 15, 1999, report high-technol-

ogy strategies for intelligence collection but say that they are not at liberty to provide the specifics. "CIA Surveillance to Storm the Residence" is cited by M. J. Zuckerman, "Point Man on Terrorism Knows Security Issues," *USA Today* (May 22, 1998), 6A.

31. Marco Zileri Dougall, "Una Cosa es Con Guitarra y Otra Con Información," *Caretas* 1700 (December 13, 2001), 74–82.

32. Communication to the author from Jeremy Bigwood, investigative journalist, March 15, 2001. Bigwood is pursuing documentation of these forces' presence.

33. Rospigliosi, *Montesinos y las fuerzas armadas,* 230–233.

34. *Ibid.,* 234–237.

35. Valuable accounts of this dispute include Luigi R. Einaudi, "The Ecuador-Peru Peace Process," in Chester A. Crocker, Fen Osler Hampson, and Pamela Aall, eds., *Herding Cats: Multiparty Mediation in a Complex World* (Washington, D.C.: U.S. Institute of Peace Press, 1999); Eduardo Ferrero Costa, "El proceso para la ejecución plena del Protocolo de Rio De Janeiro: Un testimonio (1)," *Análisis Internacional* 15 (July–December 1998), 7–56; Gabriel Marcella and Richard Downes, eds., *Security Cooperation in the Western Hemisphere: Resolving the Ecuador-Peru Conflict* (Miami: North-South Center Press, 1999); David Scott Palmer, "Peru-Ecuador Border Conflict: Missed Opportunities, Misplaced Nationalism, and Multilateral Peacekeeping," *Journal of Inter-American Studies and World Affairs* 99, no. 3 (fall 1997), 109–147; David R. Mares, "Deterrence Bargaining in the Ecuador-Peru Enduring Rivalry: Designing Strategies Around Military Weakness," *Security Studies* 6, no. 2 (winter 1996–1997); Eduardo Toche, "El conflicto con Ecuador y la política interna," in Eduardo Toche, Walter Ledesma, and Pierre Foy, eds., *Perú-Ecuador: entre la guerra y la paz* (Lima: DESCO, 1998), 13–50.

36. William P. Avery, "Origins and Consequences of the Border Dispute Between Ecuador and Peru," *Inter-American Economic Affairs* 38, no. 1 (summer 1984), 72.

37. Enrique Obando, "The Impact of the 1995 Conflict on Peru and Peruvian-Ecuadorian Relations," in Gabriel Marcella and Richard Downes, eds., *Security Cooperation in the Western Hemisphere: Resolving the Peru-Ecuador Conflict* (Miami: North-South Center Press, 1999), 97.

38. Obando, "The Impact of the 1995 Conflict," 103.

39. This paragraph is based largely on Obando, "The Impact of the 1995 Conflict," 104–105.

40. Gabriel Marcella and Richard Downes, "Introduction," in *Security Cooperation,* 2.

41. Palmer, "Peru-Ecuador Border Conflict," 118–121, and Toche, Ledesma, and Foy, *Perú-Ecuador,* 180.

42. Marcella and Downes, "Introduction," in *Security Cooperation,* 1. Official acknowledgments of 158 Peruvian deaths and 104 Ecuadorian deaths were reported, but actual figures were estimated to be more than 600 by Rospigliosi, *Montesinos y las fuerzas armadas,* 163.

43. David R. Mares, "Political-Military Coordination in the Conflict Resolution Process: The Challenge for Ecuador," in Marcella and Downes, *Security Cooperation*, 183–184.

44. Personal interview, Luigi Einaudi, Washington, D.C., November 19, 1999.

45. Personal interview, Eduardo Ferrero, Lima, July 19, 1999.

46. Jorge Valdéz, in a presentation at the Inter-American Dialogue, Washington, D.C., November 17, 1999.

47. *Debate* XXI, no. 106 (June-August 1999), 39.

48. Personal interview, Luigi Einaudi, Washington, D.C., November 19, 1999.

49. Colonel Glenn R. Weidner, "Peacekeeping in the Upper Cenepa Valley: A Regional Response to Crisis," in Marcella and Downes, *Security Cooperation*, 45–64.

50. Palmer, "Peru-Ecuador Border Conflict," 123.

51. Einaudi, "The Ecuador-Peru Peace Process," 8.

52. See Chapter III, footnote 93 for sources.

53. Author's interview with Luigi Einaudi in Washington, D.C., on November 19, 1999.

54. "Vladivideo" 1, "Reunión Dr. [Montesinos]—Rusos," July 4, 1998, pp. 11–12; and author's interview with former foreign minister Eduardo Ferrero, in Washington, D.C., on January 22, 2002.

55. Personal interview, Enrique Obando, Washington, D.C., November 18, 1999, and off-the-record interviews.

56. Personal interviews in Iquitos, April 6, 2001.

57. "A Creative Peace for Ecuador and Peru," *Peace Watch* V, no. 3 (April 1999), 6.

58. *Ibid.*

59. The survey was by the Peruvian firm Apoyo in both Peru and Ecuador; see *La República* (October 22, 1999), 5. The percentages for Ecuador were similar. Earlier surveys in the two countries were by different companies but suggested less support; see *Resumen Semanal* XX, no. 992 (October 28-November 3, 1998), 5–6. See also *Latin American Weekly Report* (May 18, 1999), 224.

60. President Alberto Fujimori, "Speech by the President of the Republic of Peru at the Meeting with Members of the Inter-American Defense College," February 3, 1999 (mimeograph).

61. Among the analysts advancing this interpretation was Enrique Obando, in an author's interview in Washington, D.C., November 18, 1999.

62. Larry Rohter, "Andes Battle: Right vs. Left vs. Civilians vs. Troops," *New York Times* (March 26, 1999), A3.

63. Angel Páez and Fabio Castillo, "Una Jugada a varias bandas," *El Espectador* (Colombian publication, May 13, 2001), available at www.elespectador.com/2001/20010513/judicial/nota1.htm. See also "Vladivideo" 1487, a videotape dated April 21, 1999, in which Montesinos is meeting with media magnate Genaro Delgado Parker.

64. Author Vallas was reporting extensively on Plan Colombia for a Peruvian periodical at this time, and this was his impression. It was also the impression of several knowledgeable U.S. journalists with whom McClintock communicated in 2000 and 2001, including in particular Sharon Stevenson, July 26, 2001, in Lima.

65. Audiotape A15, as reported in *La República* (October 18, 2001).

66. Juan O. Tamayo, "CIA's Andean Spying Under Attack: Planes Monitor More Than Drugs," *Miami Herald* (May 20, 2001), A1.

67. Author's interview with Arturo Valenzuela, in Washington, D.C., December 20, 2001.

68. This possibility was widely rumored among Peruvians in September through December 2000 but has rarely been mentioned in U.S. circles. U.S. journalists perceived more respect than fear in the relationship between the U.S. government and Montesinos. One exception is Sebastian Rotella, "Ghosts of Fujimori Stalk Peru," *Los Angeles Times* (November 22, 2000), A1.

69. This possibility is raised by Mirko Lauer, "El Plan Colombia fue mas fuerte que Montesinos," *Observador* (September 25, 2000).

70. Among the various persons interviewed on this issue, the most informed in the author's judgment was U.S. journalist Sharon Stevenson. Based in Peru since the late 1980s, Stevenson was very knowledgeable about the U.S. Embassy in Lima. Author's interview, July 26, 2001, in Lima.

71. Kevin G. Hall, "Jailed Spy Chief of Peru Drags CIA into Defense," *San Jose Mercury News* (August 3, 2001), A4.

72. In an article by William C. Rempel and Sebastian Rotella, "Arms Dealer Implicates Peru Spy Chief in Smuggling Ring," *Los Angeles Times* (November 1, 2000), arms dealer Soghanalian indicates a date only a month or two after the weapons were dropped. July 1999 is the month reported in Angel Páez, "Montesinos ofreció cena a Sarkis por venta de armas," *La República* (November 2, 2000), and his numerous other articles on the topic. "Spring" 2000 is reported by Tim Golden, "C.I.A. Links Cited on Peru Arms Deal That Backfired," *New York Times* (November 6, 2000), A3.

73. Golden, "C.I.A. Links Cited," A3. Golden's report was confirmed in several personal interviews.

74. Such a preliminary account was Páez and Castillo, "Una jugada a varias bandas," www.elespactador.com/2001/20010513/judicial.not1.htm.

75. Author's interview with Angel Páez, in Lima, July 27, 2001. Páez is the author of various articles indicating a CIA role; see, for example, Angel Páez, "La CIA le bajó por trafico de armas," *La República* (October 11, 2000). He is also the source for the Peru section of the special report "U.S. Military Aid to Latin America Implicated in Human Rights Abuses" by the International Consortium of Investigative Journalists, available at www.public-i.org/story_01_071201_text.htm., which makes this argument at length. However, Páez said that his key source had in fact been an official at the U.S. embassy in Lima. A second Peruvian analyst, Felipe de Lucio Pezet, also sug-

gested a CIA role in his article "La CIA y Montesinos," *Gestión* (July 10, 2001), but in an author's interview in Lima on July 31, 2001, he too said that he was in fact far from certain about this role.

CHAPTER V

1. Valuable overviews include John Crabtree, *Peru Under García: An Opportunity Lost* (Pittsburgh: University of Pittsburgh Press, 1992), 25–68 and 121–151, and James D. Rudolph, *Peru: The Evolution of a Crisis* (Westport, CT: Praeger, 1992), 101–150.

2. "President Alan García's Inaugural Address to Congress, July 28, 1985," *The Andean Report* (August 1985), 11.

3. Interview with Russell Graham, Economic Section, U.S. Information Service, August 19, 1987, in Lima.

4. Paul Glewwe and Gilette Hall, "Poverty, Inequality, and Living Standards During Unorthodox Adjustment: The Case of Peru, 1985–1990," *Economic Development and Cultural Change* 42 (July 1994), 715.

5. *Perú económico* 13 (August 1990), 1–6.

6. Cynthia McClintock, *Revolutionary Movements in Latin America: El Salvador's FMLN and Peru's Shining Path* (Washington, D.C.: U.S. Institute of Peace, 1998), 165–166.

7. On these measures and their political context, see Carlos Boloña, "The Viability of Alberto Fujimori's Economic Strategy," in Efraín Gonzales de Olarte, ed., *The Peruvian Economy and Structural Adjustment: Past, Present, and Future* (Miami: North-South Center Press, 1996), 183–264; Sally Bowen, *The Fujimori File: Peru and Its President, 1990–2000* (Lima: Peru Monitor, 2000), 75–83; and *The Andean Report* XVIII, no. 10 (October 1991), 157.

8. The Economist Intelligence Unit, "Country Profile: Peru, 1999–2000" (London, 1999), 22.

9. Bowen, *The Fujimori File*, 83.

10. *Latin American Weekly Report* 91, no. 37 (September 26, 1991), 7.

11. Author's interview with Ambassador Ricardo Luna, Peru's ambassador to the United States, July 23, 1999, in Washington, D.C.

12. Bowen, *The Fujimori File*, 171; *Resumen Semanal* 708 (March 3–9, 1993), 1.

13. *Latin America Weekly Report* 39, no. 19 (May 20, 1993), 223.

14. Sebastian Edwards, "The Andean Community Reforms: How Much Progress? How Far to Go?" in Miguel Rodríguez Mendoza, Patricia Correa, and Barbar Kotschwar, eds., *The Andean Community and the United States: Trade and Investment Relations in the 1990s* (Washington, D.C.: Organization of American States, 1998), 20. The other country was Argentina.

15. http://database.townhall.com/heritage/index/pastScores.cfm.

16. Efraín Gonzales de Olarte, *El Neoliberalismo a la Peruana: Economía Política del Ajuste Estructural, 1990–1997* (Lima: Instituto de Estudios Peruanos, 1998), 44.

17. On the agreement, see the Economist Intelligence Unit, "Country Profile: Peru, 1996–1997," 44–45.

18. Author's interview with Luis Quesada, chargé d'affairs, Peruvian embassy to the United States, July 30, 1999, in Washington, D.C.

19. Carlos Boloña and Javier Illescas, "Trade and Investment Between Peru and the United States," *The Andean Community and the United States*, 209. See also Andean Development Corporation, "Annual Conference: Trade and Investment in the Americas," Washington, D.C., September 2000, 61.

20. "Effort to Rescue Full ATPA Extension," *Latin American Andean Group Report* (December 11, 2001), 4.

21. Richard Webb and Graciela Fernández Baca, *Perú en Números 2000* (Lima: Cuánto, 2000), 1253.

22. *Ibid.*

23. Jaime A. García Díaz, "Evolución del comercio exterior y las inversiones entre el Perú y Estados Unidos de América," *Política Internacional*, no. 53 (Julio-septiembre 1998), 67–68.

24. During most of the 1990s, the U.S. share of imports was higher than the share of exports. Boloña and Illescas, "Trade and Investment," 200–202. For earlier decades, see Rosemary Thorp, *Progress, Poverty, and Exclusion: An Economic History of Latin America in the 20th Century* (Baltimore: Johns Hopkins University Press, 1998), 349.

25. The Economist Intelligence Unit, "Country Report: Peru, April 2000," 5.

26. *Ibid.*, and The Economist Intelligence Unit, "Country Profile: Peru, 1998–99," 33.

27. Rosemary Thorp and Geoffrey Bertram, *Peru 1890–1977: Growth and Policy in an Open Economy* (New York: Columbia University Press, 1978), 40 and 208; Richard Webb and Graciela Fernández Baca, *Perú en Números 1990* (Lima: Cuánto, 1990), 832–833; and Webb and Fernández Baca, *Perú en Números 2000*, 1254.

28. Thorp and Bertram, *Peru 1890–1977*, 40 and 208; Webb and Fernández Baca, *Perú en Números 2000*, 1254.

29. *Ibid.*

30. *Ibid.*

31. Commission for the Promotion of Private Investment (COPRI), "Peru: A Country on the Move," Lima, 1999, 31, and "U.S. Direct Investment Abroad: Country Detail for Selected Items," International Investment Data, Bureau of Economic Analysis, U.S. Government (www.bea.doc.gov/bea/di/lonctyx.htm, May 13, 1999). The spirit of the era of major privatizations is described in Bowen, *The Fujimori File*, 171–175.

32. http://database.townhall.com/heritage/indexoffreedom.cfm.

33. Oscar Ugarteche, "Cleaning Up After Fujimori: Peruvian Panel Probes 'Economic Crimes' Linked to Privatization," *NACLA Report on the Americas* XXXV, no. 4 (January–February 2002), 43.

34. AmCham Peru InfoCenter, "Inversión Americana en el Perú 1999," Lima, 2000.

35. "U.S. Direct Investment Abroad," Bureau of Economic Analysis.

36. AmCham Peru InfoCenter, "Inversión Americana."

37. *Ibid.*

38. The Economist Intelligence Unit, "Country Report: Peru, April 2000," 22, and the Economist Intelligence Unit, "Country Profile: Peru, 2000," 30.

39. Richard Webb and Graciela Fernández Baca, *Perú en Números 2001* (Lima: Cuánto, 2001), 1238–1239.

40. "Inversión American en el Perú 1999," a fact sheet from the AmCham Peru InfoCenter, based on data from CONITE and elaborated by the American Chamber of Commerce in Peru, courtesy of the American Chamber of Commerce in Peru, and Jorge L. Daly and Rebecca Lee Harris, "Private Capital Flows to the Andean Region," in *The Andean Community and the United States,* 52.

41. "Peru: Investment Statistics," International Trade Administration. Available on May 13, 1999 at www.stat-usa.gov/ccg.nsf/.

42. Economic Commission for Latin America and the Caribbean, *Preliminary Overview of the Economies of Latin America and the Caribbean 1998* (Santiago: CEPAL, 1998), 83.

43. Economic Commission for Latin America, *Preliminary Overview 1998,* 85.

44. The Economist Intelligence Unit, "Country Report: Peru, January 2002," 5.

45. Among Peruvian analysts' criticisms of the free-market model as implemented by the Fujimori government, see Humberto Campodónico, "Entre el 2000 y los Límites dela Ortodoxia," *QueHacer* 116 (November 1998-January 1999), 30–33, and Dennis Falvy, "Cómo va la Economia?" *La República* (June 6, 1999), 15.

46. The Economist Intelligence Unit, *Latin America at a Glance: A Comprehensive Guide to the Region's Markets and Operating Environment* (New York: The Economist Intelligence Unit, 2001), 48.

47. The Economist Intelligence Unit, *Latin America,* 48. Figures are from a U.S.-based source, not a Peru source (in contrast to the figures in Table V.1).

48. The Economist Intelligence Unit, "Country Profile: Peru, 2000," 24.

49. Andean Development Corporation, "IV Annual Conference on Trade and Investment in the Americas," Washington, D.C., September 2001, 33.

50. Andean Development Corporation, "IV Annual Conference," 8, and World Bank, *World Development Indicators 2000* (Washington, D.C.: World Bank, 2000).

51. Business Monitor International, *Peru: Quarterly Forecast Report* (July 2001), 22.

52. Webb and Fernández Baca, *Perú en Números 2000,* 1253.

53. *Ibid.*

54. CEPAL, *Balance preliminar de las economías* (Santiago: CEPAL, 1999), 93, and Shane Hunt, "Economic Interview," *The Peru Report and Peru Business Digest* (November 18, 1997), 23.

55. Consultandes, "Key Indicators 01–35," November 25-December 2001, 4. The data source is INEI (National Statistics and Information Institute).

56. Richard Webb and Graciela Fernández Baca, *Perú en Números 1999* (Lima: Cuánto, 1999), 1269.

57. CEPAL, *Balance Preliminar*, 92, and Webb and Fernández Baca, *Perú en Números 1999*, 568.

58. *Latin American Andean Group Report* 3 (April 2001), 5. In 2001–02, it was indicated that the Fujimori government had falsified data on poverty and other economic indicators.

59. Webb and Fernández Baca, *Perú en Números 1999*, 1271.

60. Surveys by IDICE published in *La República*, July 23, 1999, 7, and November 25, 1999, 5.

61. Webb and Fernández Baca, *Perú en Números 1999*, 1271.

62. Juan Aste Daffós, "Mining Lessons for Alejandro Toledo," *Peru Solidarity Forum* 33 (November 2001), 3.

63. *Ibid.*, 10–11.

64. Joaquin Vial, "A Limited Success Story: Foreign Trade in Latin America in the 1990s," paper presented at the Andean Development Corporation, "IV Annual Conference on Trade and Investment in the Americas," Washington, D.C., September 2001, Table A.2.

65. Vial, "A Limited Success Story," Table A.2.

66. Webb and Fernández Baca, *Perú en números 2000*, 1267.

67. Author's interview, John Youle (head of the consulting firm Macroconsult and president of the American Chamber of Commerce in Peru), July 20, 1999, in Lima; and author's interview, Liliana Honorio, foreign trade manager, Lima Chamber of Commerce, July 19, 1999, in Lima.

68. José Bravo, "En 10 años de fujimorismo 22 mil pequeñas empresas quebraron," *La República* (July 31, 2001), 21.

69. The Economist Intelligence Unit, "Country Profile: Peru, 1999–2000," 22.

70. The Economist Intelligence Unit, "Country Report: Peru, October 2001," 20; see also Humberto Campodónico, "Ampay! Gobiernos dictatoriales para administrar la pobreza," *QueHacer* 124 (May–June 2000), 8.

71. "Trend Report," *The Peru Report* (September 17, 1999), 5.

72. Rafael Hidalgo, "Acotaciones al Margen," *Caretas* (August 23, 2001), 24C.

73. http://database.townhall.com/heritage/index/indexoffreedom.cfm.

74. *Ibid.*

75. The Economist Intelligence Unit, "Country Profile: Peru, 1998–1999," 16.

76. Guillermo Perry, "The Andean Community: Where We Are," data presented at the Andean Development Corporation, "IV Annual Conference on Trade and Investment in the Americas," September 2001.

77. The Economist Intelligence Unit, "Country Report: Peru, April 2000," 18.

78. The Economist Intelligence Unit, "Country Report: Peru, 1st Quarter 2000," 28.

79. "Sour Winds Blowing into Foreign Investment Climate," *Peru Monitor Monthly* (formerly *The Peru Report*, February 25, 2000), 7.

80. The Economist Intelligence Unit, "Country Profile: Peru, 2000," 19.

81. Author's interview with John Youle, July 20, 1999, in Lima; Pedro-Pablo Kuczynski, "The Investment Panorama for Peru," *The Peru Report* (July 23, 1999), 8; Humberto Campodónico, "Entre el 2000 y los límites de la ortodoxia," *QueHacer* 116 (November 1998-January 1999), 33; "Political Interview with a Top Behind-the-Scenes Presidential Advisor," *The Peru Report* (September 15, 1998), 9–10; and "Focus Report: Camisea—Behind the Pull-Back," *The Peru Report* (July–August 1998), 27.

82. "Focus Report: Camisea," *The Peru Report* (July–August 1998), 27.

83. The Economist Intelligence Unit, "Peru: 4th Quarter 1998," 24.

84. The Economist Intelligence Unit, "Peru: 2nd Quarter 2000," 18–19, and "Gobierno tiene PBI 'bamba,'" *La República* (November 21, 1999), 3.

85. "Economic Interview with Richard Webb," *The Peru Report* (November 19, 1999), 23. Carlos Boloña was also reported to have criticized the government's data in "Cifras macroeconómicas verdaderas se conocerán después de elecciones," *La República* (October 4, 1999), 3.

86. The increase in social expenditure is reported by Campodónico, "Ampay!," 7.

87. The United States provided about $70 million in food aid to Peru annually during 1995–1999—about double the sum that the U.S. had provided Peru under the García government and more than double the sum it provided any other Latin American nation during this period. In the mid- to late 1990s, U.S. food aid was reaching almost 10 percent of the Peruvian population. See the U.S. Agency for International Development, *U.S. Overseas Loans and Grants and Assistance from International Organizations* (Washington, D.C.: U.S. AID, 1999). For the percentage of Peruvians receiving U.S. food aid, see usaid.gov/pubs/cp2000/lac/peru.html.

88. Among the numerous analyses, see Campodónico, "Ampay!" 8 and "Row Over Critical World Bank report," *Latin American Weekly Report* (October 19, 1999), 485.

89. *Peru Monitor Monthly* (formerly *The Peru Report*), "Trend Report" (April 25, 2000), 8.

90. These criticisms of the tax process were made regularly in Peru during 1998–2000. See, for example, "Trend Report: Is It a Bird? Is It a Plane? No, It's Supertaxman!" *The Peru Report* (March 19, 1998), 1–8.

91. Foremost among these analysts was John Youle; see the report on his presentation at a Washington, D.C., conference in "Peace and Democratization in Peru: Advances, Setbacks, and Reflections on the 2000 Elections," report on a conference sponsored by the George Washington University Andean Seminar and the Washington Office on Latin America (Washington, D.C.: Washington Office on Latin America, 2000), 19–20. See also "Trend Report: Sour Winds Blowing into Foreign Investment Climate," *Peru Monitor Monthly* (February 25, 2000), 5–9. On the lack of professionalism in Peru's judiciary and civil service as of the mid-1990s, see Edwards, "The Andean Community Reforms," 28–29.

92. With respect to U.S. executives, author's interview with George Bomgaarden, Director of Latin American affairs at the German Foreign Ministry (and recent participant in meetings about Peru with the U.S. Chamber of Commerce), June 10, 1999, in Washington, D.C.; and author's letter from Abraham F. Lowenthal, December 22, 1999, reporting that a group of Atlanta-based businessmen were pro-Fujimori. With respect to Peruvian executives, see Francisco Durand, "El 2000 y las Opciones Empresariales," *QueHacer* 119 (July–August 1999), 38–41. Only two of fourteen Peruvian businessmen interviewed by Durand were not planning to vote for Fujimori in 2000.

93. Coletta Youngers, "La percepción estadounidense del caso Fujimori," *QueHacer* 117 (March–April 1999), 19. Youngers's comment is about Treasury Department officials.

94. "Economic and Political Interview with Fred Levy," *The Peru Report* (February 18, 1998), 11–12.

95. Observation by a World Bank official at "Interpreting Peru's 2000 Elections," The George Washington University Seminar on Andean Culture and Politics, June 6, 2000, in Washington, D.C.

96. This informal survey is reported by Katey Downs, "Words from Washington: Island of Calm in the Andes," *Contact Peru*, 5, no. 1 (January–February 2000), 14–15.

97. *Ibid.*

98. *Ibid.*

99. "Economic Interview with Carlos Janada," *The Peru Report* (September 15, 1998), 16–19.

100. Heather Draper and John Accola, "Tape shows corruption in Peru, lawyers say," *Rocky Mountain News* (June 6, 2002).

101. Heather Draper and John Accola, "Newmont denies corruption," *Rocky Mountain News* (June 8, 2002).

102. *Ibid.*

103. Draper and Accola, "Tape shows corruption."

104. "No U-Turn in Fiscal Policy but Swerving to Continue through Elections," *The Peru Report* (December 17, 1999), 7.

105. Downs, "Words from Washington," 14–15 and Francisco Durand, "Las elites del poder y la búsqueda del orden," *QueHacer* 122 (January–February 2000), 85–89.

CHAPTER VI

1. On the points and data in this paragraph, see especially Diego García-Sayan, "Las Relaciones del Perú con los Estados Unidos: Derechos Humanos, Seguridad, y Narcotráfico," in Eduardo Ferrero Costa, ed., *Relaciones del Perú con los Estados Unidos* (Lima: CEPEI, 1987), 133–135, and Richard B. Craig, "Illicit Drug Traffic: Implications for South American Source Countries," *Journal of InterAmerican Studies and World Affairs* 29 (summer 1987), 13.

2. On the points in this paragraph, see especially García-Sayan, "Las Relaciones," 137–138.

3. On UMOPAR, see García-Sayan, "Las Relaciones," 139–140.

4. Mateen Thobani, "Peru: Agricultural Policies for Economic Efficiency," Washington, D.C.: World Bank, 1991, 68. Precise figures vary, but the trend is not in question.

5. García-Sayan, "Las Relaciones," 136.

6. William O. Walker III, "Drug Control and U.S. Hegemony," in John D. Martz, ed., *United States Policy in Latin America: A Decade of Crisis and Challenge* (Lincoln: University of Nebraska Press, 1995), 311.

7. For antinarcotics policy during the García administration, see Cynthia McClintock, "The War on Drugs: The Peruvian Case," *Journal of InterAmerican Studies and World Affairs* 30 (summer–fall 1988), 127–142, and the Bureau of International Narcotics Matters, U.S. Department of State, *International Narcotics Control Strategy Report* (Washington, D.C., March 1989), 85–90, and other annual reports.

8. Joseph B. Treaster, "On Front Line of Drug War, U.S.-Built Base Lags in Peru," *New York Times* (October 31, 1989), A1 and A10. Some U.S. Army Special Forces were probably also involved; see Kenneth Roberts and Mark Peceny, "Human Rights and United States Policy Toward Peru," in Maxwell A. Cameron and Philip Mauceri, eds., *The Peruvian Labyrinth: Polity, Society, and Economy* (University Park: Pennsylvania State University Press, 1997), 213.

9. Bureau of International Narcotics Matters, *International Narcotics Control Strategy Report* (March 1989), 90.

10. This was said to be the case by U.S. ambassador Luigi Einaudi, in an address to a symposium at CEPEI, November 6, 1990, and by U.S. ambassador Anthony C. E. Quainton, addressing the conference "Peruvian Counternarcotics Efforts: A Contextual View," at the Meridian International Center, January 11, 1993. Roberto MacLean, Peruvian ambassador to the United States 1991–1992, had the same impression; see *The Peru Report* V (February 1991), 4.

11. James Brooke, "U.S. Will Arm Peru to Fight Leftists in New Drug Push," *New York Times* (April 23, 1990), 1 and 18; and an interview with U.S. ambassador to Peru Anthony C. E. Quainton, "Las Condiciones de la Ayuda," *Caretas* (April 30, 1990), 16–17 and 32 (among other sources).

12. Lawrence A. Clayton, *Peru and the United States: The Condor and the Eagle* (Athens: University of Georgia Press, 1999), 279–285, and McClintock, "The War on Drugs," 130–139.

13. Quoted in Peter Andreas, "Peru's Addiction to Coca Dollars," *The Nation* (April 16, 1990), 515.

14. Cynthia McClintock, *Revolutionary Movements in Latin America* (Washington, D.C.: U.S. Institute of Peace Press, 1998), 241.

15. *Ibid.*, and Palmer (1992: 72–74).

16. Cogent critical statements include the Washington Office on Latin America, *Clear and Present Dangers* (Washington, D.C.: Washington Office on Latin America, 1991) and Congressman Peter H. Kostmayer, "Opening Statement: The Andean Ini-

tiative (Part II)," Subcommittee on Western Hemisphere Affairs, U.S. Congress, June 20, 1990.

17. McClintock, *Revolutionary Movements*, 241.

18. Ambassador Anthony C. E. Quainton, in an address to the conference "Peruvian Counternarcotics Efforts: A Contextual View," Meridian International Center, January 11, 1993.

19. McClintock, *Revolutionary Movements*, 397–398.

20. *Ibid.*, 241.

21. The best account is Douglas Waller, "A Spy Mission Gone Wrong," *Newsweek* (May 31, 1993), 34–35.

22. Thomas W. Lippman, "Peru Pays Compensation for Attack on U.S. Plane," *Washington Post* (December 10, 1993), A49.

23. *Ibid.*

24. Anthony Faiola and Scott Wilson, "U.S. Took Risks in Aiding Peru's Anti-Drug Patrols," *Washington Post* (April 29, 2001), A20.

25. *Ibid.*

26. Raphael F. Perl, "Clinton's Foreign Drug Policy," *Journal of InterAmerican Studies and World Affairs* 35, no. 4 (1993–1994), 143–152; Coletta Youngers, "Andean Initiative: Legislative Update" (Washington, D.C.: Washington Office on Latin America, August 1993); "All the President's Fault?" *The Economist* (September 14, 1996), 26–27.

27. *Ibid.*

28. Office of National Drug Control Policy, *National Drug Control Strategy: 2001 Annual Report* (Washington, D.C.: Office of National Drug Control Policy, 2001), 119.

29. Quoted in Peter Zirnite, *Reluctant Recruits: The U.S. Military and the War on Drugs* (Washington, D.C.: Washington Office on Latin America, 1997), 26. See also Coletta Youngers, "Política Antidrogas: No Hay Consenso en Washington," *Ideele* 70 (November 1994), 39–41.

30. Gustavo Gorriti, "The Betrayal of Peru's Democracy: Montesinos as Fujimori's Svengali," *Covert Action* 49 (summer 1994), 55.

31. Charles Lane, "'Superman' Meets Shining Path: Story of a CIA Success," *Washington Post* (December 7, 2000), A29.

32. Gorriti, "The Betrayal," 55, and "Political and Economic Trends," *The Peru Report* VI, no. 6 (July 1992), 2.

33. Gorriti, "The Betrayal," 55.

34. *Ibid.*

35. On Montesinos as the Peruvian architect of this plan, see Faiola and Wilson, "U.S. Took Risks," A1; and "The Struggle to Exterminate a Much-Loved Andean Shrub," *The Economist* (May 26, 2001), 35.

36. James Risen and Christopher Marquis, "Officials Long Debated Risks of Anti-Drug Patrol in Peru," *New York Times* (May 22, 2001), A8.

37. On this meeting, see Dan Baum, *Smoke and Mirrors: The War on Drugs and the Politics of Failure* (Boston: Little, Brown, 1996), 239.

38. Joshua Cooper Ramo, "America's Shadow Drug War," *Time* (May 7, 2001), 36.

39. Risen and Marquis, "Officials Long Debated," A8, and Faiola and Wilson, "U.S. Took Risks," A20.

40. A mention of action against "aircraft" appears for the first time in the BINM report of March 1992. The mention is in the "statistical tables"; under the rubric of "seizures," the word "aircraft" appears, with "items" as the unit of measurement. No explanation is provided. See also Faiola and Wilson, "U.S. Took Risks," A20.

41. Ricardo Soberón, "Entre cuarteles, caletas y fronteras . . ." *QueHacer*, no. 102 (July–August 1996), 53–54.

42. U.S. officials routinely indicated that the air bridge denial program began in early 1995; for example, author's interview with Rob Raymer, deputy, Narcotics Affairs Section, U.S. embassy, Lima, June 9, 1998.

43. Soberón, "Entre cuarteles," 55.

44. On the information in this paragraph, see Patrick L. Clawson and Lee W. Rensselaer III, *The Andean Cocaine Industry* (New York: St. Martin's, 1998), 229; Risen and Marquis, "Officials Long Debated," A8; and Faiola and Wilson, "U.S. Took Risks," A20.

45. Clawson and Rensselaer, *The Andean Cocaine Industry*, 229.

46. Risen and Marquis, "Officials Long Debated," A8; Faiola and Wilson, "U.S. Took Risks," A20; Cooper Ramo, "America's Shadow Drug War," 40.

47. Bureau of International Narcotics Matters, U.S. Department of State, *International Narcotics Control Strategy Report* (Washington, D.C.: Government Printing Office, 1994), 118–122.

48. Bureau of International Narcotics Matters, U.S. Department of State, *International Narcotics Control Strategy Report* (Washington, D.C.: Government Printing Office, 1995), 99.

49. Peruvian ambassador Ricardo Luna in his presentation "U.S.-Peruvian Relations 1992–1999: Assessment and Prospects for the Future," sponsored by the George Washington University Seminar on Andean Culture and Politics and the Washington Office on Latin America, May 27, 1999.

50. For McCaffrey's statements, see Theo Roncken, ed., "The Drug War in the Skies: The U.S. 'Air Bridge Denial' Strategy: The Success of a Failure," Findings of the Research Project of the "Drugs and Democracy" Program, Acción Andina, Transnational Institute, Cochabamba, Bolivia, May 1999, 36. For evaluations by other antinarcotics officials, see Bureau of International Narcotics and Law Enforcement Affairs, U.S. Department of State, *International Narcotics Control Strategy Report March 1998* (Washington, D.C.: U.S. Department of State, 1998), 100, as well as the bureau's reports for 1999 and 2000. The only factor cited by U.S authorities as important to the decline in coca cultivation besides air bridge denial was eradication.

51. The most rigorous critical assessment is Roncken, "The Drug War in the Skies." Contributing to this analysis were top experts on the drug war, including Colombia's Ricardo Vargas Mesa and Peru's Ricardo Soberón Garrido.

52. On McCaffrey's role, see Bradley Graham, "Drug Control Chief Won't Let Pentagon Just Say No," *Washington Post* (November 24, 1997), A17.

53. General Barry R. McCaffrey, "Memorandum for Record: Peru Trip, 1–3 November 1994," United States Southern Command, Department of Defense, November 7, 1994, 2. (Memorandum obtained through Freedom of Information Act request.)

54. General Barry McCaffrey, at a talk at the Woodrow Wilson Center, Washington, D.C., May 1, 1997.

55. Office of National Drug Control Policy, *2001 Annual Report*, 119.

56. The information in this paragraph is based on the annual editions of *Just the Facts: A Civilian's Guide to U.S. Defense and Security Assistance to Latin America and the Caribbean* (Washington, D.C.: Latin America Working Group and Center for International Policy). See also www.ciponline.org/facts/pe/htm. The $80 million figure for Peru for 2000 is also reported by Cooper Ramo, "America's Shadow Drug War," 41.

57. This change in the Peruvian military's attitude is discussed in Soberón, "Entre cuarteles," 53. The change was cited by U.S. officials as well, including Robert E. Brown Jr., assistant deputy director, Office of Supply Reduction, Office of National Drug Control Policy, in author's interview on June 3, 1999, in Washington, D.C.

58. Faiola and Wilson, "U.S. Took Risks," A21; Risen and Marquis, "Officials Have Long Debated," A8.

59. Faiola and Wilson, "U.S. Took Risks," A21.

60. *Ibid.*, Risen and Marquis, "Officials Have Long Debated," A8.

61. Clifford Krauss, "Pentagon to Help Peru Stop Drug-Base Shipping on Rivers," *New York Times* (February 3, 1997), A3.

62. There is no disagreement on this point. See, for example, Anthony Faiola, "U.S. Allies in Drug War in Disgrace," *Washington Post* (May 9, 2001), A28.

63. Coletta A. Youngers, "Collateral Damage: U.S. Drug Control Efforts in the Andes," paper prepared for delivery at the Latin American Studies Association Meeting, Washington, D.C., September 6–8, 2001, 15.

64. Faiola, "U.S. Allies," A28.

65. Coletta A. Youngers, "Deconstructing Democracy: Peru Under President Alberto Fujimori," Washington, D.C.: Washington Office on Latin America (February 2000), 89.

66. Youngers, "Collateral Damage," 16.

67. Anonymous, "U.S. Drug Czar in Peru Amid Andes Narcotics Crisis," CNN, August 26, 1999 (from www.rose-hulman.edu/~delacova/peru/narcotics.htm); anonymous, "Castañeda Support Threatens Fujimori," *Latin American Weekly Report* 99, no. 34 (August 31, 1999), 405; Douglas Farah, "Coca Crop Shrinking in Key Andean Nations," *Washington Post* (January 7, 1999), A21.

68. Bureau for International Narcotics and Law Enforcement Affairs, U.S. Department of State, *International Narcotics Control Strategy Report* (Washington, D.C.: Government Printing Office, 1996), 99–105.

69. Among the many accounts, see Anthony Faiola, "As Coca Market Goes, So Shall They Reap," *Washington Post* (November 18, 1997), A1 and Roberto Suro, "Lack of Air Support Hindering Drug War," *Washington Post* (March 13, 2000), A10.

70. Faiola, "As Coca Market Goes," A15.

71. Douglas Farah, "Pentagon Helps Peru Fight Drugs," *Washington Post* (April 22, 1998), A1.

72. Hugo Cabieses, "Erradicación de la coca: política bobo," *Ideele* 120 (July 1999), 68. Similar figures are presented in other sources, including Roncken, "The Drug War in the Skies," 51.

73. Carlos Basombrío Iglesias, "El Plan Colombia y el Perú," paper prepared for the meeting of the Latin American Studies Association, Washington, D.C., September 6–8, 2001, 19.

74. Christopher S. Wren, "Phantom Numbers Haunt the War on Drugs," *New York Times* (April 20, 1997), 4; also, General (retired) Alberto Arciniega and Dr. Jim Jones, speakers at the George Washington University and Washington Office on Latin America Seminar on Andean Culture and Politics, "The Fujimori Government's 'War against Drugs': The Facts, the Fantasies, and the Lessons," May 31, 2001.

75. Among other sources, see Faiola and Wilson, "The Struggle to Exterminate a Much-Loved Andean Shrub," 36.

76. Anonymous, "Hay 33,000 Hectareas Dedicadas a la Coca, Segun Dudosas Cifras Oficiales," *Diario Liberación*, February 27, 2001 (electronic communication without page number).

77. "Drugs in the Andes: Spectres Stir in Peru," *The Economist* (February 16, 2002), 33.

78. Roncken, "The Drug War in the Skies," 53–54.

79. This issue has been rigorously researched by scientist and photojournalist Jeremy Bigwood. See http://jeremybigwood.net/Lectures/GWU-WOLA-JB/GWUNov2000.htm. Also, e-mail correspondence to the author from Jeremy Bigwood, July 4, 2001. See also anonymous, "Has the U.S. Already Been Using Fusarium as a Biological Weapon?" *Latin American Weekly Report* 00, no. 29 (July 25, 2000), 337.

80. Roncken, "The Drug War in the Skies," 47–54.

81. Author's calculation from data in Roncken, "The Drug War in the Skies," 52. The data are said to underestimate the increase in coca cultivation in Colombia prior to 1995, but we are unable to assess the validity of this criticism.

82. Basombrío, "El Plan Colombia y el Perú," 16.

83. Robert E. Brown Jr., assistant deputy director, Office of Supply Reduction, in author's interview, Washington, D.C., June 3, 1999. See also Ricardo Soberón, "Drug Trafficking in Perú, A Successful Model?" *Peru Solidarity Forum* 25 (April 1999), 10–13.

84. U.S. Department of State, *International Narcotics Control Strategy Report 1999* (March 2000), sections on Bolivia, Colombia, and Peru.

85. Bureau of International Narcotics and Law Enforcement Affairs, *International Narcotics Control Strategy Report 1999* (Washington, D.C.: U.S. Department of State, 2000), xxxiv. See also Clifford Krauss, "Desperate Farmers Imperil Peru's Fight on Coca," *New York Times* (February 23, 2001), A4; Molly Moore, "Cocaine Seizures by U.S. Double in Pacific Ocean," *Washington Post* (September 3, 2000), A24.

86. Omar Terrones Carrera, "Fiscal denuncia a Montesinos por tráfico de drogas," *Latin American Times* (January 25, 2002), 12.

87. Faiola, "U.S. Allies," A28.

88. Sebastian Rotella, "Peru Spy Chief's Fall Reminiscent of Noriega Saga," *Los Angeles Times* (October 3, 2000). Available at http://pqasb.pqaarchiver.com/latimes/main/doc/000000061638810.h.

89. Faiola, "U.S. Allies," A28.

90. Krauss, "Desperate Farmers," A4, and "EE.UU. dará al Perú 150 millones de dólares para lucha antidrogas," *El Comercio* (October 8, 2001). Figures for U.S. support for alternative development were not provided in the annual reports of either the Bureau of International Narcotics and Law Enforcement Affairs or the Office of National Drug Control Policy. U.S. AID provides figures for aid for antinarcotics purposes, but these figures include aid for coca eradication. A problem in the calculation of funding for "alternative development" is that the concept is not clear. For example, the provision of social services and infrastructure in coca-producing areas benefits peasants; but is it "alternative development"? Is it classified under several rubrics?

91. http://www.state.gov/g/inl/rls/nrcrpt/2000, 30, and Bureau for International Narcotics and Law Enforcement Affairs, *International Narcotics Control Strategy Report 1999* (Washington, D.C.: U.S. Department of State, 1999), xxxiv.

92. These figures are the sums of the numbers in the Bureau for International Narcotics and Law Enforcement Affairs, *International Narcotics Control Strategy Report* issued in March 1998 and the report issued in March 2000.

93. This and subsequent information in this paragraph are based on Bureau for International Narcotics and Law Enforcement Affairs, *International Narcotics Control Strategy Report 1999*.

94. Nicole Bonnet, "Special Report—the Apurímac River Valley," *The Peru Report and Peru Business Digest* (February 18, 1998), 29–37.

95. *Ibid.;* Clifford Krauss, "Peru's Drug Successes Erode as Traffickers Adapt," *New York Times* (August 19, 1999), A3; and Krauss, "Desperate Farmers," A4.

96. Diego García-Sayan, quoted in Bonnet, "Special Report," 29.

97. The problem described in this paragraph is acknowledged by the U.S. government. See Bureau of International Narcotics and Law Enforcement Affairs, *International Narcotics Control Strategy Report 1998*, 103.

98. Anthony Faiola, "Drug War on the Home Front: Latin America, Long an Exporter, Fights Growing Addiction," *Washington Post* (September 15, 1999), A18.

99. PromPerú, *Latinobarometer 97: Public Opinion in Latin America* (Lima: PROMPERÚ, 1998), 15. The question was asked in December 1997.

100. Juan O. Tamayo, "CIA's Andean Spying Under Attack; Planes Monitor More Than Drugs," *Miami Herald* (May 20, 2001), 1A. Also, author's interview with Jeremy Weinstein, Ph.D. candidate in government at Harvard University, February 27, 2002, in Washington, D.C. Weinstein carried out dissertation research in the Upper Huallaga Valley in 2001.

CHAPTER VII

1. The definitive study is Thomas Carothers, *In the Name of Democracy: U.S. Policy Toward Latin America in the Reagan Years* (Berkeley: University of California Press, 1991).

2. Telephone interview with Jane Stanley, Peru office, U.S. Agency for International Development, Washington, D.C., March 14, 2000, and interview with Carrie Thompson, deputy chief of democratic initiatives and training for U.S. AID/Peru, June 9, 1998, in Lima; see also www.usaid.gov/pubs.

3. Public-opinion polls on this question are cited in Cynthia McClintock, *Revolutionary Movements in Latin America* (Washington, D.C.: U.S. Institute of Peace Press, 1998), 110–112.

4. *Ibid.,* 112–120.

5. U.S. Department of State, *Country Reports on Human Rights,* annual editions.

6. Alan Riding, "Peru's Twin Crises Raise Coup Rumors," *New York Times* (January 15, 1989), 6.

7. See, for example, "Embajador Watson: Diálogo en el Estribo," *Caretas* (July 3, 1989), 16–20, and also the interpretation of U.S. policy by Peruvian ambassador Roberto MacLean, *The Peru Report* 5 (February 1991), 4–6. Also, author's interviews with Ambassador Alexander Watson, December 6, 1987, and July 6, 1989, in Lima; Ambassador Anthony Quainton, April 21, 1999, in Washington, D.C.; U.S. deputy chief of mission John Youle, July 14, 1986, in Lima; Peruvian minister of foreign relations Alan Wagner, July 25, 1986, in Lima; and numerous other officials.

8. Author's telephone interview, Margaret Sarles, Head, Democracy and Human Rights Office for Latin America and the Caribbean, U.S. AID, February 26, 2000.

9. Calculation on the basis of recent data and information provided by Coletta Youngers, Washington Office on Latin America, August 27, 2001. See also Juan Forero, "Where the Bodies Are Buried in Peru," *New York Times* (February 18, 2002), A3.

10. McClintock, *Revolutionary Movements,* 114–119.

11. Felipe Zegarra, "Derechos Humanos y Construcción de la Paz," *Páginas* 130 (December 1994), 6–7.

12. Anonymous, "La pifia de Belaúnde," *Caretas* 762 (1983), 13, and anonymous, "Nada que investigar?" *Caretas* 767 (1983), 14.

13. Information in this paragraph is based on U.S. Department of State, *Country Reports on Human Rights Practices,* annual reports.

14. In 1986, for example, in the wake of the summary executions in Lima's prisons, "the Reagan administration was silent." See The Watch Committee, *The Reagan Administration's Record on Human Rights in 1986* (New York: The Watch Committee, 1987), 105.

15. McClintock, *Revolutionary Movements,* 239.

16. Cynthia McClintock, "The Decimation of Peru's Sendero Luminoso," in Cynthia J. Arnson, ed., *Comparative Peace Processes in Latin America* (Stanford, CA: Stanford University Press, 1999), 238–239.

17. U.S. Department of State, *Country Reports on Human Rights Practices for 1989* (Washington, D.C.: U.S. Department of State, 1990), 710.

18. Anonymous, "Perú: derechos humanos en un clima de terror," *Ideele* 32–33 (December 1991), 33–36.

19. Coletta Youngers, "Peru Under Scrutiny: Human Rights and U.S. Drug Policy" (Washington, D.C.: Washington Office on Latin America, 1992); Kenneth Roberts and Mark Peceny, "Human Rights and United States Policy Toward Peru," in Maxwell A. Cameron and Philip Mauceri, eds., *The Peruvian Labyrinth* (University Park: Pennsylvania State University Press, 1997), 214–217; anonymous, "Ayuda internacional y derechos humanos," *Ideele* 29 (September 1991), 17–25.

20. Youngers, "Peru Under Scrutiny," 3–7; anonymous, "Para el Departamento de Estado: Los derechos humanos ya están casi o.k.," *Ideele* 34 (February 1992), 10–11.

21. U.S. Ambassador Anthony Quainton, "Memorandum from U.S. Embassy in Lima #05426," April 1992 (precise date not given) (made available through Freedom of Information Act), 1–3.

22. U.S. Ambassador Anthony Quainton, "Memorandum from U.S. Embassy in Lima #05167," April 7, 1992 (made available through Freedom of Information Act), 2.

23. Ambassador Viron Vaky in comments at the conference The Constitutional Crisis Is Guatemala: The Response of the OAS and Civil Society in Defending Democracy, U.S. Institute of Peace, July 26, 1993.

24. One Peruvian military officer told a U.S. official that SOUTHCOM supported the autogolpe, and Ambassador Quainton was sufficiently concerned that he asked SOUTHCOM to call the Peruvian officer to correct his view. U.S. ambassador Anthony Quainton, "Memorandum from Lima #05339," April 10, 1992 (obtained from Freedom of Information Act), 2. Also, it is rumored that the CIA station chief in Lima had been alerted to the autogolpe.

25. Letter from Michael W. Cotter, director, Office of Defense Relations and Security Assistance, to the director of operations at the Defense Security Assistance Agency, April 7, 1992. The letter was sent to me courtesy of Jeremy Bigwood, who received it through a Freedom of Information Act request.

26. John M. Goshko, "U.S. Puts Hold on Aid After Peruvian Fiat," *Washington Post* (April 7, 1992), A20.

27. Eugene Robinson, "U.S. Stance on Peru Mixed," *Washington Post* (April 10, 1992), A41.

28. David Scott Palmer, "Peru: Collectively Defending Democracy in the Western Hemisphere," in Tom Farer, ed., *Beyond Sovereignty* (Baltimore: Johns Hopkins University Press, 1996), 273, and Robinson, "U.S. Stance," A41. Humanitarian aid amounted to about $121 million.

29. Washington Office on Latin America, "Andean Initiative: Legislative Update," July 1992, 5.

30. Stokes, "Peru: The Rupture of Democratic Rule," in Jorge I. Domínguez and Abraham F. Lowenthal, eds., *Constructing Democratic Governance: South America in the 1990s* (Baltimore: Johns Hopkins University Press, 1996).

31. Ferrero Costa, "El ámbito global," 40.

32. On the OAS response, see Rubén M. Perina, "El Régimen Democrático Interamericano: El Papel de la OEA," in Arlene B. Tickner, ed., *Sistema Interamericano y Democracia: Antecedentes Históricos y Tendencias Futuras* (Bogotá, Colombia: Universidad de los Andes, 2000), 321–322.

33. U.S. ambassador Anthony Quainton, "Memorandum from U.S. Embassy in Lima #05866," April 18, 1992 (made available through Freedom of Information Act), 1. See also *The Economist* (July 11, 1992), 42.

34. Eduardo Ferrero Costa, "Peru's Presidential Coup," *Journal of Democracy* 4, no. 1 (January 1993), 36.

35. *Resumen Semanal* (15–23 April 1992), 1.

36. On the U.S. and Latin American positions at this meeting, see Thomas L. Friedman, "U.S. Is Shunning Sanctions Against Peru," *New York Times* (April 14, 1992), A8.

37. Quoted in Ferrero Costa, "Peru's Presidential Coup," 35.

38. Among the valuable accounts of these negotiations and the meeting in the Bahamas, see Palmer, "Peru: Collectively Defending Democracy," 273–276; Ferrero Costa, "El ámbito global," 42–43; Perina, "El Régimen Democrático InterAmericano," 322.

39. U.S. ambassador Anthony Quainton, "Memorandum from U.S. Embassy in Lima #06112," April 24, 1992 (made available through Freedom of Information Act), 2.

40. "The President's Peruvian Approach," *U.S. News and World Report* (May 4, 1992), 16.

41. Author's inference from the U.S. embassy memorandums cited herein. On April 22, a U.S. spokesperson declared that the U.S. would "continue to deal with the government of Fujimori because that's the current government"—provoking consternation among the Peruvian opposition. See Anthony Quainton, "Memorandum from U.S. Embassy in Lima #05989," April 22, 1992 (made available by Freedom of Information Act), 2.

42. CIA documents made available to Jeremy Bigwood through the Freedom of Information Act. These documents are dated from November 14, 1992, through mid-January 1993, and are numbered from 531068 through 531131.

43. "Discurso del Señor Presidente de la República del Perú, Ing. Alberto Fujimori, en la Asamblea de Cancilleres ante la O.E.A.," in Eduardo Ferrero Costa, ed., *Proceso de Rertorno a la Institucionalidad Democrática en el Perú* (Lima: CEPEI, 1992), 191–202.

44. "Trend Report," *The Peru Report* 7 (February 1993), 6.

45. Lee Hockstader, "Peruvian President Takes Case to OAS," *Washington Post* (May 18, 1992), A12.

46. "Resolución MRE/RES. 2/92 de la Reunión Ad Hoc de Ministros de Relaciones Exteriores del 18 de mayo de 1992," in *Proceso de Retorno a la Institucionalidad Democrática en el Perú*, 203–204.

47. Statement by Deputy Secretary of State Lawrence S. Eagleburger at the OAS meeting of foreign ministers on Peru, Nassau, Bahamas, May 18, 1992 (Washington, D.C.: General Assembly of the Organization of American States).

48. *Ibid.*

49. "Peru Savours Return of Global Goodwill," *Financial Times* (December 1, 1992), 3. See also Chapter V.

50. Cynthia McClintock, "Peru's Fujimori: A Caudillo Derails Democracy," *Current History* 92 (March 1993), 118–119.

51. Domingo E. Acevedo and Claudio Grossman, "The Organization of American States and the Protection of Democracy," in Tom Farer, ed., *Beyond Sovereignty* (Baltimore: Johns Hopkins University Press, 1996), 141.

52. Stokes, "Peru: The Rupture of Democratic Rule," p. 65.

53. These charges began soon after the event. See Eugene Robinson, "Peruvians Look for Answers in Massacre of 16," *Washington Post* (November 20, 1991), A29, and Coletta Youngers, "Policy Guidelines for Peru," February 12, 1993, memorandum to Richard Feinberg.

54. U.S. Department of State, *Country Reports on Human Rights Practices for 1991*, 710–711, and *Country Reports on Human Rights Practices for 1992*, 474.

55. David Scott Palmer, "Las Relaciones Entre Estados Unidos y Perú Durante Los Gobiernos de Presidente Clinton," in Andrés Franco, ed., *Estados Unidos y los países andinos, 1993–1997: poder y desintegración* (Bogotá: Facultad de Ciencias Politicas y Relaciones Internacionales de la Pontificia Universidad Javeriana, 1998), 116; Peruvian ambassador Ricardo Luna, speaking on "U.S.-Peruvian Relations, 1992–1999: Assessment and Prospects for the Future," at George Washington University, June 10, 1999; Coletta Youngers, "After the *Autogolpe:* Human Rights in Peru and the U.S. Response" (Washington, D.C.: Washington Office on Latin America, 1994), 38, and Roberts and Peceny, "Human Rights and United States Policy," 218.

56. Palmer, "Las Relaciones entre Estados Unidos y Perú," 116–117.

57. Author's interview with U.S. Department of State personnel Anne Patterson and Ann Hall at the U.S. Department of State, January 19, 1993.

58. Youngers, "After the *Autogolpe*," 37–50.

59. U.S. Agency for International Development, *U.S. Overseas Loans and Grants*, annual editions.

60. See, for example, U.S. ambassador Alvin Adams, "Statement," in Instituto de Estudios Internacionales, ed., *Working Seminar Towards a New Convergence in Peru-United States Relations* (Lima: Pontificia Universidad Católica del Perú, 1994), 11–20.

61. U.S. Agency for International Development, *U.S. Overseas Loans and Grants*, annual editions.

62. Latin American Studies Association Delegation, *The 1995 Electoral Process in Peru* (Pittsburgh: Latin American Studies Association, 1995), 6–7.

63. U.S. State Department, *1994 Report on Human Rights for Peru*, Section 3.

64. An excellent report on the issues in this paragraph is Catherine M. Conaghan, "Troubled Accounting, Troubling Questions: Looking Back at Peru's Election," *LASA Forum* XXVI (summer 1995), 9–12.

65. Fernando Tuesta Soldevilla, *Perú Político en Cifras 1821–2001* (Lima: Friedrich Ebert Stiftung, 2001), 456. In earlier publications, the figure was 52 percent, and the percentage of invalid votes 41 percent.

66. Conaghan, "Troubled Accounting," 9; *Latin American Weekly Report* 4 (February 2, 1995), *Latin American Weekly Report* 11 (March 23, 1995).

67. Although different reasons for Transparencia's actions were provided to the authors by different analysts, the explanation that its focus had been on the presidential and not the congressional was the most persuasive. This explanation was offered by Susana Villarán, in an interview in Lima, June 19, 1998; Jorge del Castillo, in an interview in Washington, March 1, 1999; and Eduardo Stein, in an interview in Washington, January 10, 2002, among others.

68. Tuesta Soldevilla, *Perú Político en Cifras*, 456, 505–506, and 531–532.

69. At first, criticisms were muted; see, for example, Transparencia, "Informe del Conteo Rapido y la Observación Electoral de las Elecciones Generales de 1995" (Lima: Transparencia, 1995), 75–76. Gradually, however, they became sharper; see, for example, "Pérez de Cuéllar Criticises Count," *Latin America Weekly Report* (May 18, 1995), 213. By 2000, it was the conventional wisdom that these results had been manipulated; see Eduardo Stein, "La Memoria del Observador," *El Comercio*, June 16, 2001, 1.

70. Unit for the Promotion of Democracy, "Executive Summary: Electoral Observation Peru 1995" (Washington, D.C.: Organization of American States, 1997), 28–29. In the Peru report of the U.S. Department of State's *Country Reports on Human Rights Practices for 1995*, the problems in the legislative race were mentioned in one sentence.

71. More cases against Peru were before the Court than against any other country. *Latin American Andean Group Report* (July 27, 1999), 2.

72. Catherine M. Conaghan, "Making and Unmaking Authoritarian Peru: Re-election, Resistance, and Regime Transition," *The North-South Agenda Papers* 47 (June 2001), 4.

73. See, for example, the U.S. Department of State, *Country Report on Human Rights Practices for 1996, Peru Report,* Section 3.

74. Conaghan, "Making and Unmaking," 5–6.

75. Coletta A. Youngers, "Deconstructing Democracy: Peru Under President Alberto Fujimori," Washington, D.C.: Washington Office on Latin America (February 2000), 53. After the demise of the Fujimori government, "Vladivideos" revealed that bribes had been given for votes on the referendum.

76. An excellent discussion of these abuses is Youngers, "Deconstructing Democracy."

77. See, for example, Jett's statements on the topic as he prepared to leave Peru in *La República* (June 8, 1999), 4.

78. *Washington Post* (February 4, 1999), A26.

79. Catherine M. Conaghan, "Fear, Loathing, and Collusion: Press and State in Fujimori's Peru," paper delivered at the Latin American Studies Association Meeting, Chicago, September 24–26, 1998.

80. Isaías Rojas, "La Crisis de la Libertad de Prensa y (También) El Caso Lúcar," *Ideele* 118 (May 1999), 18–21.

81. This paragraph is based on author's interviews with U.S. ambassador Dennis Jett, political counselor Jim Wagner, and political officer Dan Lawton, in Lima, June 9, 1998, and with Principal Deputy Assistant Secretary of State for Inter-American Affairs Jack Leonard and the director of the South America and Mexico Office of the Latin American and Caribbean Division at the U.S. Agency for International Development, Thomas Cornell, in Washington, D.C., June 2, 1999.

82. Luis Peirano and Carlos Reyna, "Estados Unidos y La Triple 'D'" [interview with Ambassador Dennis Jett] *QueHacer* 107 (May-June 1997), 30–38. See also the U.S. Department of State *Country Report on Human Rights Practices 1998* for Peru.

83. Interviewed officials were unanimous that Jett's role had been judged counterproductive within the U.S. Department of State. Among these officials are former acting assistant secretary Peter Romero, in a telephone interview, January 7, 2002, and former National Security Council senior director Arturo Valenzuela, December 20, 2001, in Washington, D.C. On the Fujimori government's strategy of severing communications to protest criticisms, see Mauro, citing U.S. Department of State official Ted Piccone, "Peru Documents Fuel Anger at U.S.," Associated Press, February 3, 2002.

84. See discussion and sources in Chapters III and V.

85. DeYoung, "The Doctor," A22.

86. U.S. ambassador Anthony Quainton, speaking at the panel discussion "Governance in Peru," Center for Strategic and International Studies, January 31, 2002.

87. Anonymous, "Gobierno emplazó a embajador de Estados Unidos," *Cambio* (April 20, 2000), 7.

88. The authors' analysis is shaped by their participation in many of the events described in this chapter. On sabbatical for the academic year 1999–2000, McClintock was a coorganizer of an international conference about the Peruvian elections in January 2000 and a member of Transparencia's election-monitoring delegation for the April 2000 first round, and attended and participated in a large number of meetings and conferences about the elections, both in Peru and the United States. She interviewed numerous U.S. officials who were involved in policy making toward Peru during 1999–2000, including Ambassador John Hamilton, February 7, 2000, in Lima; Morton H. Halperin, director, Policy Planning Staff at the U.S. Department of State, April 19, 2000; former U.S. official at the Department of State in the Office of Policy Planning Theodore J. Piccone, December 13, 2001; National Security Council senior director Arturo Valenzuela, December 20, 2001; and former acting assistant secretary Peter Romero, January 7, 2002 (by telephone). Relevant comments were also provided by U.S. ambassador to the OAS, Roger Noriega, at the panel "U.S. Policy Toward Latin America at the Onset of the Twenty-First Century," September 6, 2001, and in a telephone interview with *Washington Post* journalist Karen DeYoung, December 14, 2000.

89. See Chapter III. Also, there are no references to Peru in a collection of comments by Secretary Albright, "Focus on the Issues: The Americas" (Washington, D.C.: Bureau of Public Affairs, U.S. Department of State, March 2000).

90. Author's telephone interview with Peter Romero, January 7, 2002.

91. For example, Romero was invited to speak at the January 27, 2000, conference "Peace and Democratization in Peru: Advances, Setbacks, and Reflections on the 2000 Elections," organized by the George Washington University Seminar on Andean Culture and Politics and the Washington Office on Latin America, and for a follow-up event with an elite group of Peruvian opposition leaders the next day, Coletta A. Youngers and the author had difficulty securing high-level U.S. official participation.

92. U.S. Department of State, "Decision of Peru's President Fujimori to Seek Third Term," released on December 28, 1999.

93. The conference was "Peace and Democratization in Peru: Advances, Setbacks and Reflections on the 2000 Elections," organized by the George Washington University Seminar on Andean Culture and Politics and the Washington Office on Latin America, in Washington, D.C., January 27, 2000.

94. www.state.gov/www/global/human_rights/1999_hrp_report/Peru, 2.

95. Hamilton was asked the question, "A critique of this government is that it is not very democratic. Do you see any changes in that area?" Hamilton's answer was: "I see, and saw when I was here before, a very fragmented political society. In the time

that I have been gone there has been a further decomposition of the traditional political parties and the rise of political movements. I see Peru still in a transition period. The main challenge was and is strengthening democratic institutions. In my initial conversations this seems to be an area the government is very much aware of and I sense a positive attitude toward these issues. I certainly hope that during my time here I can develop a relationship that encourages and strengthens the possibilities in this area." "Interview: A Decade of Changes," *Contact Peru* 4, no. 6 (October-November 1999), 14.

96. Author's interview with Ambassador Hamilton, February 7, 2000, in Lima.

97. "Los extranjeros que ejercen mayor poder en el Perú," *Debate* 114 (November-December 2001), 36.

98. "Vladivideo" No. 1792, taped on November 26, 1999.

99. Author's interview with Gustavo Gorriti (a top advisor to Toledo during 2000), July 31, 2002, in Lima.

100. Data courtesy of Joseph L. Dorsey, Peru Desk, U.S. Agency for International Development, June 24, 2002.

101. Barry Steven Levitt, "Beyond Fraud: The 2000 (and 2001) Elections in Peru," paper presented at the Latin American Studies Association meeting, Washington, D.C., September 6–8, 2001.

102. Data courtesy of Elizabeth Spehar, Unit for the Promotion of Democracy, Organization of American States, June 30, 2002.

103. "Movements," *Peru Monitor Monthly* (March 24, 2000), 13.

104. For further description, see Cynthia McClintock, "Explaining the Breakdown of Democratic Regimes in Latin America at Century's Turn: The Case of Fujimori's Peru," paper presented at the annual meeting of the American Political Science Association, August 31-September 3, 2000, in Washington, D.C., 8–9.

105. Scott Wilson, "Camera Has Turned on Peru's TV Stations," *Washington Post* (December 18, 2001), A23.

106. "Statement of the NDI/Carter Center December 1999 Pre-Election Delegation to Peru," Lima, December 3, 1999. Available at www.ndi.org/perurep1.htm. In November 1999, concern about Peru's media was expressed by the U.S. Senate in Resolution 209.

107. Off-the-record interviews. As of 2001, Toledo was said to blame U.S. skepticism of his candidacy on Ambassador Hamilton.

108. "Vladivideos" Nos. 1568 and 1569 (meeting between Montesinos and Dr. Luis Bedoya de Vivanco), June 12, 1999, and Audiotape No. 1475 (meeting between Montesinos and Eduardo Calmell), April 13, 2000.

109. Audiotape No. 1475.

110. Eduardo Stein, "La memoria del observador," *El Comercio*, June 16, 2001, A4. Among scholars, this view was articulated particularly clearly by Maxwell A. Cameron in the discussion of his paper, "Elections in a Hybrid Regime: Civil-Military Relations and Caesarism in Peru," presented at the Latin American Studies Associa-

tion meeting, Miami, March 16–18, 2000, and is also implied by Conaghan, "Making and Unmaking," 10.

111. Clifford Krauss, "Insurgent in Peru Calls for Election Boycott," *New York Times* (May 20, 2000), A5.

112. On the points in this paragraph, see Anthony Faiola, "U.S. Calls Peruvian Election Invalid," *Washington Post* (May 30, 2000), A1 and A4; Christopher Marquis, "U.S. Retreats on Peru Vote; Assessment Not 'Final,'" *New York Times* (May 31, 2000), A5; and John Lancaster, "U.S. Softens Tone on Peruvian Election," *Washington Post* (May 31, 2000), A23.

113. Peter Hakim, "U.S. in Latin America: Good Deeds or Intervention?" *Christian Science Monitor,* (May 27, 2000), 21.

114. Arturo Valenzuela, senior director for Western Hemisphere Affairs, in a report on a manuscript submitted to the *Journal of Democracy* (August 2001).

115. Andrew F. Cooper and Thomas Legler, The OAS in Peru: A Model for the Future?" *Journal of Democracy* 12, no. 4 (October 2001), 128.

116. See, for example, "Peru: A Bad Start," *The Economist* (August 5, 2000), 36.

117. Coletta Youngers, "Peru: Democracy and Dictatorship," *Foreign Policy in Focus* 5 (October 2000): 2.

118. "Hamilton: Se restauraría ayuda en lucha antidrogas," *Expreso* (Lima), July 25, 2000.

119. For the tone of this period, see "Fujimori Still Enjoying 'Moral High Ground': Toledo's Backing Evaporates," *Latin American Weekly Report* 00–01 (August 8, 2000), 361.

120. Among the many comments to this effect were those by Thomas A. Shannon, 2000–2001 U.S. deputy permanent representative to the OAS and currently director of Andean affairs at the U.S. Department of State, at the Center for Strategic and International Studies, Washington, D.C., April 16, 2002 and by John T. Fishel (of the National Defense University), "Fujimori's Peru: the Rise and [Apparent] Fall of a Quasi-Democratic Regime," paper prepared for delivery at the Latin American Studies Association Meeting, Washington, D.C., September 6–8, 2001, 2. This view was also held by other observers; see, for example, Carmen Rosa Balbi and David Scott Palmer, "'Reinventing' Democracy in Peru," *Current History* 100, no. 643 (February 2001), 65 and Ernesto García Calderón, "Peru's Decade of Living Dangerously," *Journal of Democracy* 12, no. 2 (April 2001), 46.

121. DeYoung, "'The Doctor,'" A22.

122. *Ibid.*, and authors' interviews, as indicated above.

123. This survey was conducted by Monica Villalobos, using random route methodology in various parts of Lima.

124. Survey conducted by Monica Villalobos.

125. On the question of U.S. support for Montesinos's flight and the explanations for it discussed in this paragraph, see Larry Rohter, "Peru Spy Chief Flies to Panama

Looking for Asylum," *New York Times* (September 25, 2000), A8; Anthony Faiola, "Peruvian Spy Chief Arrives in Panama," *Washington Post* (September 25, 2000), A14; Christopher Marquis, "U.S. Says Asylum in Panama Helped Avert a Coup in Peru," *New York Times* (September 26, 2000), A8. Among these sources is discussion of Peruvian military sectors' dismay with Montesinos. Also valuable to the author's assessment was an interview with Gustavo Gorriti, July 31, 2002, in Lima, and attendance at a meeting in Washington, D.C. in late September 2000 at which a mid-level U.S. government official made off-the-record comments about the reasons for U.S. support for Montesinos's flight.

126. "Fujimori's grey eminence bows out," *Latin American Regional Report– Andean Group* (October 3, 2000), 2–3.

127. "As Montesinos flees judicial reckoning, Peru's opposition suspects a big scam," *Latin American Weekly Report* (September 26, 2000), 445. For further discussion of the possibility of a deal around Montesinos's videotapes, see "Montesinos, It Is Said, Has Videos, Too," *Washington Post* (September 29, 2000), A28; and "A spy departs," *The Economist* (September 30, 2000), 40. In an author's interview in Lima on July 26, 2001, journalist Sharon Stevenson reported her view—echoed by others—that CIA officials had taken a lead role in negotiating the departure of Montesinos.

128. Anthony Faiola, "Tough Road Ahead for Peru's Fujimori," *Washington Post* (September 30, 2000), A14.

129. For an excellent description of this comic search, see Conaghan, "Making and Unmaking," 25.

130. See, for example, Luigi Einaudi, "The Peruvian Transition and the Role of the International Community," in Cynthia Arnson, ed., *The Crisis of Democratic Governance in the Andes* (Washington, D.C.: Latin American Program of the Woodrow Wilson International Center for Scholars, 2001), 128–129. Indeed, in the view of the President of the U.S. Chamber of Commerce, "The United States has become Fujimori's most important prop." John J. Youle, "Political and Economic Summary— October–November 2000" (Newsletter from Lima written and distributed electronically by John J. Youle, on November 8), 1.

131. Adrian Karatnycky, "Flat-Footed in Peru," *Washington Post* (October 25, 2000), A31.

132. In the Villalobos survey, a plurality (41 percent) judged U.S. policy during the Fujimori-Montesinos government to be "regular." Among Peruvians, *regular* means "so-so" or "fair"—a C grade in the United States. Another 33 percent judged it "bad," and 7 percent "very bad." However, 4 percent did rate it "very good" and 16 percent "good."

CHAPTER VIII

1. See, for example, "The Once and Current President," *Time* (May 7, 2001), 8.

2. For a refutation of the criticism, see Samuel R. Berger, "A Foreign Policy for the Global Age," *Foreign Affairs* 79 (November–December 2000), 22–39.

3. At the Latin American Studies Association panel "U.S. Policy Toward Latin America at the Onset of the Twenty-First Century," held on September 6, 2001, in Washington, D.C., the question of U.S. support for the Fujimori regime was raised. Ambassador Roger Noriega, U.S. Ambassador to the OAS, responded that the reason had been "stability."

4. Lars Schoultz, *Beneath the United States: A History of U.S. Policy Toward Latin America* (Cambridge, MA: Harvard University Press, 1998).

POSTSCRIPT

1. Angel Páez, "Embargan 2 mil millones de red de Montesinos," *La República* (August 15, 2001), 16–17.

2. Supplement "La Gaceta" of the Congress of the Republic, *La República* (November 4, 2001), 7. Estimates of the total sum stolen by Fujimori and his network—separate from Montesinos and his close allies—are as high as $1 billion; see Catherine M. Conaghan, "Making and Unmaking Authoritarian Peru: Reselection, Resistance, and Regime Transition," *The North-South Agenda Papers* 47 (June 2001), 27.

3. "Peru Approves Charges Against Fujimori," *Washington Post* (November 1, 2001), A32.

4. Anthony Faiola, "Peruvian Investigators Pursue Fujimori," *Washington Post* (November 26, 2000), A20.

5. *El Comercio* (September 29, 2001), A10.

6. "La Purga de David," *Caretas* 1702 (December 28, 2001), 14–15.

7. "Reducen de 2,400 a 400 el número de personas que trabajan en el SIN," *La República* (October 10, 2001).

8. "Ley de Sistema de Inteligencia Nacional (SINA)," *El Peruano* (Lima: Editora Perú, 2001), 204311.

9. Silvia Rojas, "Bush se compromete desclasificar más rápido documentos secretos," *La República* (March 24, 2002), 4.

10. The National Security Archive, "Peru in 'the Eye of the Storm,'" Declassified U.S. Documentation on Human Rights Abuses and Political Violence, available at www.gwu.ed/~ensarchiv.

11. "Faltó la carne," *Caretas* 1703 (January 10, 2002), 18–19.

12. "Cuba: El Cuento del Tío Sam," *Caretas* 1716 (April 11, 2002), 30–31.

13. Elizabeth Bumiller, quoting Secretary of State Colin Powell, "In El Salvador, Bush Talks of Trade and Criticizes Democrats," *New York Times* (March 25, 2002), A6.

14. "Pricier Coca May Reverse Eradication Gains," *Latin American Weekly Report* (April 9, 2002), 164.

15. Clifford Krauss, "Desperate Farmers Imperil Peru's Fight on Coca," *New York Times* (February 23, 2001), A4.

16. "Pricier Coca May Reverse Eradication Gains," 164.

17. Joseph Contreras, "Turning the Clock Back to Chaos?" *Newsweek International* (March 18, 2002), 60.

18. The Economist Intelligence Unit, "Country Report: Peru," January 2002," 5 and 11.

19. Minister Pedro-Pablo Kuczynski, in a speech at the North American Peruvian Business Council, in Washington, D.C., April 22, 2002.

20. "Bid to Extend and Enhance the ATPA," *Latin America Regional Report Andean Group* (January 22, 2002), 7.